Lecture Notes in Artificial Intelligence 13128

Subseries of Lecture Notes in Computer Science

Series Editors

Randy Goebel
University of Alberta, Edmonton, Canada

Wolfgang Wahlster
DFKI, Berlin, Germany

Zhi-Hua Zhou
Nanjing University, Nanjing, China

Founding Editor

Jörg Siekmann
DFKI and Saarland University, Saarbrücken, Germany

More information about this subseries at https://link.springer.com/bookseries/1244

Koen H. Van Dam · Nicolas Verstaevel (Eds.)

Multi-Agent-Based Simulation XXII

22nd International Workshop, MABS 2021
Virtual Event, May 3–7, 2021
Revised Selected Papers

Editors
Koen H. Van Dam ⓘ
Imperial College London
London, UK

Nicolas Verstaevel ⓘ
Toulouse 1 Capitole University
Toulouse, France

ISSN 0302-9743   ISSN 1611-3349 (electronic)
Lecture Notes in Artificial Intelligence
ISBN 978-3-030-94547-3   ISBN 978-3-030-94548-0 (eBook)
https://doi.org/10.1007/978-3-030-94548-0

LNCS Sublibrary: SL7 – Artificial Intelligence

This Springer imprint is published by the registered company Springer Nature Switzerland AG
The registered company address is: Gewerbestrasse 11, 6330 Cham, Switzerland

Preface

This volume presents selected papers from the 22nd International Workshop on Multi-Agent-Based Simulation (MABS 2021), a workshop hosted by the 22nd International Conference on Autonomous Agents and Multi-Agent Systems (AAMAS 2021), originally planned to be held in London, which took place as a fully virtual event during May 3–7, 2021.

The meeting of researchers from multi-agent systems (MAS) engineering and the social/economic/organizational sciences is recognized as a source of cross-fertilization, and it has undoubtedly contributed to the body of knowledge produced in the MAS area. The excellent quality of this workshop has been recognized since its inception and its proceedings have been regularly published in Springer's Lecture Notes in Artificial Intelligence series. More information about the MABS workshop series may be found at https://www.pcs.usp.br/~mabs/.

The goal of the workshop is to bring together researchers interested in MAS engineering with researchers aiming to find efficient solutions to model complex social systems from areas such as economics, management, organization science, and social sciences in general. In all these areas, agent theories, metaphors, models, analyses, experimental designs, empirical studies, and methodological principles all converge in simulation as a way of achieving explanations and predictions, exploration and testing of hypotheses, and better designs and systems.

In this edition, 23 submissions were received from which we selected 18 for presentation (near 78% acceptance) and 14 for the post-proceedings (60% acceptance). The papers presented in the workshop have been revised and reviewed again in order to become part of this post-proceedings volume.

We are truly grateful to all authors for their contribution. We are also very grateful to all the members of the Program Committee for their hard work.

May 2021

Koen H. Van Dam
Nicolas Verstaevel

Organization

Program Chairs

Koen H. Van Dam	Imperial College of London, UK
Nicolas Verstaevel	University of Toulouse, France

MABS Steering Committee

Frédéric Amblard	University of Toulouse, France
Luis Antunes	University of Lisbon, Portugal
Paul Davidsson	Malmö University, Sweden
Emma Norling	Manchester Metropolitan University, UK
Mario Paolucci	National Research Council, Italy
Jaime Simão Sichman	University of São Paulo, Brazil
Samarth Swarup	University of Virginia, USA
Takao Terano	Tokyo Institute of Technology, Japan
Harko Verhagen	Stockholm University, Sweden

Program Committee

Frederic Amblard	Toulouse 1 Capitole University, France
Johan Barthelemy	University of Wollongong, Australia
Joao Balsa	University of Lisbon, Portugal
Sung-Bae Cho	Yonsei University, South Korea
Paul Davidsson	Malmö University, Sweden
Frank Dignum	Umeå University, Sweden
Benoit Gaudou	Toulouse 1 Capitole University, France
Luis Gustavo Nardin	National College of Ireland, Ireland
Rainer Hegselmann	Bayreuth University, Germany
Jean-Pierre Muller	CIRAD, France
Paulo Novais	University of Minho, Portugal
Mario Paolucci	Institute of Cognitive Sciences and Technologies, Italy
Juliette Rouchier	CNRS-LAMSADE, France
Ruth Meyer	Manchester Metropolitan University, UK
Samarth Swarup	University of Virginia, USA
Natalie Van Der Wal	Vrije Universiteit Amsterdam, The Netherlands
Harko Verhagen	Stockholm University, Stockholm
Neil Yorke-Smith	Delft University of Technology, The Netherlands

Contents

Social Simulation for Non-hackers

H. Van Dyke Parunak(✉) ⓘ

Parallax Advanced Research, Beavercreek, OH 45431, USA
van.parunak@parallaxresearch.org

Abstract. Computer simulation is a powerful tool for social scientists, but popular platforms require representing the semantics of the model being simulated in computer code, leading to models that are either expensive to construct, inefficient, or inaccurate. We introduce SCAMP (Social Causality using Agents with Multiple Perspectives), a social simulator that uses stigmergy to execute models that are written as concept maps and spreadsheets, without requiring any programming expertise on the part of the modeler. This Repast-based framework has been extensively exercised in the DARPA Ground Truth program to generate realistic social data for analysis by social scientists.

Keywords: Social simulation · Stigmergy · Polyagent · Repast

1 Introduction

Social simulation is a two-edged sword. On the one hand, computer simulation of social scenarios opens new research perspectives. On the other, computer programming and the social sciences involve complementary skills that can be difficult to integrate. There are three approaches to constructing a social simulation, each with drawbacks:

1. An expert programmer and a social scientist can work closely together to build the model. This approach is expensive and poses challenges of knowledge acquisition analogous to those experienced in the early days of expert systems.
2. The social scientist can learn some programming, typically in a platform such as NetLogo, and program the model personally. While some social scientists have commendably and creditably pursued this path, the effort needed to learn advanced programming idioms and testing disciplines is onerous and distracts the researcher from the social science aspects of the problem.
3. An experienced programmer may construct the model based on an intuitive understanding of the problem, again risking inaccuracy, this time by missing the social and psychological nuances of the scenario.

SCAMP (Social Causality using Agents with Multiple Perspectives) is a framework constructed in Repast [1] whose models are external to the computer code, rather than embedded in it. Social scientists construct these models using concept maps, a drawing program, and a spreadsheet, model.xlsx. The key to moving the model outside of the code is stigmergy, inspired by social insects [8] but well documented in human systems as well [17], and a central technique of "swarm intelligence" [25]. Swarming agents move

© Springer Nature Switzerland AG 2022
K. H. Van Dam and N. Verstaevel (Eds.): MABS 2021, LNAI 13128, pp. 1–14, 2022.
https://doi.org/10.1007/978-3-030-94548-0_1

over these external models, coordinating their actions by leaving and sensing changes to them. While stigmergic techniques are common for modeling subcognitive behaviors, in SCAMP these techniques capture sophisticated psychological and social features [19], including preferential choice, goal-based reasoning, dynamic social affiliations that modulate agent preferences, non-deterministic decision-making, mental simulation, and bounded rationality. SCAMP's combination of event-driven causality, geospatial interactions, goal-based reasoning, and social networks draws on our earlier work on multi-perspective modeling [4, 21].

We[1] developed SCAMP for the DARPA Ground Truth program [26]. It was one of four simulators that generated socially realistic data that social scientists used to test methods for extracting causality from data. The known causal structure of each simulation then allowed evaluation of the analysis methods. A forthcoming issue of *Computational and Mathematical Organization Theory (CMOT)* will document each facet of the overall program. SCAMP's model represented a civil conflict inspired by recent events in Syria, and was constructed entirely by professional geopolitical analysts with no programming experience, demonstrating the point of this paper.

Section 2 describes the SCAMP stigmergic architecture, while subsequent sections document the various components of the model that social scientists construct, using a toy model for clarity: definitions of the social groups active in the scenario (Sect. 3), a causal event graph (CEG) (Sect. 4), the geospatial context of the scenario (Sect. 5), a set of hierarchical goal networks (HGNs) (Sect. 6), and discontinuous changes to agents (Sect. 7). SCAMP exposes a very large parameter space to users, but a default mechanism (not discussed here for lack of space) reduces the complexity of bringing up a new model. Section 8 describes the data produced by SCAMP and summarizes the full conflict model used in Ground Truth, and Sect. 9 concludes.

2   The SCAMP Architecture[2]

A SCAMP agent repeatedly chooses among accessible alternatives, based on their features and its own preferences. Alternatives are nodes in a graph and are accessible if they are adjacent to an agent's current location. The central graph is a directed graph of the *types of events* in which an agent may participate, and the outgoing edges from one event type indicate others that an agent could coherently choose next. Thus every path through this graph is a valid *narrative* about the domain. Some events are geospatial requiring an agent to move spatially, and lead the agent to a *geospatial lattice*, on which agents can move from one location to any adjacent one.

Each agent has a home group. The groups in our conflict scenario are an oppressive *Government*, neutral *People*, an *Armed Opposition* seeking to replace the government with democratic institutions, *Violent Extremists* with strong ideological motives, *Relief Agencies*, and the *Military*, initially affiliated with the Government.

---

[1] In addition to the author, the SCAMP team included J.A. Morell of 4.699 LLC; L. Sappelsa of ANSER LLC; J. Greanya and S. Nadella of Wright State Research Institute (now Parallax Advanced Research). Kathleen Carley of CMU consulted on social network issues.
[2] An ODD protocol for SCAMP is available [14].

Each node that an agent can choose carries a vector in an underlying *feature space* with three kinds of features.

Some features describe *intrinsic characteristics* of the choice, in $[-1, 1]$. A geospatial node might be characterized by its terrain and gradient, while an event is marked by its impact on the physical, psychological, and economic wellbeing of participating agents.

Some features summarize the *recent presence* of agents by group (one feature per group), in $[0, 1]$. Agents augment these features as they traverse the graph, like insects depositing pheromones. Like pheromones, presence features evaporate over time.

Some features describe the *urgency* of a node for achieving each group's goals, in $[0, 1]$. Urgency features vary over time, depending on the state of the system.

Each group has a baseline set of scalar *preferences* in $[-1, 1]$ over the feature space. When agents are initialized, they draw their preferences from distributions whose means are defined by their group's baseline.

At any moment, an agent is participating in one event and has a set of accessible alternatives. To make its choice, it computes the inner product, between its preference vector and the feature vector of each accessible alternative, exponentiates these values (to make them positive), and normalizes them to form a roulette wheel. This fundamentally stochastic decision process recognizes recent research in decision making [16] showing that the basis for human choice is not deterministic preference, but a probability $Pr(A, B)$ of choosing A over B. SCAMP is heavily influenced by the decision field model [2] of stochastic decision theory. Modelers can adjust the degree of determinism by exponentiating the roulette segments and renormalizing. An exponent of 0 makes all segments equal, yielding random choice, while an exponent larger than 1 biases the choice toward the strongest alternative.

People make decisions using mental simulations [12, 13], a mental rehearsal of possible story trajectories to decide how to proceed. SCAMP implements this insight by representing each active entity as a set of agents, a *polyagent* [23]. One agent, the *avatar*, is persistent, and manages a population of transient *ghosts* that simulate its possible future courses of action to a limited horizon. Each ghost explores one possible future, using preferences and features. As it moves, it augments the presence features for the groups with which its avatar is affiliated. Collectively, the ghosts develop a field over alternative trajectories. To simulate a scenario, the avatar selects from its alternatives, weighting its choice by the presence features on each accessible alternative.

SCAMP's accessibility to non-programmers is evident by comparing it with the other three social simulations in the Ground Truth program, each using a different agent-based social modeling technology. In the huge space of social simulations (e.g., [3, 5–7]), these three offer a particularly apt comparison because they were all constructed for the same purpose: generate realistic social data to test analysis methods in the social sciences. SCAMP's social expressivity is comparable to them.

George Mason University, Tulane University, and the University of Buffalo produced a model of Urban Life [36] in the MASON modeling toolkit [15] and its GeoMASON extension [35]. Numerous aspects of the model are generated algorithmically, including the agent population, the geospatial map, and the social network among the agents. The system provides a pre-defined set of triggers (sensitive to both internal and external factors), behaviors to which they lead, actions that make up behaviors, and goals that determine when actions stop. Defining new triggers, behaviors, actions, and goals require programming, but a drag-and-drop interface allows modelers to assemble and parameterize these components to define a scenario..

Raytheon BBN produced ACCESS [28] in the Repast framework. The model highlights the interactions among individual agents, groups to which they belong, and the overall population or "world." ACCESS models space as a list of locations, but without orientation or distances, so there is no "map" for a user to enter, and the individual behaviors are determined by equations embedded in the code.

USC ISI produced a disaster world [27] in their PsychSim social simulation framework. Agents are driven by partially observable Markov decision processes (POMDPs) and can reason recursively about one another. PsychSim provides one interface that allows social scientists to create simulation models directly, and another allowing them to manipulate the parameters governing the simulation. However, both interfaces abstract over the full complexity of a PsychSim model (e.g., limiting the types of probability distributions and reward functions), so specifying arbitrary probability and utility models requires sufficient programming ability to use the PsychSim API.

GMU and ISI both support non-programmers who wish to modify a scenario, but still require programmers to modify details, and introduce proprietary interfaces. SCAMP allows non-programmers to define new groups, actions, and goals and their relations, using tools with which they may already be familiar.

3 Group Definitions

The modeler defines the model's groups in the *groups* tab of model.xlsx. SCAMP also supports an impersonal *Environment* group whose agents generate background events not modeled in detail, such as drought and economic collapse.

Agents have a home group, but can affiliate with other groups, if their preference vector is close enough to the baseline vector of those groups.

The user provides each group with an ID number, a descriptive name, and a short abbreviation used in defining other parameters that refer to the group (in our scenario, Gov, Peo, AO, VE, RA, Mil, and Env). For each group, the user defines.

- A baseline *preference vector* in $[-1, 1]^n$, specifying the group's preference for each feature in the n-dimensional feature space. -1 indicates that the group's agents are strongly repelled from the feature; $+1$ indicates that they are strongly attracted to it.
- *Starting locations* in geospace where agents in the group should begin.
- Overall *speed* of geospatial movement of agents in the group.
- Parameters governing how agents in a group *affiliate* with other agents:

  - Do group members affiliate with other groups?
  - Does the group accept affiliations from agents in other groups, and if so, how close must they be to its baseline preference vector? A high threshold (close to 1) characterizes an exclusive group, while a low one (close to 0) marks an open one.

- How much *variation* is applied when sampling individual agents from the group baseline? Groups can range from highly homogeneous group to more diverse.

- Does the group reason strategically by using a *hierarchical goal network* (HGN)?
- *How many agents* in the group should SCAMP initially generate?

Some execution parameters governing the polyagent simulation can also vary by group, including how many ghosts the avatar sends out, how far they explore into the future, and how many iterations they perform before reporting. In our work so far, these have been set by system developers rather than by modelers, but an area of future work is deriving them from variables that are meaningful to modelers.

4 Causal Event Graph

SCAMP's central modeling construct is the Causal Event Graph (CEG), a directed graph whose nodes represent different types of events, based on our previous work on narrative spaces [24, 30]. The CEG is inspired by narrative graphs in common use in intelligence analysis [9], cyber security planning [33], discrete event simulation [31], analysis of social disagreement [32], computer games [14] and the study of natural-language texts [29], among other applications. In all these formalisms,

- Nodes are event types, not the variables used in other causal formalisms.
- A directed edge between two nodes indicates a causal relation between event types.
- Every trajectory through the graph represents a possible narrative.
- The graph summarizes many possible narratives.

Most event types make sense only for members of some groups. Those groups "have agency" for those events, and agents can choose to participate in events for which their groups (home or affiliated) have agency. As a result, the CEG is a collection of group-specific subgraphs, though some event types support participation by multiple groups. In particular, the CEG has a single START node and a single STOP node for which all groups have agency. Figure 1 illustrates a simple CEG for a well-known children's rhyme:

Little Miss Muffet sat on a tuffet/eating her curds and whey.

Along came a spider and sat down beside her/and frightened Miss Muffet away.

Alternative paths through the CEG generate not only the canonical version of the poem, but a version that ends, "and she ate that too," another that ends, "and they began to play," and others as well.

An *event* in SCAMP occurs when agents participate in an event type over a continuous period. Multiple events of the same type can occur during a simulation run.

Time in SCAMP is an integer, representing units of domain time (hour, day, week, …) appropriate to the domain. Each event type has a transit time (how long an agent participates in the event before selecting another) and an effect time (how long the event's presence features remember the agent's participation). The modeler specifies nominal values for these variables in the *events* tab of models.xlsx based on each event's semantics. SCAMP samples the actual times for each participating agent from an exponential distribution, reflecting interarrival times of a Poisson process.

CEGs have two kinds of edges.

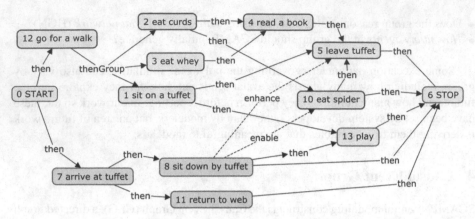

Fig. 1. CEG for Little Miss Muffet

Agency edges (solid arrows in Fig. 1) capture an agent's possible choices. These reflect the subjective choices made by the modeler. For example, in Fig. 1, the modeler has decided that eating a spider (node 10) only makes sense after eating curds (another solid food), not after eating (actually, drinking) the liquid whey, while either 2 or 3 can be followed by reading a book.

The agency edges labeled "then" connect an antecedent event to a single successor, while the "thenGroup" multiedge specifies a group of events that execute concurrently. Such a group of events behaves like a single event with the following constraints:

1. It can have at most one event type that requires geospatial movement (it makes sense for an agent to walk and chew gum, but not to walk from A to B while driving from A to C).
2. The transit time for the set of events is the maximum of the events in the group.
3. The set of event types accessible to the agent after completing the group is the union of the successor events of the event types in the group. (Thus in this case, the agent may well choose to eat the spider after eating whey, but the causal precondition is eating the curds, which will also be complete.)

Agency edges define the narrative trajectories available to agents. Every event type must fall on at least one trajectory from START to STOP, subject to two restrictions and one exception. The restrictions are:

1. Each agency edge must define a coherent snippet of narrative, so that it makes sense for an agent on the first event type to participate subsequently in the second one. As a result, any path of agency edges through the CEG is a meaningful narrative.
2. An agency edge can only join two events if the same group has agency for both.

The exception is that the agent change system described in Sect. 7 can move agents discontinuously across the CEG, providing an exit from event types that are not connected to STOP and an entrance to event types that are not connected to START.

Influence edges (dashed edges in Fig. 1) capture causal influences among event types between which agents do not move directly (for example, an impersonal Environment event type such as a drought causing People agents to move from the countryside into the city). The effect of an influence edge depends on the level of participation in the influencing event type (that is, the total presence feature on the influencing node in the CEG). An influence edge adjusts the segments in the roulette wheel corresponding to the influenced event type, based on the total presence features on the influencing event type (that is, the degree of recent participation in the influencing event).

The hard influences *prevent* and *enable* probabilistically exclude or include an event type's segment in the roulette, depending on the total presence features on the influencing event. Soft influence edges, *enhance* and *inhibit*, adjust the size of the influenced event's segment, based on the influencer's presence features.

Modelers construct the CEG, with its events, agency edges, and influence edges, using CMapTools, a concept mapping tool [11]. The *events* tab in model.xlsx records.

- The groups that have *agency* for the event type;
- The values in [−1, 1] of the *intrinsic features* in the event type's feature vector, for each group that has agency for the event type;
- The nominal values of the *transit time and effect time* for the event type;
- For event types that involve geospatial movement, a *destination* in geospace for each group that has agency in the event type;
- Whether or not the event type can be immediately *repeated*.

5 Geospatial Context

Some event types (e.g., "go to the post office") require physical movement. When an agent participates in such an event type, it drops into geospace (a hexagonal lattice) and moves through it until it reaches its destination, at which point its participation in the event ends, and it chooses another event type. The transit time for a geospatial event depends on the length of the agent's geospatial journey. Participation in an event moves an agent through time. Geospatial events also move agents through space.

Figure 2 shows successive steps in Miss Muffet's movement, starting with her initial location (1). Superimposed on the terrain map are her home (magenta, lower left), the tuffet (green, center), and the spider web (yellow, upper right). For example, event 12 "go for a walk" has a destination of the tuffet, so to complete this event, Miss Muffet must drop into geospace (3), move from her current location at home to the tuffet (4), and then return to the event node (5).

Hexagonal tiles in geospace, like events in event space, have feature vectors. Intrinsic features reflect the gradient of the underlying terrain. Presence features record the recent presence of agents of different groups. Urgency features record the proximity of the tile to the destination for each group, while the wellbeing features record the gradient of the local terrain. The transit time for an agent to move through one hex depends on the movement speed defined for its group, and the local terrain (it takes longer to cross water than to travel on land).

Modelers construct the geospatial model using the GIMP drawing program [35], which represents an image as a stack of layers. A required *heightmap* layer (the grayscale background in Fig. 2) shows the local elevation over the region of the map, while distinctive features (such as rivers, road networks, cities, and national boundaries) are distinguished by the layer in which they are represented and the colors used to depict them. The *regions* tab of model.xlsx identifies regions that can be specified as initial locations for groups and as destinations for events. For each region, it specifies.

- An *identifier* (e.g., R003) used to refer to the region in the *events* and *groups* tabs
- A *descriptive name* for the region (e.g., "rivers," "capital city")
- The name of the GIMP *layer* containing the region
- The GIMP name of the *color* used to represent the regions
- The region's *falloff*, indicating how far away it is detectable by agents in geospace (falloff = 1 means that a gradient leading to the region is defined everywhere, while 0 means that an agent must stumble across the region before knowing where it is)
- A *speed modifier* for each group, indicating how that region impacts speed of agents of that group in moving across the region.

SCAMP reads the GIMP file saved in the OpenRaster file format. Mechanisms for movement of agents through geospace guided by polyagents in SCAMP are refined from methods we demonstrated in earlier projects [18, 22].

The modeler determines for each event type whether it involves geospatial movement. In our conflict model, of 467 event types, 360 do not involve movement. In addition, while the transit time of a geospatial event is determined dynamically as the agent moves through geospace, the modeler can define a nominal transit time to be used if the geospatial processing is turned off (by a Repast parameter). Thus SCAMP readily accommodates non-geospatial scenarios.

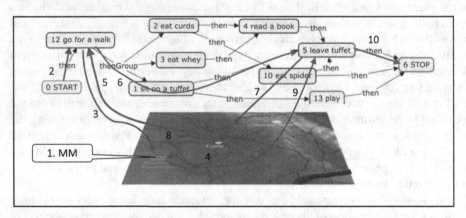

Fig. 2. Agent movement between CEG and geospace (Color figure online)

6 Hierarchical Goal Networks

Human decisions reflect not only the immediate characteristics of available alternatives, but also the actors' long-range goals. SCAMP supports a hierarchical goal network

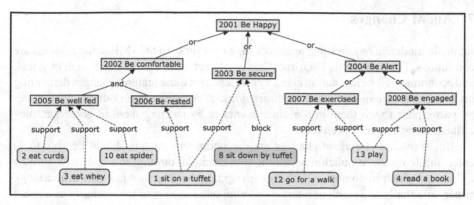

Fig. 3. HGN for Miss Muffet

(HGN) [34] for each group, capturing the group's high-level goal and its decomposition into subgoals. The lowest level subgoals are "zipped" to events in the CEG that either support or block them [20]. Figure 3 shows an HGN for Miss Muffet, zipped to events in Fig. 1. Agents do not move over the HGN as they do over the CEG and geospatial lattice, but the HGN modulates their movement in event space.

Each goal maintains two scalar variables in [0, 1]: its *satisfaction*, and its *urgency*. Satisfaction accumulates through a sigmoid, so it saturates at 1. At the root, `urgency` $= 1 -$ `satisfaction`. The root determines its satisfaction by querying its subgoals recursively. Satisfaction propagates upward through *or* relations as the maximum of the satisfaction levels of the subgoals, and through *and* relations as the minimum. The lowest-level subgoals determine their satisfaction from the presence features of events in the CEG. Once the root goal knows its satisfaction, it propagates its urgency to its subgoals. The urgency of a higher-level goal is passed directly to subgoals that support it via *and*. Subgoals joined by an *or* subtract their own urgency from that of their parent goal. This process is inspired by quality in TÆMS [10], as implemented in our earlier work [20].

Satisfaction and urgency are thus driven by agent participation (reflected in presence features) in CEG events zipped to the HGN. The presence features on CEG events determine satisfaction of leaf subgoals, while urgency on those subgoals modifies the urgency features of events zipped to them. The HGN converts agent presence on events in the CEG into the urgency of those events for the strategic objectives of each group.

An event for which one group has agency can change the satisfaction of goals of other groups, and also respond to the urgency levels in other HGNs, if it is zipped to subgoals in those HGNs. As a result, agents can modulate their decisions by the desire to advance or hinder the goals of other groups.

Domain experts capture HGNs in CMapTools. The HGNs and the zip relations can be included in the same CMap file containing the CEG. It is also possible to generate separate HGNs and capture the zips between events and leaf-level subgoals in the *zips* tab of model.xlsx.

7 Agent Changes

Realistic modeling requires that agents change over time. In SCAMP, some changes are continuous. For instance: 1) Each event has an impact on an agent's emotional, physical, and economic well-being, and an agent's preference for these features changes depending on its current state in each of these dimensions. 2) As agents meet other agents, either by participating with them in the same events or by meeting them in geospace, they influence one another's preferences.

But some realistic agent changes are discontinuous. Agents should be able to 1) enter and leave the simulation as it runs (for example, through influx of new foreign fighters, or death in combat); 2) change group membership (not just side affiliations), either voluntarily as a result of interactions with other agents, or involuntarily as a result of abduction and forced indoctrination; 3) change location discontinuously (for example, when protestors injured in a street protest are moved to a hospital); or 4) suspend and resume involvement in the scenario (for example, by being taken prisoner and then later released). The *groupChanges* tab of model.xlsx provides a powerful facility for discontinuous changes. It allows the modeler to specify.

- The event type or geospatial location that *triggers* the change, when an agent enters it;
- The *maximum number* of affected agents;
- The before-and-after *home group* of affected agents;
- The before-and-after *location* (either in event space or geospace) of affected agents;
- If the transition *depends on the presence of agents* of some group at some location, the groups and locations involved;
- The *probability* that the change will actually happen if triggered;
- *Groups that increase (promoters) or hinder (blockers)* the probability of the transition, and where they must be located to have this effect.

To enable birth and death of agents, SCAMP recognizes the pseudo-group Guf (named for the repository of souls in Jewish mysticism). An agent that changes from Guf to one of the regular groups is born at that point, while one that changes from a regular group to Guf is removed from the simulation.

To enable suspension of agents, SCAMP supports pseudo-events of the form L*nnn* (for "Limbo"). If a rule moves an agent from a CEG node to a Limbo node, the agent ceases to participate in the simulation until execution of another rule moves it from the Limbo node back to some CEG node.

8 SCAMP's Data

SCAMP uses Repast's user interface to display the total presence pheromone on each CEG node and geospatial hex and the satisfaction on each HGN goal in real time, but it also generates several logs that can be analyzed after a run and compared across different parameter settings. These include:

- *Agent state* over time, including event participation, group affiliations, physical location, preference vector, meetings with other agents, group membership and location changes, and emergent social networks
- The number and total length of agents' *pairwise meetings* on events and in geospace
- Presence pheromone *entropy* over events, by group and total, over time
- The *strength of influence edges* over time
- The *satisfaction level* at the root of each group's HGN over time.

From these logs, we can construct answers to many questions that an interviewer might ask research subjects in a real scenario. Here are some examples that we answered.

- What were you doing on a given date?
- What was the last thing you were doing before your present activity?
- What other options did you consider at that time?
- What influenced your choice of this option?
- What options are you considering next, and how would you prioritize them?
- Whom have you met recently?
- How strong is your relation to those people?
- How satisfied are you with your achievement of your objectives?
- How happy are you about your current economic, physical, psychological state?
- How sympathetic are you to a specific group (e.g., the government)?

Additional logs of internal SCAMP variables can easily be added.

The full conflict model has a CEG with 467 event types involving six groups (Fig. 4). The HGNs for these groups have a total of 77 goals and subgoals, zipped to 253 events (of which 177 are distinct). Figure 5 shows geospace, which includes four countries and their borders, numerous cities, and diverse terrain. Our forthcoming *CMOT* paper [26] reports on results generated by this model, including variations in group satisfaction as the scenario evolves, maps

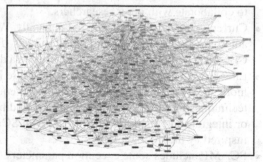

Fig. 4. CEG for conflict model. Node colors show which groups have agency for each event type.

showing the interactions of agents in geospace, and population changes over time, in addition to results of the experiments with the social science teams in the program.

9 Discussion and Next Steps

The capabilities described in this report evolved during the 30 months of the Ground Truth program, driven both by the needs of modelers to capture the social dynamics of a complex scenario and by the information requests posed by the social scientists. By the end of the program, SCAMP had matured into a robust, flexible system. Parsing the wide range of data that modelers can define externally necessarily results in a complex code base, but it is supported with thorough unit tests and commented to trace its behavior to the underlying causal metamodel of the system. Our experience with two different teams of modelers without

Fig. 5. Geospace for conflict model

programming experience shows that non-hackers can indeed construct complex models in SCAMP. The largest drawback is the large number of parameters that they must specify, though a system of defaults can reduce this considerably. The model graphs and spreadsheet can have bugs, just as code can (e.g., undefined locations, dead-ends in the CEG), but every time a model revision encountered a new bug, we added tests for it in the code, so that SCAMP itself now flags a wide range of possible model flaws.

A number of future directions for SCAMP are possible.

- Our success in representing a complex social situation in the Ground Truth program suggests that the system will be useful in providing decision-makers with planning insight in other domains. We are exploring opportunities, and welcome opportunities to collaborate with other researchers.
- Currently, models are constructed manually. We are exploring techniques that would automate the partial construction of models (for example, the basic structure of the CEG) from archival materials that describe a domain of interest.
- Like any agent-based model that can capture human cognition, SCAMP runs much more slowly (on a per-agent basis) than an equation-based model. We are exploring techniques to address this challenge, including hybrid models that either alternate or integrate an equation-based model with SCAMP, and a renormalization approach inspired by theoretical physics.
- SCAMP includes some execution parameters (e.g., pheromone deposit and evaporation rates) that in their present form are not meaningful to modelers and must be set by developers. If we can map these to variables that are psychologically and socially meaningful, we can reduce the involvement of programmers even further.

Acknowledgements. The development of SCAMP was funded by the Defense Advanced Research Projects Agency (DARPA), under Cooperative Agreement HR00111820003. The content of this paper does not necessarily reflect the position or the policy of the US Government, and no official endorsement should be inferred.

References

Papers by the author are available at https://www.abcresearch.org/abc/papers

1. Argonne National Laboratory: Repast Agent Simulation Toolkit. Argonne National Laboratory (2007). http://repast.sourceforge.net/
2. Busemeyer, J.R., Townsend, J.T.: Decision field theory: a dynamic-cognitive approach to decision making in an uncertain environment. Psychol. Rev. **100**(3), 432–459 (1993)
3. Cioffi-Revilla, C.: Introduction to Computational Social Science, 2nd edn. Springer, Cham (2017). https://doi.org/10.1007/978-1-4471-5661-1
4. Crossman, J., Bechtel, R., Parunak, H.V.D., Brueckner, S.: Integrating dynamic social networks and spatio-temporal models for risk assessment, wargaming and planning. The Network Science Workshop, West Point, NY (2009)
5. de Marchi, S.: Computational and Mathematical Modeling in the Social Sciences. Cambridge University Press, Cambridge (2005)
6. Epstein, J.M.: Generative Social Science. Princeton University Press, Princeton (2006)
7. Gilbert, N., Troitzsch, K.G.: Simulation for the Social Scientist, 2nd edn. Open University Press, Buckingham (2005)
8. Grassé, P.-P.: La reconstruction du nid et les coordinations interindividuelles chez*Bellicositermes natalensis* et*Cubitermes sp.* la théorie de la stigmergie: Essai d'interprétation du comportement des termites constructeurs. Ins. Soc. **6**, 41–84 (1959). https://doi.org/10.1007/BF02223791
9. Heuer, R.J., Jr., Pherson, R.H.: Structured Analytic Techniques for Intelligence Analysis. CQ Press, Washington, DC (2010)
10. Horling, B., et al.: The TÆMS White Paper. Multi-Agent Systems Lab, University of Massachusetts, Amherst (2004). http://mas.cs.umass.edu/pub/paper_detail.php/182
11. IHMC: IHMC CmapTools – Download, Pensacola, FL (2013). https://cmap.ihmc.us/cmaptools/
12. Kahneman, D., Tversky, A.: The simulation heuristic. In: Kahneman, D., Slovic, P., Tversky, A. (eds.) Judgment Under Uncertainty: Heuristics and Biases, pp. 201–208. Cambridge University Press, Cambridge (1982)
13. Klein, G.A.: Sources of Power: How People Make Decisions. MIT Press, Cambridge (1998)
14. Lindley, C.A.: Story and narrative structures in computer games. In: Bushoff, B. (ed.) Developing Interactive Narrative Content. High Text Verlag, München (2005)
15. Luke, S., Cioffi-Revilla, C., Panait, L., Sullivan, K., Balan, G.: MASON: a multiagent simulation environment. Simulation **81**, 517–527 (2005)
16. Mosteller, F., Nogee, P.: An experimental measurement of utility. J. Polit. Econ. **59**, 371–404 (1951)
17. Parunak, H.V.D.: A survey of environments and mechanisms for human-human stigmergy. In: Weyns, D., Parunak, H.V.D., Michel, F. (eds.) E4MAS 2005. LNCS (LNAI), vol. 3830, pp. 163–186. Springer, Heidelberg (2006). https://doi.org/10.1007/11678809_10

18. Parunak, H.V.D.: Real-time agent characterization and prediction. In: International Joint Conference on Autonomous Agents and Multi-Agent Systems (AAMAS 2007), Industrial Track, Honolulu, Hawaii, pp. 1421–1428, ACM (2007)
19. Parunak, H.V.D.: Psychology from stigmergy. In: Computational Social Science (CSS 2020), vol. (forthcoming). CSSSA, Santa Fe (2020)
20. Parunak, H.V.D., et al.: Stigmergic modeling of hierarchical task networks. In: Gennaro Tosto, H., Parunak, D. (eds.) MABS 2009. LNCS (LNAI), vol. 5683, pp. 98–109. Springer, Heidelberg (2010). https://doi.org/10.1007/978-3-642-13553-8_9
21. Parunak, H.V.D., Bisson, R., Brueckner, S.A.: Agent interaction, multiple perspectives, and swarming simulation. In: Proceedings of the International Joint Conference on Autonomous Agents and Multi-Agent Systems (AAMAS 2010), pp. 549–556. IFAAMAS (2010)
22. Parunak, H.V.D., Brueckner, S.: Synthetic pheromones for distributed motion control. In: Proceedings of DARPA-JFACC Technical Symposium on Advances in Enterprise Control, DARPA (1999)
23. Parunak, H.V.D., Brueckner, S.: Concurrent modeling of alternative worlds with polyagents. In: Antunes, L., Takadama, K. (eds.) MABS 2006. LNCS (LNAI), vol. 4442, pp. 128–141. Springer, Heidelberg (2007). https://doi.org/10.1007/978-3-540-76539-4_10
24. Parunak, H.V.D., Brueckner, S., Downs, E.A., Sappelsa, L.: Swarming estimation of realistic mental models. In: Giardini, F., Amblard, F. (eds.) MABS 2012. LNCS (LNAI), vol. 7838, pp. 43–55. Springer, Heidelberg (2013). https://doi.org/10.1007/978-3-642-38859-0_4
25. Parunak, H.V.D., Brueckner, S.A.: Engineering swarming systems. In: Bergenti, F., Gleizes, M.-P., Zambonelli, F. (eds.) Methodologies and Software Engineering for Agent Systems, pp. 341–376. Kluwer (2004)
26. Parunak, H.V.D., Greanya, J., Morell, J.A., Nadella, S., Sappelsa, L.: SCAMP's stigmergic model of social conflict. Comput. Math. Organ. Theory (2021). https://doi.org/10.1007/s10588-021-09347-8
27. Pynadath, D.V., et al.: Disaster World: Decision-theoretic agents for simulating population responses to hurricanes. Comput. Math. Organ. Theory (2021). (forthcoming)
28. Rager, S., Leung, A., Pinegar, S., Mangels, J., Poole, M.S., Contractor, N.: Groups, governance, and greed: the ACCESS world model. Comput. Math. Organ. Theory. (2021). https://doi.org/10.1007/s10588-021-09352-x
29. Richards, W., Finlayson, M.A., Winston, P.H.: Advancing computational models of narrative. MIT-CSAIL-TR-2009–063, MIT CSAIL, Cambridge (2009)
30. Sappelsa, L., Parunak, H.V.D., Brueckner, S.: The generic narrative space model as an intelligence analysis tool. Am. Intell. J. **31**(2), 69–78 (2014)
31. Savage, E.L., Schruben, L.W., Yücesan, E.: On the generality of event-graph models. INFORMS J. Comput. **17**(1), 3–9 (2005)
32. Shapiro, B.P., van den Broek, P., Fletcher, C.R.: Using story-based causal diagrams to analyze disagreements about complex events. Discourse Process. **20**(1), 51–77 (1995)
33. Sheyner, O.M.: Scenario graphs and attack graphs. Thesis at Carnegie Mellon University, Department of Computer Science Department (2004)
34. Shivashankar, V.: Hierarchical goal networks: formalisms and algorithms for planning and acting. Thesis at University of Maryland, Department of Computer Science (2015)
35. Sullivan, K., Coletti, M., Luke, S.: GeoMASON: Geospatial support for MASON. George Mason University, Fairfax (2010). https://www.researchgate.net/publication/235955903_GeoMason_Geospatial_Support_for_MASON
36. Züfle, A., et al.: Urban life: a model of people and places. Comput. Math. Organ. Theory (2021). https://doi.org/10.1007/s10588-021-09348-7

Using Causal Discovery to Design Agent-Based Models

Stef Janssen, Alexei Sharpanskykh, and S. Sahand Mohammadi Ziabari(✉)

Delft University of Technology, Delft, The Netherlands
{s.a.m.janssen,O.A.Sharpanskykh,s.s.mohammadiziabari}@tudelft.nl

Abstract. Designing agent-based models is a difficult task. Some guidelines exist to aid modelers in designing their models, but they generally do not include specific details on how the behavior of agents can be defined. This paper therefore proposes the AbCDe methodology, which uses causal discovery algorithms to specify agent behavior. The methodology combines important expert insights with causal graphs generated by causal discovery algorithms based on real-world data. This causal graph represents the causal structure among agent-related variables, which is then translated to behavioral properties in the agent-based model. To demonstrate the AbCDe methodology, it is applied to a case study in the airport security domain. In this case study, we explore a new concept of operations, using a service lane, to improve the efficiency of the security checkpoint. Results show that the models generated with the AbCDe methodology have a closer resemblance with the validation data than a model defined by experts alone.

Keywords: Causal discovery · Agent-based modelling · Airport security

1 Introduction

Agent-based models have shown to be useful in a variety of areas, ranging from urban planning to ecology and security [1]. Some guidelines exist to aid (new) modelers in their model development, and they share some similarities [2, 3]. Most of these guidelines are quite high-level, and do not go beyond a description of which elements have to be defined. A notable exception is the 'overview, design concepts, and details'(ODD) protocol, which has been used widely in literature [4, 5]. It provides a detailed set of steps, along with guidelines, to design agent-based models and individual-based models. The ODD protocol has evolved over time. Firstly, it was observed that there was a lack of decision-making features in the ODD protocol; the protocol did not support the definition of human behavior that contains decisions, adaptation, and learning. This leads to a revised version of ODD, the ODD+D (Decision) protocol [6]. However, the lack of properly incorporating data in the empirical models was an important issue with ODD+D. Therefore, ODD+2D (ODD + Decision + Data) [7] was introduced to solve this lacking. While this method added structure to incorporating data in agent-based models, the creativity of the modeler remains a central component. With more and more data becoming available over the last decades, methods to interpret and understand this

© Springer Nature Switzerland AG 2022
K. H. Van Dam and N. Verstaevel (Eds.): MABS 2021, LNAI 13128, pp. 15–28, 2022.
https://doi.org/10.1007/978-3-030-94548-0_2

data became better as well. Numerous methods to find these patterns and relationships exist, of which regression, neural networks, and clustering are three examples [8]. A particularly promising method to find relationships between variables is that of causal inference [9]. These causal graphs show the causal relationships between variables and identify structure in the dataset. In this work, we propose the Agent-based Causal discovery Design methodology (AbCDe), a novel methodology that aids the development of agent-based models using causal discovery.

This paper is structured as follows. In Sect. 2, related work in the areas of designing agent-based models and causal discovery are reviewed. Then, the AbCDe methodology as proposed in this work is outlined in Sect. 3. The case study is outlined in Sect. 4. Finally, the work is concluded in Sect. 5.

2 Related Work

Designing agent-based models is a complex task. An agent-based model has three main components: agents, environment, and interactions. Klugl and Bazzan [3] state that agent-based models are an appropriate choice when a system meets a set of six different conditions. These conditions for instance include the existence of local interactions and heterogeneity in states and behavioral rules. However, the work lacks a proper method to describe how agents can be defined. It is recognized by the community that a uniform framework or methodology for designing agent-based models is lacking [2]. To design a conceptual model or model a software program, there are two popular standards, the Unified Modeling Language (UML) and the 'overview, design concepts, and details' (ODD). UML is used to represent different classes in object-oriented programming and the connection between them [29].

The ODD protocol has been used widely in literature [4, 5]. While the ODD protocol contains detailed steps to design agent-based models, no insights on how to design the behavioral properties of agents are provided. With the right dataset, data-driven methods may be useful in specifying the behavioral properties of agents. These methods find relationships between variables in a dataset, which could determine relationships between actions of agents and the outcomes in the environment. The successor of the ODD protocol, the ODD+2D protocol, consists of two major steps: 1) data preprocessing, and 2) linking data [7]. The link between data components and agent-based modeling elements in ODD+2D consists of three main sections: 1) overview, 2) design concepts, and 3) details.

While the ODD+2D adds structure to incorporating data in agent-based models, it remains up to the modeler how to use this data. This topic was explored in detail in [10]. In that work, behavioral properties of agents are learned from data by applying machine learning techniques, such as support vector machines. While these more traditional machine learning techniques are effective tools to learn behavioral properties, they do not reveal the structure of relationships between variables related to agents. A particularly promising method to reveal this structure is that of causal discovery.

Traditionally, mathematical analysis is used to find relationships between variables. However, a relationship between two variables does not necessarily mean that one variable causes the other. In the field of causality, causal relationships between variables are found by using causal graphs [9, 11]. Causal graphs can be created using two main methods. In the first method, experts use their knowledge to manually create a graph, while in the second method causal graphs are generated using data. An example of manually creating a causal graph using expert knowledge is discussed in [12]. The second method, which is also applied in this work, uses causal discovery algorithms. These algorithms can broadly be categorized into two categories: score-based methods [13] and constraint-based methods [14]. Score-based methods assign a score to a set of potential graphs and then select the graph with the highest score. Constraint-based methods define constraints on causal graphs based on statistical independence of variables. In the constraint-based category, the PC algorithm [16] is very popular, while in the score-based category, the GES algorithm [22] is frequently used in literature.

The most extensive work in the interaction of agent-based modelling and causality is by Casini and Manzo [15], who provide a technical report on the differences and similarities of agent-based modeling and causality. However, their work only focuses on analyzing agent-based models, and not on designing them. Then, Kvassay et al. [16] provide a method, based on causal partitioning, to analyze causal relationships relating to emergence in agent-based models. This work also focuses on analyzing agent-based model behavior and does not cover designing them either. Guerini and Moneta [17] cover the topic of agent-based model validation. They estimate time-series of economic models using structural vector autoregressive (SVAR) models. Using causal discovery algorithms, they generate two SVAR models: one based on results generated by the designed agent-based model, and the other based on actual data. When the two SVAR models are similar enough, the agent-based model is considered validated. This work only covers agent-based model validation and does not cover designing agent-based models. Finally, Janssen et al. [18] developed a methodology that uses causal discovery algorithms to analyze emergent behavior in agent-based models. They show that causal graphs can he experts to interpret and identify emergent behavior in agent-based models. To overcome the lack of work using causal discovery algorithms to design agent-based models, we introduce the AbCDe methodology below

3 Methodology

This section outlines the novel Agent-based Causal discovery Design methodology, called AbCDe, which is used to design agent-based models with the aid of causal discovery algorithms. The methodology includes all aspects needed to design agent-based models, and uses causal discovery algorithms in one of its steps.

The methodology exploits the ever-growing availability of data to design agent-based models. Using data on the behavior of agents, a causal graph is generated using causal discovery algorithms. This graph is then, with the aid of experts, translated into behavioral properties of agents. These properties ultimately determine the dynamics of the model, leading to insights into the phenomenon that is modeled. Causal discovery algorithms provide a more structured method to develop agent-based models than relying on experts alone. However, experts are still needed in many aspects of the methodology to ensure that the model is of high quality. This combination of causal discovery algorithms and experts can lead to better models than models created by experts alone.

The AbCDe methodology contains five steps, which are graphically outlined in Fig. 1. As with many modelling studies, in the first step of AbCDe, the purpose of the model is specified, research questions are formulated and hypothesis are formulated. Then, in the second step of the methodology the scope of the model is determined. This specifies what elements will be included in the model and what will not be included. Once the scope is clarified, a conceptual model is formalized. The conceptual model forms the basis for the remainder of the methodology. In this model, agents are identified first. An agent, in this work, is defined as an entity that perceives its environment through sensors and acts upon that environment through effectors [19]. In this step, we specifically focus on the identification of the agents to be modeled, along with their characteristics and the behavior that they can exhibit. Only the higher-level behavior that the agent exhibits is specified (i.e., what the agent can do); the full specification of the behavior (i.e., how the agent does it) will be done in step 4.

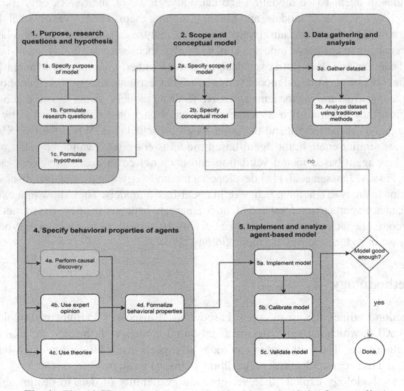

Fig. 1. The AbCDe methodology as used in this work. (Color figure online)

After identifying the agents and specifying the environment, data is collected about the behavior and characteristics of the agents in the model in step 3. This data is obtained by observing agents, their actions, and the consequences of these actions in the real world. This will later be used to specify behavioral properties of agents. Depending on what is modeled, different types of data can be collected. The collected data that will be used to generate behavioral properties is always on the agent-level (and not population-level), and should therefore contain as much detail about the characteristics of the agent (as defined in the conceptual model of the previous step), its behavior and the results of this behavior. Data is therefore in the form of characteristics of agents, actions performed by agents, effects of agent actions on the environment and effects of agent actions on other agents. The collected data is then analyzed following standard data analysis techniques, such as clustering, regression, and statistical tests. This provides early insights into the behavior of agents and will be useful for the next step of the methodology.

In step 4, behavioral properties are formalized based on two sources: causal discovery and expert input. This step includes the unique contribution of this paper in which causal discovery is used to define behavioral properties (green box of Fig. 1). Both causal discovery and expert input are discussed in detail below, combined with a discussion on how to translate them into behavioral properties.

Causal discovery algorithms (see also Sect. 2) are used to infer a causal structure from the gathered data of step 3. Before applying the algorithm, the data has to be preprocessed. This preprocessing is done to ensure that only individual agent behavior is found, and not collective emergent effects. These emergent effects should be part of the model, but not explicitly coded into the behavior of agents. It should emerge from the behavior and interaction of agents in the model (see also the work of Janssen et al. [18]).

Furthermore, the dataset has to be organized such that a single causal graph for a single agent is produced. Data of other agents can be included in the dataset for the agent under consideration, so that observable behavior, such as communication and alterations of the environment, can be found by the causal discovery algorithms as well.

After preprocessing, a causal discovery algorithm is applied to the dataset, leading to a causal graph representing the behavior of an agent in the model. The generated graphs relate characteristics of agents to exhibition of their behavior by means of including an arrow between them. Results of the behavior of other agents or properties of environmental objects are included in the graph following the same standard.

After generating the causal graphs, an expert provides input for two purposes. While causal discovery is useful, applying it still requires some level of expert knowledge [23]. The expert checks the graph that was generated for inconsistencies with their knowledge and the original data analysis that was performed in the previous step. These inconsistencies are then fixed in the graph. Second, the expert provides additional insights based on theories from literature or their experience. These insights can be used to compensate for missing data in the dataset, and provide another means to specify behavioral properties in the next step. After obtaining both the causal graph and the input of experts, the behavioral properties are specified. These properties can be obtained from the graph (enhanced by the expert) by selecting a variable to be used as a behavioral property and using its parents as building blocks to specify the behavior.

Finally, in step 5, the defined model is implemented, calibrated, and validated. When the model sufficiently resembles validation data, the AbCDe methodology is finished. When this is not the case, the methodology returns to step 2.

4 Case Study

We apply the AbCDe methodology to a case study in the field of airport security. In airport terminals, the security checkpoint is the most important bottleneck for passengers (leading to unwanted waiting time) and an important source of costs for airport management. As airport passenger numbers are projected to increase in the future, security checkpoints have to be operated efficiently. In this case study, we explore a new concept of operations, using a service lane, to improve the efficiency of the security checkpoint. Service lanes process passengers that are expected to be slow, and the other open lanes (defined as normal lanes) process the remaining passengers. A standard lane is a lane in which no experiment took place, and all passengers are processed. This concept of operations is projected to improve the overall throughput of the system, as faster passengers do not have to wait for slower passengers in front of them. Slow passengers also receive extra help from experienced security officers, potentially increasing the throughput as well.

We design an agent-based model following the AbCDe methodology to determine the effects of implementing a service lane on the throughput of the security checkpoint, as compared to a standard setup.

The purpose of the model is to determine the effects of implementing a service lane on the throughput of the security checkpoint, as compared to a standard setup. The scope of this experiment is to find passengers behavioral traits in the collect and drop section at the security checkpoint in the airport, while disregarding cognitive behavior of the passengers. Now that the scope of the model is clarified, we specify the conceptual model (step 2 of AbCDe). This conceptual model is specified in more detail in a technical report [28], but the most important elements are provided below. We identify the environmental objects that are modeled first. These are outlined below.

- **Luggage.** Luggage is owned by a passenger and has a specific threat level. This is a real value between 0 and 1.
- **Box.** Object in which luggage is dropped. Luggage can be dropped into multiple boxes.
- **Walk-through metal detector (WTMD).** Randomly specifies passengers that require an explosive trace detection (ETD) test or patdown.
- **Flight.** Abstract concept that has an associated flight time. Passengers are associated with exactly one flight.
- **Queue separator.** Physical objects that are used to form queue areas for passengers.

Now that the environment of the model is specified, we specify the agents of the model.

- **Passenger.** Agent that is associated with a flight, moves through the security checkpoint.
- **X-ray operator.** Uses the X-ray sensor to determine if luggage needs an extra check, and communicates this with the luggage check operator.
- **Luggage check operator.** Checks luggage when requested by the X-ray operator.
- **Patdown operator.** Performs patdowns and ETD checks.

We collected data of passengers moving through the security checkpoint at Rotterdam The Hague Airport [26] (step 3 of AbCDe). Data for a total of 2277 passengers, flying to 16 different destinations was gathered. Three types of lanes were considered: standard, normal and service lanes. Data for standard lanes were gathered between 23 February 2018 and 17 April 2018, while data for normal and service lanes were collected on the experimental days: 17 December 2018 and 18 December 2018. A service lane was used to process passengers that are expected to be slow, while the normal lanes processed the other passengers. As mentioned in earlier, the scope of this paper is based on the generation of behavioral properties on the drop and collect behavior of passengers. We use the data of the standard lanes to generate the behavioral properties of the agent, while we use data of the service lane experiment to validate the models.

To generate the graphs, we combine the score-based GES [22] algorithm and the constraint-based PC algorithm [16], following the work of Janssen et al. [18] (see also Sect. 2). We use the following variables from the dataset to generate the graph for the characteristics model: *drop*, *collect* (the time a passenger takes to drop/collect luggage on/from the belt), *boxes* (the number of boxes the passenger uses at the security checkpoint), *type* (the type of passenger, see Table 2 and 3), and *group size* (the size of the group the passenger travels with, see Table 2). These variables are a combination of the characteristics of the agent, and the two behavioral properties that we are interested in (*drop* and *collect*) and are used to generate the causal graph that we will refer to as the characteristics model.

The same variables are used for a causal model that we define as the extended model. However, the following variables are additionally used in the extended model: $drop_p$ (the drop time of the previous passenger in line), $wait\ I_p$ (the time the previous passenger waited between dropping luggage and going through the WTMD), $boxes_p$, $type_p$, and $group\ size_p$ (the boxes, type, and group size of the previous passenger respectively). It is important to note that these consist of the observable behavior and characteristics (i.e. observable by the passenger) of the passenger in front of the passenger for which the behavioral properties are defined.

Figure 2a and Fig. 3a show the graphs that were generated by the causal discovery algorithm for the characteristics model and the extended model respectively. Based on expert insights, these graphs are translated to their final versions, as shown in Fig. 2b and Fig. 3b. This procedure of using expert insight to update the graphs is aided by the work of Shrier and Platt [12].

The graph generated for the characteristics model shows that both *ETD* (the time the passenger receives an Explosive Trace Detection) and *patdown* (the time the passenger receives a patdown) are not connected to any other variable in the graph. That means that these are independent variables that will be generated in the model independently as well. Both *boxes* and *type* show a causal relationship with both drop and collect. This implies that these characteristics combined are of influence on the speed in which passengers drop and collect luggage. The generated graph additionally shows that boxes is caused by both drop and collect. Based on expert advice, we assume this link to be unidirectional in the direction of drop and collect. Finally, the size of the group influences *collect*, but not *drop*. In a security checkpoint, passengers traveling in groups often wait for each other to finish collecting their luggage. In this way, they can continue their journey to the gate together. This is not the case for dropping luggage, as passengers can only pass through the WTMD individually.

The extended model is based on a generated graph that contains five more variables and is therefore more complex. This shows that some variables related to the previous passengers are closely related to the same variables of the passenger under consideration. To allow for a fair comparison between the two models, we assume that both the group size and the type of agent are independently generated. The arrows between variables show the causalities between them.

To this end, we remove the links $group_p \leftrightarrow group$, $type_p \leftrightarrow etd$, $type_{ep} \leftrightarrow type$ and $drop_p \longrightarrow group$. Another important factor that we use to correct the graph, is the assumption that the passenger under consideration cannot influence the characteristics or behavior of the passenger that is next in line.

(a) The generated graph for the char. model.   (b)The expert-based corrected graph for the char. model.

Fig. 2. The generated graph for the characteristics model, along with the expert-based corrections. Gray variables are characteristics of passengers, while white variables are observable behaviors.

The links $drop \longrightarrow drop_p$, $boxes \longrightarrow boxes_p$ and $type \longrightarrow boxes_p$ are therefore removed. Finally, we reverse the direction of the arrow $drop \longrightarrow boxes$ to correct the direction of causality.

Now that the graphs are complete, we transform them into agent behavior (step 4d of the AbCDe methodology). This is done by fitting distributions of a variable using its parent variables in the causal graph. For the characteristics model (Fig. 2b), we generate conditional random distributions for the time the passenger takes to drop luggage (based on *boxes* and *type*), and collect luggage (additionally based on the *group size*). To fit these distributions, we use data of all passengers in the calibration set that possess the right characteristics. Equations 1–2 below show the *drop* and *collect* distributions for a *business* passenger traveling alone with one box worth of luggage.

$$drop = GeneralizedExtremeValueDistribution(43.95, 19.81, -0.07) \quad (1)$$

$$collect = NormalDistribution(36.12, 20.93) \quad (2)$$

where the Normal distribution is parameterized by its mean (first param.) and standard deviation (second param.), and the Generalized Extreme Value distribution is parameterized by its location (1st param.), scale (2nd param.) and shape (3rd param.).

A similar procedure as above is followed for the extended model. However, the parent variables that specify the drop and collect distribution are continuous, as compared to discrete and categorical variables in the characteristics model. We therefore use a method to fit a generalized linear model [25], based on maximum likelihood estimation (MLE), for the drop and collect distributions. We use the Poisson distribution as a basis for both the *drop* and *collect* variables, and a linear combination of their respective parent variables to specify the parameter λ of the Poisson distribution. Equations 3–6 show the distributions for *drop* and *collect*.

$$\lambda_1 = 3.30 + 0.24 \times boxes + 0.009 \times drop_p - 0.001 \times (boxes \times drop_p) \quad (3)$$

$$drop_p = PoissonDistribution(exp \, \lambda_1) \quad (4)$$

$$\lambda_2 = 3.86 + 0.006 \times drop - 0.002 \times waitI_p - 2.18e^{-5} \times (drop \times waitI_p) \quad (5)$$

$$collect = PoissonDistribution(exp \, \lambda_2) \quad (6)$$

The *boxes* parameter is based on the passenger *type*, the number of boxes that the previous passenger used (*boxesp*) and the time between dropping luggage and going through the WTMD of the previous passenger (*waitIp*). When collecting data, we observed that passengers will take longer to drop their luggage if they cannot continue to the WTMD yet. For instance, they realize they have their belts still on and use an extra box to put that in, or take off their shoes and put that in a new box. This may explain the relationship between the number of boxes and these parameters.

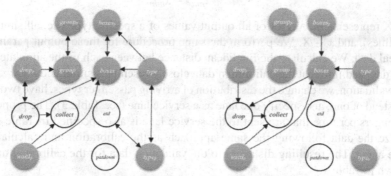

(a) The generated graph for the extended model. (b) The corrected graph for the extended model.

Fig. 3. The generated graph for the extended model, along with the expert-based corrections.

We follow a generalized linear modeling approach to specify the boxes distribution in the extended model as well. However, as *type* is a categorical variable, we specify a distribution for each passenger type individually. Equations 7–8 show the distribution for the business passenger; other passenger types are defined similarly.

$$\lambda_3 = 0.9 - 0.03 \times boxes_p - 0.01 \times waitI_p + 0.003 \times (boxes_p \times waitI_p) \qquad (7)$$

$$drop = PoissonDistribution(exp \, \lambda_3) \qquad (8)$$

We have implemented these two models in the AATOM simulator, an agent-based airport terminal operations simulator [25], as well as a model based on expert-input alone. For calibration, we focus our analysis on a setup with a single standard lane open. For validation, we focus the analysis on a single service lane and a single normal lane open. We calibrated the model with the data that was collected for the nine standard lanes. All important parameters, their descriptions, and their calibrated values can be found in Tables 1, 2 and 3. We ran a total of N = 1,000 simulations for all three models, and extracted the following four output values for each simulation run: *wait I time*, *wait II time* (time between WTMD passage and collecting luggage of passengers), *throughput* (number of passengers processed per hour) and *occupation* (mean number of passengers in the security checkpoint). We perform linear normalization for each of these output values, using the following functions.

$$\sigma = sd(X) \qquad (9)$$

$$x_{min} = mean(X) - 2\sigma \qquad (10)$$

$$x_{max} = mean(X) + 2\sigma \qquad (11)$$

$$x_{norm} = \frac{x - x_{min}}{x_{max} - x_{min}} \qquad (12)$$

Where X represents the vector of all output values of a specific type (i.e. all simulated *wait I* times), and $x \in X$. We perform the same procedure for these output parameters in the real data. We calculate the Euclidean distance between each of the simulated and the real data and find that the calibration data closely resembles simulated data.

For validation, we change the distribution of arriving passenger types, have two lanes open instead of one, and specify one lane as a service lane (see Table 3). The proportion of passengers per type that are sent to the service lane is also specified in Table 3. We normalize the data following the same approach as the calibration and calculate the distance again. The resulting distances to the validation data for the calibrated models are shown in Table 4.

Table 1. The calibrated parameters of the model (simplified table).

Parameter	Description	Calibrated value
Passenger		
desiredSpeed	The desired speed (in m/s) that the passenger moves through the checkpoint	Calibrated based on the data that was collected for the nine standard lanes
groupSize	The size of the group the passenger travels with	Based on groupSizeDistribution (Table 2)
Operator		
WTMDCheckDistribution	The distribution of patdown times	GeneralizedExtremeValueMathDistribution (19.19, 9.35, −0.01);
Flight		
arrivalDistribution	The distribution in which passengers arrive	20% (first half hour), 60% (second), 20% (third), 0% (last) based on the expert knowledge at the airport
Passenger distribution		
passengerTypeDistribution	The distribution of passenger types in the population	Table 3
groupSizeDistribution	The distribution of group sizes in the population	Table 2
serviceLaneDistribution	The proportion of passengers per type that will be directed to the service lane	Table 3

Results show that the extended model has the lowest distance to validation data. It is followed by the expert model and finally the characteristics model. These results indicate that building a model with our methodology can improve the accuracy of the models over models developed by experts alone. While more work is needed to show the (dis)advantages of the methodology, these initial results are promising.

Table 2. The distribution of group sizes for the different passenger types.

	Group size 1	Group size 2	Group size 3
Business	0.75	0.16	0.09
Senior	0.12	0.67	0.21
Young	0.02	0.15	0.83
Family	0.33	0.52	0.27
PRM	0.16	0.58	0.26
Regular	0.34	0.50	0.16

Table 3. The proportion of passengers.

	Calibration	Validation	Service lane
Business	0.15	0.17	0.21
Senior	0.17	0.23	0.60
Young	0.15	0.13	0.41
Family	0.11	0.07	0.76
PRM	0.012	0.004	1.00
Regular	0.41	0.37	0.51

Table 4. The calibrated models along with their distances to the validation data.

Model	desiredSpeed	Distance
Expert	1.4	3.6071
Characteristics	1.4	3.6486
Extended	1.5	3.4862

5   Discussion and Conclusion

Causal discovery algorithms translate data into a directed causal graph that reveals the causal structure among variables. In this paper, we investigated how these algorithms can be incorporated in the design process of agent-based models. We proposed an agent-based model-design methodology, called AbCDe, that uses causal discovery algorithms and the growing availability of data to specify behavioral properties. This methodology combines traditional expert-based model design techniques with causal graphs to design better models. We applied the methodology to a case study in the airport domain. The models that were generated with the AbCDe methodology show closer resemblance to validation data than an existing expert-based model. Future work can also focus on developing dedicated causal discovery algorithms for agent-based model development, instead of adapting existing algorithms for that purpose.

An important issue that occurred during the generation of causal graphs is that different algorithms and parameters produce quite diverse causal graphs. By integrating the PC algorithm with the GES algorithm, this problem is partially addressed, but certainly not solved. Further developments in the field of causality will address this problem.

A major advantage of our methodology is that it provides modelers with a toolbox to design agent-based models. In cases where agent-specific data can be gathered, such as our example of airport security checkpoint, our methodology can impact the final quality of the developed model.

References

1. Janssen, S., Sharpanskykh, A., Curran, R.: Agent-based modelling and analysis of security and efficiency in airport terminals. Transp. Res. Part C Emerg. Technol. **100**, 142–160 (2019)
2. Klugl, F., Oechslein, C., Puppe, F., Dornhaus, A., et al.: Multi-agent modelling in comparison to standard modelling. Simul. News Europe **40**, 3–9 (2004)
3. Klugl, F., Bazzan, A.L.: Agent-based modeling and simulation. AI Mag. **33**(3), 29 (2012)
4. Grimm, V., et al.: A standard protocol for describing individual based and agent-based models. Ecol. Model. **198**(1–2), 115–126 (2006)
5. Grimm, V., Berger, U., DeAngelis, D.L., Polhill, J.G., Giske, J., Railsback, S.F.: The odd protocol: a review and first update. Ecol. Model. **221**(23), 2760–2768 (2010)
6. Muller, B., et al.: Describing human decisions in agent-base models- odd + D, an extension of the odd protocol. Environ. Model. Softw. **48**, 37–48 (2013)
7. Laatabi, A., Marilleau, N., Nguyen-Huu, T., Hbid, H., Babram, M.A.: Odd+2D: an odd based protocol for mapping data to empirical ABMs. J. Artif. Soc. Soc. Simul. **21**(2), 9 (2018)
8. Witten, I.H., Frank, E., Hall, M.A., Pal, C.J.: Data Mining: Practical Machine Learning Tools and Techniques. Morgan Kaufmann, San Francisco (2016)
9. Pearl, J.: Causality. Cambridge University Press, New York (2009)
10. Kavak, H., Padilla, J.J., Lynch, C.J., Diallo, S.Y.: Big data, agents, and machine learning: towards a data-driven agent-based modeling approach. In: Proceedings of the Annual Simulation Symposium, p. 12. Society for Computer Simulation International (2018)
11. Peters, J., Janzing, D., Scholkopf, B.: Elements of Causal Inference: Foundations and Learning Algorithms. MIT press, Cambridge (2017)
12. Shrier, I., Platt, R.W.: Reducing bias through directed acyclic graphs. BMC Med. Res. Methodol. **8**(1), 70 (2008)
13. Magliacane, S., Claassen, T., Mooij, J.M.: Ancestral causal inference. In: Advances in Neural Information Processing Systems, pp. 4466–4474 (2016)
14. Colombo, D., Maathuis, M.H., Kalisch, M., Richardson, T.S.: Learning high-dimensional directed acyclic graphs with latent and selection variables. Ann. Stat. **40**, 294–321 (2012)
15. Casini, L., Manzo, G.: Agent-based models and causality: a methodological appraisal, Linkoping University, Department of Management and Engineering, The Institute for Analytical Sociology, The IAS Working Paper Series 2016:7
16. Kvassay, M., Krammer, P., Hluchý, L., Schneider, B.: Causal analysis of an agent-based model of human behaviour. In: Complexity 2017, pp. 1–18 (2017). https://doi.org/10.1155/2017/8381954
17. Guerini, M., Moneta, A.: A method for agent-based models validation. J. Econ. Dyn. Control **82**, 125–141 (2017)
18. Janssen, S., Sharpanskykh, A., Curran, R., Langendoen, K.: Using causal discovery to analyze emergence in agent-based models. Simul. Model. Pract. Theory **96**, 101940 (2019)
19. Russell, S.J., Norvig, P.: Artificial Intelligence: A Modern Approach. Pearson Education Limited, New Delhi (2016)
20. Hauser, A., Buhlmann, P.: Characterization and greedy learning of interventional Markov equivalence classes of directed acyclic graphs. J. Mach. Learn. Res. **13**, 2409–2464 (2012)
21. Spirtes, P., Zhang, K.: Causal discovery and inference: concepts and recent methodological advances. Appl. Inform. **3**, 3 (2016)
22. Tisue, S., Wilensky, U.: NetLogo: a simple environment for modeling complexity. In: International Conference on Complex Systems, Boston, MA, vol. 21, pp. 16–21 (2004)
23. Luke, S., Cioffi-Revilla, C., Panait, L., Sullivan, K., Balan, G.: MASON: a multiagent simulation environment. Simulation **81**(7), 517–527 (2005)

24. North, M.J., et al.: Complex adaptive systems modeling with repast symphony. Complex Adapt. Syst. Model. **1**, 1–26 (2013)
25. Janssen, S., Sharpanskykh, A., Curran, R., Langendoen, K.: AATOM: an agent-based airport terminal operations model simulator. In: Proceedings of the 51st Computer Simulation Conference, SummerSim 2019, Berlin, Germany, 22–14 July 2019
26. Janssen, S., van der Sommen, R., Dilweg, A., Sharpanskykh, A.: Data-driven analysis of airport security checkpoint operations. Aerospace **7**(6), 69 (2020)
27. Daniel, W.W.: Kolmogorov-smirnov one-sample test. Appl. Nonparametr. Stat. **2** (1990)
28. Nelder, D.J.A., Wedderburn, R.W.: Generalized linear models. J. Royal Stat. Soc. Ser. A (General) **135**(3), 370–384 (1972)
29. Bersini, H.: UML for ABM. J. Artif. Soc. Soc. Simul. **15**(1), 9 (2012). http://jasss.soc.surrey.ac.uk/15/1/9.html

Multi-level Adaptation of Distributed Decision-Making Agents in Complex Task Environments

Darío Blanco-Fernández[✉][ID], Stephan Leitner[ID], and Alexandra Rausch[ID]

University of Klagenfurt, 9020 Klagenfurt, Austria
{dario.blanco,stephan.leitner,alexandra.rausch}@aau.at

Abstract. To solve complex tasks, individuals often autonomously organize in teams. Examples of complex tasks include disaster relief rescue operations or project development in consulting. The teams that work on such tasks are adaptive at multiple levels: First, by autonomously choosing the individuals that jointly perform a specific task, the team itself adapts to the complex task at hand, whereby the composition of teams might change over time. We refer to this process as self-organization. Second, the members of a team adapt to the complex task environment by learning. There is, however, a lack of extensive research on multi-level adaptation processes that consider self-organization and individual learning as simultaneous processes in the field of Managerial Science. We introduce an agent-based model based on the *NK*-framework to study the effects of simultaneous multi-level adaptation on a team's performance. We implement the multi-level adaptation process by a second-price auction mechanism for self-organization at the team level. Adaptation at the individual level follows an autonomous learning mechanism. Our preliminary results suggest that, depending on the task's complexity, different configurations of individual and collective adaptation can be associated with higher overall task performance. Low complex tasks favour high individual and collective adaptation, while moderate individual and collective adaptation is associated with better performance in case of moderately complex tasks. For highly complex tasks, the results suggest that collective adaptation is harmful to performance.

Keywords: Adaptation · Complex tasks · Agent-based modeling

1 Introduction

Disaster relief rescue operations [17], or project development in consulting firms [3] are examples of tasks that can be characterized as *complex tasks*. These and many other complex tasks have two characteristics in common: (i) A single individual alone usually cannot find a solution to complex tasks, as the capabilities required to solve them are greater in scope than the ones a single individual possesses [5], and (ii) complex tasks are formed by various subtasks that are interdependent [7].

© Springer Nature Switzerland AG 2022
K. H. Van Dam and N. Verstaevel (Eds.): MABS 2021, LNAI 13128, pp. 29–41, 2022.
https://doi.org/10.1007/978-3-030-94548-0_3

Individuals are required to coordinate and share their capabilities to solve complex tasks. We refer to this process as *team* formation [16]. Team formation often occurs autonomously, i.e., agents form teams by themselves and without the direct intervention of a central planner or decision-maker [12]. Giving individuals the possibility to autonomously organize themselves into teams can, for example, be found in firms that engage in consulting work [3], or professional service firms that are organized as a partnership (such as law or accounting firms) [6].

Teams that engage in complex problem solving might be dynamic in their composition, as they change by adapting to the particular task they face [3]. Adaptation at the team level is referred to as *collective adaptation*. However, not only the team as a collective adapts, but also the individual agents (who make up a team) adapt by learning [3] (i.e., agents go through a process of *individual adaptation*). Thus, a team that is formed to solve a complex task goes through a continuous *multi-level* adaptation process. By successfully adapting at the individual and collective level to a particular complex task, the team's performance is expected to improve [4].

Previous research indicates that individual agents adapt their capabilities to the task requirements by learning about the task they face [2], becoming more capable of performing the task, and thus improving the overall *task performance* [4]. To model individual adaptation, we consider a learning approach that can be characterized as *autonomous*. Learning is autonomous when it occurs without any interaction between agents or the intervention of a central agent who can take the role of a supervisor or a teacher. Similar approaches to autonomous learning can be found in [10, 11].

Individual agents are endowed with the ability to adapt and to autonomously form teams. Research in economics and Managerial Science often assumes that agents are homogeneous (i.e., following the concept of the *representative agent*) [1]. This assumption implies that any collective (e.g., a team) is just the aggregation of a set of homogeneous agents. This allows researchers to study collective adaptation similarly to individual learning, since teams can be treated as uniform entities that go through a process of learning [14]. However, the notion of homogeneity in agents poses a problem, as this assumption is rather unrealistic and does not reflect real-life settings properly: Individuals usually differ in their characteristics [1]. In contrast, by considering heterogeneous agents, we drop this restrictive assumption and give this research a more realistic perspective [19]. Moreover, it also allows for implementing collective adaptation as a process differing from just the aggregation of individual learning dynamics. For example, by autonomously forming and recurrently reorganizing teams, a continuous process of collective adaptation emerges by reconsidering the role of the current members of the team against other potential members with different capabilities [8]. A significant branch of the previous literature concerning team self-organization has implemented auction-based mechanisms for team formation, in which an auction is held and the highest bidders are selected to form the team [15]. We consider collective adaptation as a self-organization process which follows an auction-based approach.

It seems reasonable to think that more adaptation is always positive for performance. However, in contrast to popular belief, more knowledge can be a burden. Previous research has shown that individual learning is beneficial for task performance, but only up to a threshold [11, 13]. Moreover, researchers argue that recurrent team self-organization can be harmful to performance in certain circumstances [8]. This is related to the *exploration vs exploitation dilemma*, which states that individuals should adequately balance searching for new solutions (i.e., exploration) against building on the solutions already at their disposal (i.e., exploitation) [13]. According to [11], the emergence of new solutions is positive for performance only at early stages of task-solving. However, at later stages, acquiring new solutions instead of building on the current ones known can lead to sub-optimal situations in terms of task performance [11]. We consider a multi-level perspective on this dilemma: Exploration can be increased either by increasing individual learning or by self-organizing the team more often. Both actions imply that the team is actively looking for new solutions. Decreasing individual learning or self-organization, in turn, can be associated with more exploitation of the current solutions available.

While some researchers in Managerial Science have focused on the study of learning processes that consider the interplay between the individual level and the team level [2,13], a multi-level adaptation approach that combines both individual learning and team self-organization has not been extensively studied. There are two main reasons for this. First, as outlined previously, many researchers work under the assumption of homogeneity of agents in a team [1]. Since all agents of the model are homogeneous, there exists no incentive to look for replacements. The second reason for multi-level adaptation not being properly studied in this field is that stable team structures have been associated with higher task performance [9]. However, there is research outside the field of Managerial Science in which multi-level adaptation via individual learning and team self-organization has been studied. For example, in Physics, [8] propose an approach to adaptation in which agents freely form or break-up teams, combining it with individual learning. Results suggest that recurrent self-organization can in fact act as a mechanism for collective adaptation that improves complex task performance [8].

Given the vast range of complex tasks in real-life settings [3,17], the conflicting findings on the role of self-organization on performance [8,9], and the lack of extensive implementation of multi-level adaptation in Managerial Science research, it is important to understand the relationship between simultaneous adaptation at multiple levels and complex task performance. Due to the reasons outlined above, there is a research gap in the field of Managerial Science that we aim to fill. By implementing a multi-level adaptation approach to a practical Managerial Science problem, our objective is to understand better how simultaneous individual and collective adaptation affect task performance. To do so, we propose an agent-based model based on the *NK*-framework for Managerial Science [11] and perform a simulation study. This *NK*-framework studies decision-making using an evolutionary approach, in which complex tasks are solved by sequentially making decisions and improving task performance step-by-step [11]. This contrasts with other modeling choices such as neoclassical modeling, in which systems are modeled so the global maximum is found in the fewest possible steps [19]. The remainder of this paper is structured as follows: Sect. 2 discusses the model and its most important aspects. Results are presented in Sect. 3, and a discussion about the results is provided in Sect. 4. Finally, Sect. 5 provides a conclusion and potential avenues for future research.

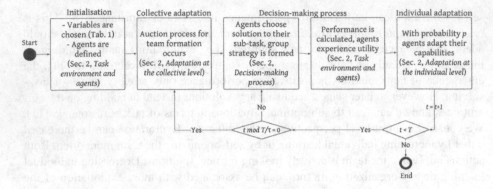

Fig. 1. Sequence of events during simulation runs

2   Model

We propose a model that serves as an abstraction of any complex decision-making task performed by humans. Figure 1 provides an overview of the events of the model sequentially. Each element of the model sequencing is discussed in detail in the following subsections. We model situations in which a population of $P \in \mathbb{N}$ agents faces a task of $N \in \mathbb{N}$ binary choices[1] (see Sect. 2, *Task environment and agents*). The agents' capabilities are limited in the following two ways: (i) Single agents cannot solve the task on their own, so they have to collaborate with other agents in a team[2] consisting of $M \in \mathbb{N} < P$ members to jointly find a solution to the task; and (ii) agents cannot evaluate the entire set of possible solutions simultaneously. To overcome limitation (i), agents are endowed with the capability of recurrently self-organizing into a team (see Sect. 2, *Adaptation at the collective level*). Concerning limitation (ii), we endow the agents with the capability of adapting to the task environment by sequentially exploring the solution space and learning new solutions in the process. We refer to this process as individual adaptation (see Sect. 2, *Adaptation at the individual level*). The model architecture is illustrated in Fig. 2. We observe for $t = \{1, \ldots, T\} \subset \mathbb{N}$ periods how individual and collective adaptation affect task performance and interact.

Task Environment and Agents. We base the task environment on the *NK*-framework [11] and formalize the complex decision problem, which agents face, by the string $\mathbf{d} = (d_1, \ldots, d_N)$, where $d_n \in \{0,1\}$ for $n = \{1, \ldots, N\} \subset \mathbb{N}$. Since agents are limited in their capabilities (see Sect. 2, *Adaptation at the individual level*), we segment the decision problem into M parts of equal size $S \in \mathbb{N} = N/M$. Within the team, agent $m = \{1, \ldots, M\} \subset \mathbb{N}$ is responsible for the subtasks $\mathbf{d}_m = (d_{S \cdot (m-1)+1}, \ldots, d_{S \cdot m})$. Each decision d_n is associated with a performance contribution $f(d_n) \sim U(0,1)$. $K \in \mathbb{N}_0$ interdependencies among decisions d_i shape the complexity of the task $\mathbf{d}$, so that performance contribution $f(d_n)$ might not only be affected by d_n but also by

---

[1] E.g., whether to enforce a dress code in the workplace or not, whether to hire a new employee or not.

[2] We assume that only one team is formed.

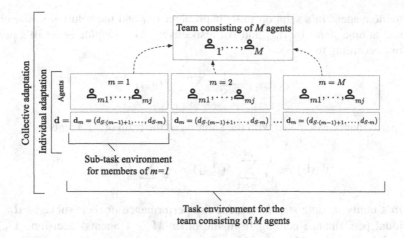

Fig. 2. Model architecture

K other decisions. K represents the *complexity* of the overall task. We formalize the corresponding contribution function by

$$f(d_n) = f(d_n, \underbrace{d_{i_1}, \ldots, d_{i_K}}_{K \text{interdependencies}}),$$ (1)

where $\{i_1, \ldots, i_K\} \subseteq \{1, \ldots, n-1, n+1, \ldots, N\}$, and $0 \leq K \leq N-1$. To compute performance landscapes[3] of different complexity based on Eq. 1, we consider the stylized interdependence structures illustrated in Fig. 3.

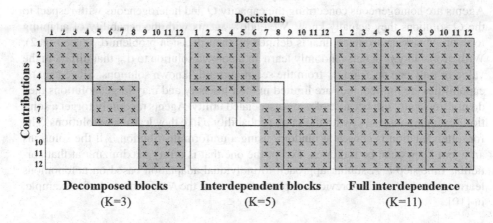

Fig. 3. Stylized interdependence structures

---

[3] For a detailed discussion of the resulting landscapes' characteristics, the reader might consult [11].

We denote agent m's solution to their problem $\mathbf{d}_m$ and the solution to the entire problem $\mathbf{d}$ at time step t by $\mathbf{d}_{mt}$ and $\mathbf{d}_t$, respectively. We compute agent m's performance in t according to

$$\phi(\mathbf{d}_{mt}) = \frac{1}{S} \sum_{d_{nt} \in \mathbf{d}_{mt}} f(d_{nt}) \qquad (2)$$

and the performance associated with the solution of the team of M agents by

$$\Phi(\mathbf{d}_t) = \frac{1}{M} \sum_{m=1}^{M} \phi(\mathbf{d}_{mt}) = \frac{1}{N} \sum_{n=1}^{N} f(d_{nt}) \ . \qquad (3)$$

Agent m's utility in time step t includes the performance of their subtasks $\mathbf{d}_m$ and the residual performance coming from the other $M - 1$ agents' decisions $\mathbf{D}_m = (\mathbf{d}_1, \ldots, \mathbf{d}_r)$, where $r = \{1, \ldots, M\}$ and $r \neq m$. Agent m's utility in t follows the linear function

$$U(\mathbf{d}_{mt}, \underbrace{\mathbf{D}_{mt}}_{(\mathbf{d}_{1t}, \ldots, \mathbf{d}_{rt})}) = \alpha \cdot \phi(\mathbf{d}_{mt}) + \beta \cdot \frac{1}{M-1} \sum_{\substack{r=1 \\ r \neq m}}^{M} \phi(\mathbf{d}_{rt}) \ , \qquad (4)$$

where $\alpha \in \mathbb{R}$ and $\beta \in \mathbb{R}$ indicate the weights for agent m's own and residual performances, respectively, and $\alpha + \beta = 1$. The objective of the agents is to maximize the utility function $U(\mathbf{d}_{mt}, \mathbf{D}_{mt})$ at each time step t.

Adaptation at the Individual Level. Since agents face binary choices, there are 2^S possible solutions for each subtask. Agents are limited as they do not know the entire solution space within their subtask. Initially, they only know a subset of $Q \in \mathbb{N} < 2^S$ solutions. Agents are homogeneous concerning the capacity Q and heterogeneous with respect to the Q solutions they actually know. We endow agents with the capability of adapting to their subtask environment that is defined by their decision problem $\mathbf{d}_m$ (see Fig. 2). With probability p, agents randomly learn an unknown solution to $\mathbf{d}_m$ that differs in the value of only one decision d_n from the set of currently known solutions. Since agents' capabilities are limited, they are limited in their memory and may forget solutions they do not frequently use because of a low associated utility. Agents randomly forget a solution from the subset of Q with the same probability p like they learn new solutions. The forgotten solution is chosen at random, using a uniform distribution. All the solutions an agent knows can be forgotten, except the one that is utility maximizing at that particular time step t. A similar approach to individual adaptation based on autonomous learning can be found in previous implementations of the *NK*-framework, for example, in [10].

Adaptation at the Collective Level. We assume that the population of P agents is equally distributed across M subtasks so that for each subtask, there are $J \in \mathbb{N} = P/M$ agents who can find a solution to this subtask. Consequently, J agents compete for a slot in the team; and all P agents autonomously organize themselves in a team finally composed of M agents. The self-organizing process follows the concept of a second-price auction and always occurs at timestep $t = 1$. Afterwards, $\tau - 1$ other auctions are held over the remaining $T - 1$ time steps in regular intervals, so for $t > 1$, auctions are held each time $t \mod \frac{T}{\tau} = 0$. This means that τ auctions take place over the considered time horizon T each $\frac{T}{\tau}$ time steps.

We implement this second-price auction process in the following way: To become a team member, agents place bids. These bids represent what agents intend to contribute to team performance. Since the selection mechanism follows a second-price auction, agents have incentives to reveal their true contributions [18]. Agents, however, cannot observe the other agents' bids and this is why they assume that the residual decisions $\mathbf{D}_{mt-1}$ will remain constant from implemented solution at $t - 1$. Agents compute the expected utilities for all their solutions to their subtasks $\mathbf{d}_m$ available in time step t according to $U(\mathbf{d}_{mt}, \mathbf{D}_{mt-1})$ (see Eq. 4). Each agent submits the highest attainable expected utility among the different solutions as their bid in t. Consequently, there are J bids for each slot in the team. Following the logic of second-price auctions, the team comprises those agents M who submit the highest proposals per slot. For being a part of the team, agents are charged the second-highest bid per slot.[4]

Decision-Making Process. In each time step t, the M team members are tasked with finding a solution $\mathbf{d}_t$ to the complex task $\mathbf{d}$. Agents are autonomous in their decisions, and there is no communication or coordination between agents. The decision-making process is a two-stage process. First, each agent m focuses on their subtask $\mathbf{d}_{mt}$ and computes the expected utility for each solution available in this particular time step. Since we do not allow for communication, the agents calculate the expected utility following the same process described earlier in Sect. 2 for each solution known. The agent chooses the solution that promises the highest utility. In the first step, each agent comes up with an S binary values vector that represents the solution to their subtask. Second, once all agents have submitted their solutions, the overall solution is computed by concatenating all of the M solutions chosen by the agents. The solution to the complex problem in t, $\mathbf{d}_t$, is thus represented by a vector of N binary values. We compute the performance of the overall solution according to Eq. 3, and agents receive the resulting utility according to Eq. 4.

3   Results

Scenarios. An overview of the model's variables and the values they can take is given in Table 1. With the values provided in Table 1 for the number of auctions that occur at each simulation, we identify three different scenarios. First, for $\tau = 1$, there is *initial* collective adaptation: The auction process occurs only at the first period, never to be repeated. Second, for $\tau = 20$, there is *moderate* collective adaptation, with the team self-organizing each $\frac{T}{\tau} = 10$ time steps. Finally, for $\tau = 200$, there is *high* collective adaptation, with the team self-organizing at each time step.

---

[4] Since agents only experience utility if they are team members, they always have incentives to participate in this process.

Table 1. Variables of the model

Type	Description	Denoted by	Values
Exogenous variable	Complexity	K	$\{3, 5, 11\}$
	Probability of individual adaptation	p	$\{0, 0.1, 0.2, 0.3, 0.4, 0.5\}$
	Number of auctions held	τ	$\{1, 20, 200\}$
Observed variable	Team performance	C_t	$\in [0, \ldots, 1]$
Other variables	Time steps	t	$\in [0, \ldots, 200]$
	Temporal horizon	T	200
	Number of decisions	N	12
	Weights of utility	α, β	0.5
	Simulation runs	R	1,500
	Number of subtasks	M	3
	Number of agents	P	30

Performance Measure. During each simulation run r and at every time step t, the team performance $\Phi(\mathbf{d}_t)$ is normalized by the highest possible performance in that simulation run, $max(\Phi_r)$. Based on this measure, we compute the average performance of the scenario for each timestep t as follows:

$$\tilde{\Phi}_t = \frac{1}{R} \sum_{t=1}^{T} \frac{\Phi(\mathbf{d}_t)}{max(\Phi_r)} . \tag{5}$$

We further condense the average distance per timestep, $\tilde{\Phi}_t$, to the total Manhattan Distance. This means that we compute the difference at each time step t between average performance $\tilde{\Phi}_t$ and the maximum performance $max(\Phi_r)$. Then each difference is summed over the T time steps[5]. We formalize the total Manhattan Distance MD as follows:

$$MD = \sum_{t=1}^{T} (1 - \tilde{\Phi}_t) \tag{6}$$

Please note that a higher Manhattan Distance MD implies a higher average distance to the maximum, and thus a lower overall performance.

In Fig. 4, we plot the Manhattan Distance for each scenario studied. The x-axis of each subplot represents the probability of individual adaptation. On the y-axis, we plot the three scenarios considered for collective adaptation. The three subplots represent the results for different complexity levels (see Fig. 3). Each point of a subplot represents a total Manhattan Distance MD for a particular configuration of individual and collective

---

[5] Note that since performance has been normalized using Eq. 5 and then averaged, maximum performance is $max(\Phi_r) = 1$.

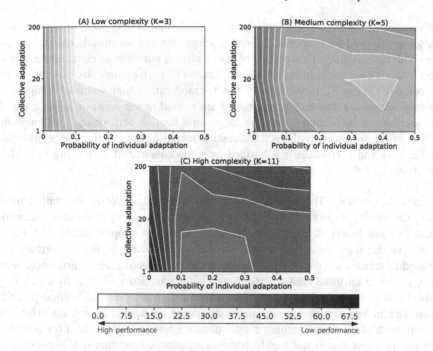

Fig. 4. Results for scattered interdependencies

adaptation. A point located in a lighter (darker) area implies lower (higher) MD, and thus a better (worse) performance.

Individual Adaptation. The results suggest that the probability of individual adaptation p has a considerable effect on task performance. In particular, there is a substantial decrease in the total Manhattan Distance MD, when agents are capable of learning, i.e., when $p > 0$. This pattern is robust across all interdependence structures under consideration (i.e., for each level of K), as shown in all three subplots of Fig. 4. The effect of individual learning on performance is highly significant. This suggests that promoting learning is beneficial for task performance even when it is very low.

Regarding $p > 0.1$, there is a decreasing marginal positive effect of individual adaptation on performance in low complexity scenarios (i.e., the subplot (A) in Fig. 4). The marginal effect is smaller when the probability of learning increases from $p = 0.1$ to $p = 0.5$ as compared to a shift from $p = 0$ to $p = 0.1$. This is true for all three collective adaptation scenarios considered. Thus, beginning to learn about a task has huge implications on performance. However, any increase in individual adaptation reduces the overall impact of individual learning on performance, even when this effect is still positive.

For higher levels of complexity (see subplots (B) and (C) in Fig. 4), this positive effect eventually turns negative. As a consequence, the overall performance declines. For example, subplot (B) in Fig. 4 (i.e., for $K = 5$) shows that a team with high collective adaptation reaches its lowest total distance of $MD = 20.00$ at a learning probability of $p = 0.1$. Further increases in individual adaptation appear to affect performance negatively, surpassing $MD = 25.00$ for $p = 0.5$. Eventual decreases in performance can also be observed for moderate collective adaptation and for initial collective adaptation (both for $p > 0.4$). This pattern of initial growth but with an eventual decline in performance is even more pronounced in scenarios of high complexity (i.e., $K = 11$, see subplot (C) in Fig. 4). Results imply that, for moderate or high levels of complexity, individual adaptation and task performance are related in the form of an inverted-U: Initial increases in individual adaptation are positive for task performance, although the marginal effect decreases with each successive increase. Eventually, the relationship turns negative and performance is harmed as a consequence of increasing individual adaptation.

Collective Adaptation. The results suggest that whether collective adaptation has a positive or negative impact on performance depends on the complexity of the scenario studied. For low levels of complexity (represented by the subplot (A) in Fig. 4), we can observe that high collective adaptation is associated with higher performance as compared to scenarios with either moderate or initial collective adaptation (except for $p = 0$, in which all three teams perform very similarly, and $p = 0.1$, in which high and moderate collective adaptation perform similarly). Moreover, the highest possible performance in low complexity scenarios considered is attained by a team exhibiting high collective adaptation, reaching a total distance below $MD = 1.00$ for $p = 0.5$. When facing a task that is not highly complex, results suggest that it is beneficial for performance to increase the effort in finding new solutions (i.e., increasing exploration), at both the individual and collective level.

However, in scenarios with medium complexity (see subplot (B) in Fig. 4), for most values of p, moderate collective adaptation leads to higher performances compared to both high or initial collective adaptation scenarios. There are two exceptions to this, which are for the extreme values of $p = 0$ (in which moderate and high collective adaptation perform very similarly) and $p = 0.5$ (in which moderate and initial collective adaptation perform very similarly). For $0 < p < 0.5$, moderate collective adaptation is associated with a higher performance than any other alternative. Moreover, the highest attainable performance in all medium complexity scenarios considered occurs for moderate collective adaptation and $p = 0.4$ and is around $MD = 15.00$. In contrast to low complexity scenarios (except for the extreme case of $p = 0$, in which agents do not learn at all), high collective adaptation is always associated with the lowest performance compared to the other two alternatives. The results suggest that increasing exploitation (exploration) by decreasing (increasing) collective adaptation can be harmful to performance. Moderate collective adaptation, in turn, improves performance in the majority of cases.

Results in scenarios of high complexity, as shown in subplot (C) of Fig. 4, suggest that increasing collective adaptation is detrimental to performance when individual learning occurs (i.e., for $p > 0$). There is an exception in the extreme case of $p = 0.5$, in which initial and moderate collective adaptation are associated with a similar performance around $MD = 43.00$. For $0 < p < 0.5$, initial collective adaptation is associated with a higher performance than any other alternative. Furthermore, the highest attainable performance for high complexity scenarios is attained by a team with initial collective adaptation and $p = 0.2$, with approximately $MD = 38.00$. When tasks are highly complex, stability in team composition seems to be a good choice, since the recurrent reorganization of a team eventually impairs task performance.

4   Discussion

Our research is concerned with multi-level adaptation and its relationship with task performance in teams. Results indicate that, in low complexity environments, putting a lot of effort into adaptation at both the collective and the individual level cannot be associated with negative effects on performance. This extends the insights about adaptation in complex environments provided by [11]: When facing a task of low complexity, high exploration does not decrease the overall task performance, because sub-optimal, long-term solutions are less likely. Since only a single level of adaptation was considered in [11], our results contribute to previous research by showing that this is also true for multi-level settings.

For moderate levels of complexity, our results show that the exploration vs exploitation dilemma can be applied in a multi-level adaptation setting, too. Also, a proper balance between exploration and exploitation is key to improving task performance in teams. These insights are in line with previous research [11, 13, 14, 20] regarding the exploration vs exploitation dilemma. Our results differ from previous research in that exploration can be increased either by increasing individual or collective adaptation. In particular, when considering moderately complex tasks, the results suggest that moderate individual learning has to be combined with moderate collective adaptation to improve performance. These findings are consistent with previous results, which indicate that recurrent self-organization of teams combined with individual learning can be associated with higher task performance [8]. In real-life settings this moderate adaptation at both levels could be achieved, for example, by allowing employees of a firm to dedicate a limited amount of working hours to self-education and training; combined with holding regular team meetings with employees outside the team to discuss the state of the task and other members' contributions.

The results for low and moderate complexity indicate that recurrent self-organization can be beneficial for task performance. These insights contrast views in the field of Managerial Science that characterize team reorganization as harmful to performance [9]. In particular, team stability has been associated with high degrees of team-level learning and, eventually, higher performance [9]. In this context, adaptation occurs just at the team level, following a learning process for the collective. This highlights the importance of considering multi-level adaptation. By considering multiple, simultaneous adaptation processes (in this case, by endowing agents with the capabilities of learning combined with recurrent team self-organization), emerging insights into topics such as team reorganization differ from those found in previous research. Since adaptation has been considered as occurring at multiple levels, for example, by [13], we believe that these findings and similar implementations help to understand better the relationship between adaptation and task solving in teams and to relate the insights to real-life problems.

Our results also contribute to the literature on multi-level adaptation and task performance when considering highly complex tasks. Previous research on multi-level adaptation and task performance (which is, in itself, not extensive) has not considered highly complex tasks (see, for example, [8]). Thus, we can consider our results as a first step in the matter of studying multi-level adaptation under high complexity. We find that, in highly complex tasks, collective adaptation is negative for performance, and that the positive effect of individual adaptation is limited considerably. As the previous literature shows, highly complex environments are associated with lower benefits for exploration, since the probability of finding sub-optimal, long-term solutions is very high [11]. Again, our results can be understood as extensions to previous insights on the exploration vs exploitation dilemma by considering multi-level adaptation.

This set of results provides an extension to approaches that consider a single level of adaptation [11, 13, 14, 20]. Our research adds to the literature in Managerial Science by providing a discussion on individual and collective adaptation, both occurring simultaneously. To our knowledge, there is a lack of an extensive implementation of a multi-level adaptation approach that considers autonomous individual learning and team self-organization in Managerial Science. By considering these two aspects, we believe that our research provides a novel approach to multi-level adaptation in this field. Our results should then be understood as both complementary to previous findings in the literature and an extension [11, 20].

5 Conclusion

Individual and collective adaptation are two factors that strongly determine the performance of a task. In particular, we have found that high individual and collective adaptation increase task performance when task complexity is low. However, this changes when complexity increases. When tasks are moderately complex, teams need to combine individual learning with moderately recurrent team self-organization up to a threshold in order to reach the highest attainable performance. If the task is highly complex, low individual learning combined with no collective adaptation is the best alternative in terms of task performance. These aspects show that the exploration vs exploitation dilemma also holds when considering multi-level adaptation.

However, our research has some limitations. For example, the importance of coordination and communication is not addressed [20]. Also, we do not consider the potential costs that individual and collective adaptation might incur in. Further extensions of the model may include endowing agents with the capabilities of choosing more or less individual adaptation [7] or breaking up the formed team [8], and including alternative mechanisms of adaptation such as social learning [2]. The implementation of these and further aspects might help in extending our research.

Another aspect that has been mentioned but not extensively studied in this paper is the role of interdependencies between the agents' decisions. We study one structure of interdependencies at three different levels (see Fig. 3). Previous research has shown that not only the level of interdependencies, but also the structure of those interdependencies (i.e., which actual decisions are interdependent with each other), can lead to different insights into task performance in groups [14]. A potential extension to this paper could consider the impact of alternative interdependence structures.

Finally, our results suggest the existence of an interaction effect between adaptation at multiple levels, as a simultaneous increase of adaptation at both levels eventually leads to "too much exploration" and a decrease in task performance. Extensions of this research may elaborate on this. Despite its limitations, we believe that our research is a first step towards the study of multi-level adaptation and its effects on performance. Moreover, it also serves as a departure point for future research on the topic of multi-level adaptation and complex task performance in teams.

References

1. Axtell, R.L.: What economic agents do: how cognition and interaction lead to emergence and complexity. Rev. Austrian Econ. **20**(2–3), 105–122 (2007)
2. Baumann, O., Schmidt, J., Stieglitz, N.: Effective search in rugged performance landscapes: a review and outlook. J. Manag. **45**(1), 285–318 (2019)
3. Creplet, F., Dupouet, O., Kern, F., Mehmanpazir, B., Munier, F.: Consultants and experts in management consulting firms. Res. Policy **30**(9), 1517–1535 (2001)
4. Eisenhardt, K.M., Martin, J.A.: Dynamic capabilities: what are they? Strateg. Manag. J. **21**, 1105–1121 (2000)
5. Funke, J., Frensch, P.A.: Complex problem solving research in North America and Europe: an integrative review. Foreign Psychol. **5**, 42–47 (1995)
6. Gershkov, A., Li, J., Schweinzer, P.: Efficient tournaments within teams. RAND J. Econ. **40**(1), 103–119 (2009)
7. Giannoccaro, I., Galesic, M., Francesco, G., Barkoczi, D., Carbone, G.: Search behavior of individuals working in teams: a behavioral study on complex landscapes. J. Bus. Res. **118**, 1–10 (2019)
8. Gomes, P.F., Reia, S.M., Rodrigues, F.A., Fontanari, J.F.: Mobility helps problem-solving systems to avoid groupthink. Phys. Rev. E **99**(3), 1–10 (2019)
9. Hsu, S.C., Weng, K.W., Cui, Q., Rand, W.: Understanding the complexity of project team member selection through agent-based modeling. Int. J. Project Manage. **34**(1), 82–93 (2016)
10. Leitner, S., Wall, F.: Multiobjective decision making policies and coordination mechanisms in hierarchical organizations: results of an agent-based simulation. Sci. World J. **2014**, 1–12 (2014)
11. Levinthal, D.A.: Adaptation on rugged landscapes. Manage. Sci. **43**(7), 934–950 (1997)
12. LiCalzi, M., Surucu, O.: The power of diversity over large solution spaces. Manage. Sci. **58**(7), 1408–1421 (2012)
13. March, J.G.: Exploration and exploitation in organizational learning. Organ. Sci. **2**(1), 71–87 (1991)
14. Rivkin, J.W., Siggelkow, N.: Patterned interactions in complex systems: implications for exploration. Manage. Sci. **53**(7), 1068–1085 (2007)
15. Rizk, Y., Awad, M., Tunstel, E.W.: Cooperative heterogeneous multi-robot systems: a survey. ACM Comput. Surv. **52**(2), 1–31 (2019)
16. Simon, H.A.: Models of Man, Social and Rational. Wiley, New York (1957)
17. Tang, J., Zhu, K., Guo, H., Gong, C., Liao, C., Zhang, S.: Using auction-based task allocation scheme for simulation optimization of search and rescue in disaster relief. Simul. Model. Pract. Theory **82**, 132–146 (2018)
18. Vickrey, W.: Counterspeculation, auctions, and competitive sealed tenders. J. Financ. **16**(1), 8–37 (1961). https://doi.org/10.2307/2977633
19. Wall, F.: Agent-based modeling in managerial science: an illustrative survey and study. RMS **10**(1), 135–193 (2014). https://doi.org/10.1007/s11846-014-0139-3
20. Wall, F.: Emergence of task formation in organizations: balancing units' competence and capacity. J. Artif. Soc. Soc. Simul. **21**(2), 6 (2018)

Fast Agent-Based Simulation Framework with Applications to Reinforcement Learning and the Study of Trading Latency Effects

Peter Belcak[✉], Jan-Peter Calliess, and Stefan Zohren

Oxford-Man Institute of Quantitative Finance, University of Oxford, Oxford, UK
peter.belcak@st-hildas.ox.ac.uk, jan-peter.calliess@oxford-man.ox.ac.uk,
stefan.zohren@eng.ox.ac.uk

Abstract. We introduce a new software toolbox for agent-based simulation. Facilitating rapid prototyping by offering a user-friendly Python API, its core rests on an efficient C++ implementation to support simulation of large-scale multi-agent systems. Our software environment benefits from a versatile message-driven architecture. Originally developed to support research on financial markets, it offers the flexibility to simulate a wide-range of different (easily customisable) market rules and to study the effect of auxiliary factors, such as delays, on the market dynamics. As a simple illustration, we employ our toolbox to investigate the role of the order processing delay in normal trading and for the scenario of a significant price change.

Owing to its general architecture, our toolbox can also be employed as a generic multi-agent system simulator. We provide an example of such a non-financial application by simulating a mechanism for the coordination of no-regret learning agents in a multi-agent network routing scenario previously proposed in the literature.

Keywords: Multi-agent systems · Reinforcement learning · Software toolbox · Model prototyping · Latency · Colocation · Simulation

1 Motivation

Complementing the classical methods of statistical analysis and mathematical modelling, agent-based modelling (ABM) of financial markets has recently been gaining traction [4,9,11,12]. In particular, applications of this paradigm to market microstructure [2] have attracted increasing attention. To name but a few, they include the study of statistical properties of limit order books [3], (non-) strategic behavior of a collective of traders [10] when modelled via the flow of their orders, as well as research into market bubbles and crashes [13]. With the ever-increasing importance of automated trading in finance and the rising popularity of artificial intelligence in academic and industrial research, the importance of the ABM approach in the study of electronic markets is likely to grow further.

© Springer Nature Switzerland AG 2022
K. H. Van Dam and N. Verstaevel (Eds.): MABS 2021, LNAI 13128, pp. 42–56, 2022.
https://doi.org/10.1007/978-3-030-94548-0_4

The diversity of use cases of ABM in finance and economics is reflected by the recent proliferation of a variety of software tools tailored to the particularities of their respective applications, as can be seen in the aforementioned sources. What is missing is an efficient code base implementing a general, all-encompassing multi-agent exchange framework that can be easily adapted to simulate scalable ABMs based on any particular exchange as a special case. Among many other conceivable use cases, such a software environment could serve as a flexible toolbox allowing its users to investigate a range of research questions. Such could include, but are not limited to, the following:

- The impact of different matching algorithms on the (learned) behaviour and revenues of (adaptive) trader agents inhabiting a given limit order book (LOB);
- The amount of strategic decision making required to explain some of the important statistical properties of these LOBs;
- The response of strategic trader agent behavior to a change in the rules of the order matching, as well as to changing infrastructural effects such as communication delays.
- Conversely to the above, the impact of different learning behaviors of the trading agents on the ensuing market dynamics.

To address the need for such a toolbox, we introduce the Multi-Agent eXchange Environment (MAXE), a general code environment for the simulation of agent-based models, with a database ready-to-use agents for simulation of electronic exchanges and other financial markets. For convenience, MAXE also provides a Python API to facilitate rapid prototyping of artificial agents. However, since the meaningfulness of ABMs often rests on the capability to simulate large agent populations, the core of the implementation was written in C++, with an eye for computational and memory efficiency, as well as for support for native multi-threading for execution of separate simulation instances (with possibly varying parameters) in parallel.

The remainder of this paper is structured as follows: After placing our toolbox into the context of previous, related simulator packages in Sect. 2, Sect. 3 proceeds with introducing the architecture of MAXE. We present different use cases of our framework. Section 4 contains an illustration of a simple study of the effects of communication delays. Section 5 shows how MAXE can be utilised in the general context of agent-based modelling, and Sect. 6 compares MAXE's performance in a simple simulation scenario to that of a contender. Concluding remarks can be found in Sect. 7.

2   Related Work

Beyond simple market replay approaches, there still is a need for publicly available ABM software sufficiently generic to be capable of simulating the markets and many other environments at scale. Our toolbox was designed to meet this demand. The most closely related toolboxes we are aware of include Adaptive

Modeler [7], Swarm [18], NetLogo [17], Repast [8], and ABIDES [5]. In what is to follow, we briefly summarise the features of these packages in relation to ours.

Adaptive Modeler [7] is a "freemium" specialized market simulator first released in 2003 and still maintained. At the core of the software is a virtual market featuring a predefined set of classes of agents that may be further adjusted by the user by changing various parameters such as the population sizes, agent wealth, or class mutation probability. Once an environment consisting of traders and traded assets is specified, the user may start the simulation whilst keeping track of outputs such as the event log, quotes, or various economic statistics. All of these functionalities are – or can easily be – implemented in MAXE as well. In addition however, MAXE also allows the creation of completely customised agents with arbitrary behavior and simulate them on an arbitrary timescale, as the unit time step is not bound to any physical measure of time and can thus be chosen to represent an arbitrarily small fraction of a second.

Swarm [18] is an open-source ABM package for simulating the interaction of agents and their emergent collective behaviour. First released in 1999, it remains maintained today. Whilst not directly designed for financial modelling, it has been used to create the Santa Fe Artificial Stock Market [14] that, for the first time, reproduced a number of stylized facts about the behaviour of traders and further emphasized the importance of modelling of financial markets. Unlike swarm, MAXE comes with an incorporated time-tracking unit that takes care of the delivery of messages between the agents involved and the advancement of simulation time. This allows for a transparent unified channel of inter-agent communication, enabling simple scheduling of agent tasks (as outlined in an example in Fig. 1) and greatly simplifying output generation and debugging.

NetLogo [17] and *RePast* [8] are general-purpose software frameworks for agent-based modelling. On top of simulation capabilities, both of these tools feature components enabling easy display of data, and have extensively been used for research in social sciences. They have been previously used for small-scale simulation of financial markets, though their distributions do not feature readily available agents for market simulation. In comparison to the extensive constraints placed on the agent interface by either, MAXE places no constraints on the design of the agent, apart from requiring that the agents conform to the minimal messaging structure, for which there are template agent classes readily available.

JADE [1] is an open-source software framework for peer-to-peer agent based applications. It is fully implemented in Java, and as such suffers from the memory limitations and reliance on garbage collecting as it exists in a managed environment. It, however, benefits from the platform of choice by being runnable on every operating system supporting the Java runtime binaries, and even allows its users to run simulations across multiple devices simultaneously.

ABIDES [5] is the newest open source market modelling tool. Released as recently as 2019, it was specifically designed for LOB simulation. Aimed to closely resemble NASDAQ by implementing the NASDAQ ITCH and OUCH messaging protocols it hopes to offer itself as a tool for facilitation of AI research on the exchange. Just as MAXE, ABIDES and allows users to implement their own agents in Python. However, since MAXE also allows specification in C++ we expect that MAXE has an edge in terms of the execution efficiency and scalability. Moreover, MAXE, being based on a compiled binary core interacting directly with the operating system allows for multi-threaded execution of simulations, which becomes an advantage when simulating a range of similar simulations differing only in a number of input parameters. Apart from that, MAXE comes with the implicit support for the trading at multiple exchanges at once and for limit order books matched with different matching algorithms, in particular pro-rata matching. MAXE is also highly modular due to the option to develop a database of agents first, and then configure a set of simulations via an XML configuration file.

3 Architecture

MAXE is based on a message-driven, incremental protocol. Its core logic steps forward time and delivers messages, and thus while it was developed with the modelling of financial markets in sight, it can easily be utilised for simulating many general multi-agent systems unrelated to finance, an example of which we give in Sect. 5. We will, nevertheless, continue to present MAXE's features mainly in the light of market simulation, believing that it will turn out to be its most popular application.

In MAXE, every relevant entity of a trading system one would wish to model (e.g. exchanges, traders, news outlets or social media) can be implemented as an agent. This is different to the usual approach to agent-based modelling of exchanges where at the centre of the simulation is the exchange concerned and the communication protocol between the entities of the trading system is made to resemble the one of the real exchange, often to ease the transition of any models developed there into production environments. As it is the case with any common implementation of message-driven frameworks, agents taking part in the simulation remain dormant at any point in simulation time unless they have been delivered a message. When a message is due to be delivered, the simulation time freezes as all agents that have been delivered at least one message begin to take turns to deal with their inbox. Each agent is given an unlimited amount of execution time to process the messages they have been delivered and to send messages on their own. Messages can be dispatched either immediately (i.e. with zero delay) or scheduled to be delivered later in the future by specifying a non-negative delay which can be used to, for example, model latency, that we will show in Sect. 4.

At the beginning of a simulation, each agent is delivered a message that allows them to take initial actions and possibly schedule a wake-up in the future by addressing a message to themselves. At the end of the simulation, a message of similar nature is sent out to all agents to allow them to process and save any data they might have been gathering up to that point for further analysis outside the simulation environment. Figure 1 shows an example communication of an agent that trades based on regular L1 quote data from the exchange.

Aside from its core, MAXE also contains a small initial repository of common agents that can be expanded upon by its users. This initial repository includes an exchange agent that can operate a number of different matching mechanism, as well as a collection of zero-intelligence and other simple agents. An overview of the top level of the hierarchy of available agents is depicted in Fig. 2. Further details on the various agents can be found in the code repository [15].

For simplicity and in order to facilitate convenient prototyping of trading system models, MAXE has been built with an interactive console interface, designed to read the simulation configurations from a hand-editable XML file, and is, despite the overall emphasis on the performance, supplemented with an additional Python interface. A user of MAXE wishing to quickly try out an idea for an agent-based model would thus proceed as follows: First, they would consider whether any of the built-in agent types fit their needs. For any agent type with custom behaviour they would write a Python script, testing it in a 'mock'

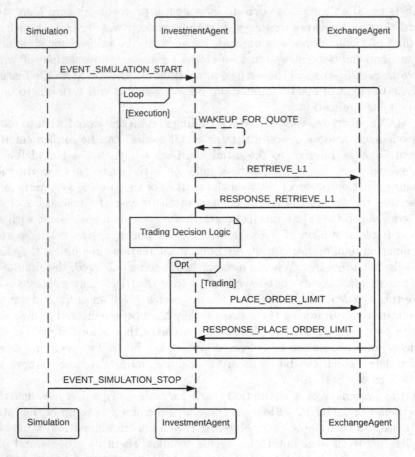

Fig. 1. A sequence diagram of an example communication between a trading agent, exchange agent, and the simulation environment.

environment API that is provided. Once satisfied with the scripted behaviour of individual agents, they would with ease set up the simulation of their model by writing an XML configuration file, and once satisfied with the overall model, they would have the option to scale up to hundreds of thousands of agents by re-implementing the behaviour first scripted in Python in C++. Some resource limits for MAXE when running solely agents implemented in C++ are discussed in Sect. 6.

4   Example Case Study – Processing Delay in Market Dynamics

As discussed previously, MAXE can serve as a simulation environment of many types of multi-agent systems. As a first example related to financial markets, we demonstrate MAXE's ability to simulate some aspects of "market physics". In particular, we utilise it to examine the effect processing or communication delays have on various statistics of the market dynamics following a large trade.

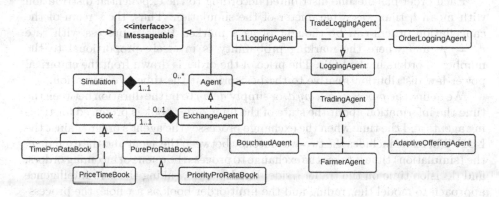

Fig. 2. The class diagram of the simulation-agent hierarchy of the simulator.

4.1   The Model

The core of the model consists of one exchange agent with a modifiable choice of matching algorithm and a population of zero-intelligence trading agents interacting with the exchange. The exchange agent maintains the limit order book and executes orders submitted by the trading agents. At the beginning of the simulation, the LOB contains two small orders, one on each side of the book with the initial bid-ask spread S_0, to serve as the indicators of the opening prices for further trading.

Following the start of the simulation, traders place orders and are given a fixed period of time to reconstruct the LOB to match the empirical average shape from [3] by placing orders in a manner described below. In the simulation runs focused on statistics not related to the study of impactful trades, the remaining time is used to measure those. The other type of simulations experiences an impact agent entering the exchange and making a large trade, following which more statistics are computed. The simulation runs over a fixed time horizon of $40000t_p$, chosen by experimentation focused on the setup appearing to have dealt with the largest of the trades used in our experiment.

The behaviour of our trading agent is similar to the behaviour presented in [3] that has been previously shown to be able to reconstruct the LOB's shape to be resembling the one of real LOBs of highly liquid stocks on the Paris Bourse. The behavior presented in [3] is further adjusted by some features of the behaviour presented in [10], which has been shown to be able to explain some of the dynamic properties of the LOB, including the variance of the bid-ask spread. For a detailed specification of the agents' behaviour we refer the reader to [15].

According to the L1 information available to the trader at the time they are making the decision (which may be outdated due to the communication delay between the trader and the exchange), each trader places both market and not immediately marketable limit orders according to a Poisson process with rate r_p, with the fraction of the market orders f_m being a parameter of the simulation.

Each order has lifetime distributed according to the exponential distribution with mean t_l that was a parameter of the simulation. Thus, the stream of the cancellation orders can be thought of as a marked Poisson process with rate $r_c = \frac{1}{l_o}$ and where the marking probability is inversely proportional to the number of orders in the LOB. The price of the order is drawn from the empirical power-law distribution relative to the best price at the time of observation.

We define the *processing delay d*, or simply *delay* to be the duration between the time the information about the state of the limit order book is produced for trading agents and the time when the exchange processes the agent's order against the LOB. This time includes the two-way latency between the agent and the exchange, the (simulation) time it takes the exchange to process the queue of incoming orders, and decision time on the trader's side. Furthermore, taking the zero-intelligence approach to model the trading and the limit order book as a whole, the processing delay can also be thought of as encapsulating the time it takes the trader to decide whether and how to trade and possibly evaluating their strategy given the information becoming available during that time, and we shall use this fact when interpreting our findings. We also define *greed g* to be the size of a large market order expressed as a fraction of the total volume (i.e., considering the volume of all price levels) in the queue it is meant to be executed against.

4.2   Findings

When simulating, we treated the placement frequency r_p as fixed and looked at the effects of the other two time-based parameters, r_c and d, relative to it. The observed effects turned out to be independent of the matching algorithm used. Perhaps somewhat more surprisingly, the cancellation rate r_c appeared not to have had any effect on the statistics considered (see below).

Notation: If Q is the quantity we are observing, let $e[Q]$ denote the empirical simulation-time-weighted mean of Q and $v[Q]$ the empirical simulation-time-weighted variance of Q.

We found that the mean bid-ask spread $e[S]$ increased linearly with the fraction of market orders f_m (with a hint of convexity), decreased with d, and appeared to converge to the bid-ask spread of the initial setup S_0, coming within a few ticks distance of S_0 for all sufficiently large delays d. The relationship between the parameters involved is depicted in Fig. 3a and fitted ($R^2 = 0.90$)

$$e[S] \approx S_0 + s_0 f_m e^{-s_1 d}.$$

The time-weighted variance of the best bid and ask prices (simply the "best" price $B(t)$ at time t as the behavior is the same for both sides of the queue, see Fig. 3c) appeared to monotonously decrease with increasing d and, to increase exponentially with increasing f_m, coming to a negligible distance from 0 for sufficiently large values of the delay d.

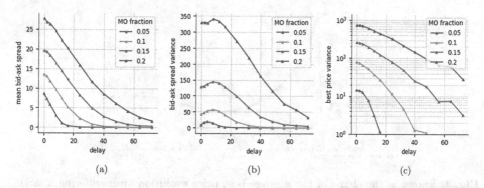

Fig. 3. Statistics of the simulation L1 data, namely the mean bid-ask spread, bid-ask spread variance, and the variance of the best price, plotted against d (in multiples of t_p) for different values of f_m.

Shape of the Average Impact Scenario. Turning our attention to the scenario of an impactful trade occurring at time t_I, we define the climb C to be the immediate increase in the best price B following a large (10-100x the size of average market order) trade against the respective order queue. We further define F to be the difference between the highest and the lowest point the best price attains after t_I, and I to be the long term impact of the trade, i.e. the difference between the equilibrium best price prior to the impactful trade and the equilibrium price to which the best price "settles" long after t_I. We expressed the volume of the large trade considered as a fraction of the volume available on the respective order queue at the time the trade is executed and denote it by g.

We have found empirically that, irrespective of the volume of the large trade affecting the best price, $e[B](t)$ seemed to exhibit the same feature of going through the phases of *fall, overreaction,* and *settlement* (see Fig. 4). The climb in the best price itself occurred almost instantly after t_I in the vast majority of cases, with the exception when a delayed limit order unaware of the sudden price movement significantly improved the new best price but was quickly eliminated by newly incoming marketable orders. The first phase, fall, exhibited a steep best price fall towards the future equilibrium and its steepness decreased with increasing latency d. The fall was succeeded by something that could described as an overreaction, a phase during which the best price dived further below the future equilibrium price and hit the absolute minimum at the time at which the bid-ask spread was also minimal. The best bid and ask prices then diverged again towards their new equilibrium in the settlement phase.

The identification of such patterns has the potential of being of practical utility. They might endow us with a method for predicting the price at which the best price will settle after a large trade given the information about the long-term variance of and current information about the values of the bid-ask spread.

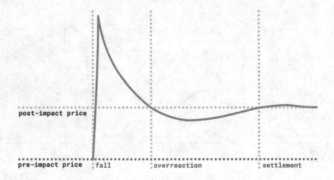

Fig. 4. Shown is the shape of the average best price evolution after suffering a large aggressing trade.

The Large Trade Scenario. We observed that both $e[C]$ and $e[F]$ decreased linearly for large delays and small delays with small values of g (Fig. 5a and Fig. 5b). In addition, large values of g seemed to allow the climb and fall to peak at a specific small delay.

The long-term impact appeared to be mostly linear with d with the downwards slope decreasing with the increasing values of greed, increases linearly with f_m (Fig. 5c). Furthermore, it did not seem to exhibit the same peak as climb and fall do, demonstrating that these two compensated for each other in the long run. Furthermore, the logarithm of the long term impact increased proportionally to the volume traded, in keeping with the results presented in [16].

We said that the best price had reached *stability* if the moving average with a fixed window of size w had fallen within the distance of $\sqrt{\frac{v[B]}{w}}$.

Whilst we found significant evidence that the impact of a large trade on the best price depends on the greed parameters, perhaps surprisingly, the mean and

variance of the time did not seem to exhibit any notable dependence on the level
of greed, i.e. the best price appears to converge to stability in time independent
of the size of the large trade nor the share of the marketable orders f_m (Fig. 6b).

Further evidence of such behavior was found when producing the results
depicted in Fig. 6c. Here, we looked at the proportion of the runs of the simulation
in which the price fulfilled the post-impact stability criterion given above before
the simulation was terminated. As can be seen from the plot, simulation runs
for higher values of the parameter f_m would see the price succeed to become
stabilised in the time horizon of the simulation more often than for the lower
values, but the greed parameter had again little to no effect on the proportion
of the runs that would become stabilised for varying values of d. This is further
supported by setting a time limit on convergence in the distant future from
the impactful trade and measuring the convergence success rate, defined as the
proportion of the simulation runs that succeeded in converging before that time
(see Fig. 6c).

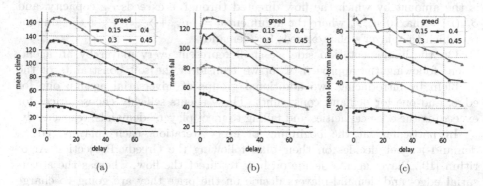

Fig. 5 Absolute mean climb, mean fall, and mean long-term impact (in price ticks)
plotted against the processing delay d (in multiples of t_p) for fixed values of f_m and
varying values of greed g.

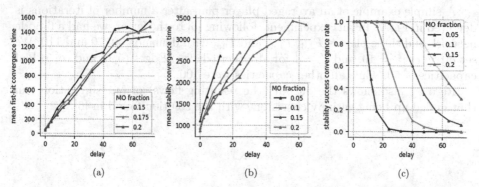

Fig. 6. Convergence statistics shown against d (as a multiple of t_p) for different values
of f_m. The time is also expressed as a multiple of the mean order placement rate r_p.

5 Example Use Case – Market-Based Coordination of Learning Agents

The generality of MAXE's architecture allows us to simulate multi-agent systems with no relation to finance at all. As a specific example we now implement the experiment presented in [6], concerning a multi-agent mechanism that, under some assumptions about agents' rationality, gives plausible solutions for routing problems.

Consider a finite directed graph $G = (V, E)$, in which each edge $e \in E$ has capacity $\gamma(e)$ and a fixed intrinsic cost c^e for each unit of flow that is to be directed through the edge. Suppose that there are players who each want to send an amount of flow d_{sr} from some vertex s to r – that is, player P_{sr} wants to direct d_{sr} from s to r and to that end has an individual plan represented by a vector $\mathbf{f}_{sr} = (f_{sr}^e)_{e \in E}$. We require the players to plan in such a way that the resulting flows through the graph conserve flow. The players' planning is influenced by two soft constraints: $\beta_e(\nu) = \max\{0, u_e \nu\}$ where $\nu = f_{sr}^e - \gamma(e)$ is the amount by which the flow directed through e exceeds e's capacity, and $\beta_{sr}(\nu) = \max\{0, u_{sr}\nu\}$ where the argument $\nu = -d_{sr} + \sum_{e \in E} f_{sr}^e$ is the amount by which the player's plan exceeds her demand.

On the implementation side we shall represent every player by an agent. Then, following the approach of [6] we transform the soft constraints of the problem by introducing two additional groups of adversarial agents: one for edge, and one for demand constraints. These agents selfishly choose prices for exceeding the edge capacities and failing to meet players' demands, respectively.

In particular, at the beginning of every iteration, each (player-, edge-, demand-) agent decides on their plan following the Greedy Projection Algorithm [19]. Player-agents decide on how to direct the flow, whereas the adversarial edge- and demand-players decide on the price they are going to charge the player-agents for their respective constraint violations. Player-agents then poll the adversarial agents on their prices and store the information for the decision-making in next iteration of the game.

A simple example of an averaged player plan after a number of iterations is depicted in Fig. 7. In this experiment, following [6] to the letter, we had a 6-node network and three players $P_{2,3}$, $P_{1,4}$, and $P_{4,6}$ with demands 30, 70 and 110. We set $c^{(2,3)}, c^{(3,2)} = 10$, and $c^e = 1$ for all other edges e. Edges $(5, 6)$ and $(6, 5)$ had capacities of 50, while all other capacities were 100.

Figure 7 also shows the output (the resulting flows) of our simulation run that ended up being entirely consistent with the solution found in [6].

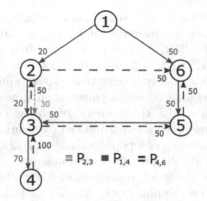

Fig. 7. A graphical representation of the experiment output consistent with the simulation run in [6].

6 A Performance Comparison

Although numerous software packages can be used for simulation of financial markets, we identified ABIDES as a top contender for MAXE, being extensible enough to allow for almost arbitrary simulation of limit order books while featuring a small group of default agent types allowing for an easy simulation setup.

MAXE and ABIDES vary fundamentally in how they approach simulation. While MAXE uses its own, general messaging protocol, ABIDES uses a combination of NASDAQ ITCH-OUCH protocols and agent wake-up scheduling. To examine how these two different approaches affect the simulation performance we considered one of the simplest multi-agent market models conceivable, in which agents require only very little computation to decide how to act.

Inspired by ABIDES' RMSC01 configuration, we thus started with a unit population for ABIDES consisting of a single market-maker and 25 ABIDES-default zero-intelligence agents, and a population for MAXE of the same size consisting of MAXE's equivalent agents. We scaled the unit population by the factors of $1, 2, 4, 8, 16$, while examining the average runtime of 1 h of simulation time over 10 attempts for factors $1, 2, 4, 8$. In the case of the 16-factor, only three runs were considered due to the large demands on memory and duration of the program run.

The results of our simulation are shown in Fig. 8. We only comment on the relative runtime performance of ABIDES and MAXE as the agent population increases.

For small agent populations there does not seem to be a significant difference in the performance of the two simulators. As the agent population grows, the runtime of MAXE becomes more clearly separated from that of ABIDES. This is most likely due to the different methods of agent communication handling employed by the two simulators. Our plot stops at 416 agents, after which the memory demand of the Python environment running ABIDES exceeded the

16 GiB of memory available in our small workstation and the operating system resorted to swapping, significantly hindering the runtime performance of ABIDES. A test run of ABIDES on 450 agents resulted in a Python *Memory error*. We noticed that ABIDES, at present, does not allow for regular flushing of trading history to the disk, and we believe that a small adjustment to the design of the simulator, coupled with the employment of an appropriate memory management strategy, could resolve the memory greediness currently limiting the feasibility of ABIDES' use when a larger number of agents is involved. For comparison, a simulation consisting of a population of 100,022 agents in MAXE with the same setup fit comfortably into 100 MiB of memory.

In summary, the plot of Fig. 8 is consistent with our intuition that the design choices made for the key components of MAXE do indeed result in marked performance improvements over alternative packages when a larger population of agents is to be simulated.

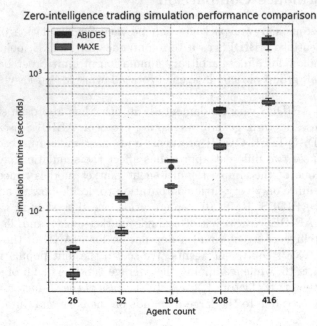

Fig. 8. A runtime comparison of MAXE and ABIDES.

7 Conclusions

We have introduced a new multi-agent simulation framework for financial market microstructure, called the Multi-Agent eXchange Environment (MAXE). There are a number of distinctive advantages MAXE offers over alternative simulation frameworks such as ABIDES [5]. Most notably, our framework was designed to be fast and flexible; it allows the modelling of different matching rules and can model latency.

We have demonstrated its potency for research into market dynamics. In particular, we utilised MAXE to showcase a mini study of the impact the delay in processing order has on a few LOB statistics and on the behaviour of the best prices after a large trade is registered with the exchange. We have also shown that MAXE is suitable for applications beyond the study of financial markets, as we used it to simulate a multi-agent reinforcement-learning network routing scenario. As our first evidence provided suggests, MAXE can be used to simulate markets and multi-agent systems more efficiently than comparable existing toolboxes. We therefore hope that it will be useful to facilitate research across different disciplines in need of simulating large-scale agent-based models.

Expanding on our illustrative case studies would be interesting in particular, given the dearth of studies utilising ABM in the context of pro-rata matching rules. We hope such inquiries would be greatly aided by our MAXE package, providing a standardised, scalable, and easily customisable toolbox to support this kind of research.

References

1. Bergenti, F., Caire, G., Monica, S., Poggi, A.: The first twenty years of agent-based software development with JADE. Auton. Agent. Multi-Agent Syst. **34**, 1–19 (2020)
2. Bouchaud, J.P., Bonart, J., Donier, J., Gould, M.: Trades, Quotes and Prices: Financial Markets Under the Microscope. Cambridge University Press, Cambridge (2018)
3. Bouchaud, J.P., Mézard, M., Potters, M., et al.: Statistical properties of stock order books: empirical results and models. Quant. Finance **2**(4), 251–256 (2002)
4. Buchanan, M.: Meltdown modelling: could agent-based computer models prevent another financial crisis? Nature **460**(7256), 680–683 (2009)
5. Byrd, D., Hybinette, M., Balch, T.H.: ABIDES: towards high-fidelity market simulation for AI research. arXiv:1904.12066 (2019)
6. Calliess, J.P., Gordon, G.J.: No-regret learning and a mechanism for distributed multiagent planning. Carnegie-Mellon Univ Pittsburgh PA Machine Learning Dept, Technical report (2008)
7. Capterra: Adaptive modeler (2019). https://www.capterra.com/p/131204/Adaptive-Modeler/. Accessed 19 Dec 2019
8. Collier, N.: RePast: an extensible framework for agent simulation. Univ. Chicago's Soc. Sci. Res. **36**, 2003 (2003)
9. Cont, R.: Volatility clustering in financial markets: empirical facts and agent-based models. In: Teyssiére, G., Kirman, A.P. (eds.) Long Memory in Economics, pp. 289–309. Springer, Heidelberg (2007). https://doi.org/10.1007/978-3-540-34625-8_10
10. Farmer, J.D., Gillemot, L., Iori, G., Krishnamurthy, S., Smith, D.E., Daniels, M.G.: A random order placement model of price formation in the continuous double auction. Econ. Evol. Complex Syst. **3**, 133–173 (2006)

11. Iori, G., Porter, J.: Agent-based modelling for financial markets (2012)
12. Luna, F., Stefansson, B.: Economic Simulations in Swarm: Agent-Based Modelling and Object Oriented Programming, vol. 14. Springer, Boston (2012). https://doi.org/10.1007/978-1-4615-4641-2
13. Paddrik, M., Hayes, R., Todd, A., Yang, S., Beling, P., Scherer, W.: An agent based model of the E-mini S&P 500 applied to flash crash analysis. In: 2012 IEEE Conference on Computational Intelligence for Financial Engineering & Economics (CIFEr), pp. 1–8. IEEE (2012)
14. Palmer, R., Arthur, W.B., Holland, J.H., LeBaron, B.: An artificial stock market. Artif. Life Robot. **3**(1), 27–31 (1999)
15. Belcak, P., Jan-Peter Calliess, S.Z.: Maxe github repository (2020). https://github.com/maxe-team/maxe. Accessed 17 Aug 2020
16. Potters, M., Bouchaud, J.P.: More statistical properties of order books and price impact. Phys. A **324**(1–2), 133–140 (2003)
17. Sklar, E.: NetLogo, a multi-agent simulation environment. Artif. Life **13**(3), 303–311 (2007)
18. Swarm: Swarm main page. http://www.swarm.org/wiki/Swarmmainpage. Accessed 19 Dec 2019
19. Zinkevich, M.: Online convex programming and generalized infinitesimal gradient ascent. In: Proceedings of the 20th International Conference on Machine Learning (ICML 2003), pp. 928–936 (2003)

On the Same Wavelengths: Emergence of Multiple Synchronies Among Multiple Agents

Sophie C. F. Hendrikse[1,2]([✉]), Jan Treur[3], Tom F. Wilderjans[1,2,4], Suzanne Dikker[1,5], and Sander L. Koole[1]

[1] Amsterdam Emotion Regulation Lab, Department of Clinical Psychology, Vrije Universiteit Amsterdam, Amsterdam, The Netherlands
{s.c.f.hendrikse,s.l.koole}@vu.nl, t.f.wilderjans@leidenuniv.nl
[2] Methodology and Statistics Research Unit, Institute of Psychology, Faculty of Social and Behavioural Sciences, Leiden University, Leiden, The Netherlands
[3] Social AI Group, Department of Computer Science, Vrije Universiteit Amsterdam, Amsterdam, The Netherlands
j.treur@vu.nl
[4] Research Group of Quantitative Psychology and Individual Differences, Faculty of Psychology and Educational Sciences, Katholieke Universiteit (KU) Leuven, Leuven, Belgium
[5] NYU – Max Planck Center for Language, Music and Emotion, New York University, New York, USA
suzanne.dikker@nyu.edu

Abstract. People spontaneously synchronize their mental states and behavioral actions when they interact. This paper models general mechanisms that can lead to the emergence of interpersonal synchrony by multiple agents with internal cognitive and affective states. In our simulations, one agent was exposed to a repeated stimulus and the other agent started to synchronize consecutively its movements, affects, conscious emotions and verbal actions with the exposed agent. The behavior displayed by the agents was consistent with theory and empirical evidence from the psychological and neuroscience literature. These results shed new light on the emergence of interpersonal synchrony in a wide variety of settings, from close relationships to psychotherapy. Moreover, the present work could provide a basis for future development of socially responsive virtual agents.

Keywords: Social agent model · Emergent synchrony patterns · Social simulations · In-Sync model

1 Introduction

People spontaneously synchronize their movements, affective responses, and verbal actions when they interact with each other. Such interpersonal synchrony has been related to a variety of positive outcomes in social settings. For instance, Miles and colleagues [20] found that synchrony was the most pronounced for minimal groups of people who were most divergent in terms of their artistic taste, suggesting that synchrony might serve as a tool to bridge social distance and intergroup differences. Elevated levels of movement

K. H. Van Dam and N. Verstaevel (Eds.): MABS 2021, LNAI 13128, pp. 57–71, 2022.
https://doi.org/10.1007/978-3-030-94548-0_5

synchrony have further been shown to foster social affiliation [10], cooperation [45] and compassion [39]. Moreover, interpersonal synchrony has been suggested to be a key component of a good therapeutic alliance, or working relationship, between patients and therapists in psychotherapy [19].

Crucially, interpersonal synchrony has mostly been examined separately in the fields of movement science, psychophysiology and (cognitive) linguistics, respectively, without relating them to each other, e.g. [17, 26, 29]. Nevertheless, it is plausible that associations between these different types of interpersonal synchrony exist [4, 18, 21, 24, 33]. To date, only a few theories have attempted to integrate the different modalities of interpersonal synchrony into one model. One of these theories is the Interpersonal Synchrony (In-Sync) model [18]. The In-Sync model seeks to explain how two actors mutually synchronize their behaviors and experiences (for example, patient and therapist during psychotherapy). At its core, the model supposes that higher-level synchrony processes of language and emotion regulation are affected by more elementary synchrony processes of movement and physiology.

The present paper presents computational simulation experiments in which two agents synchronize with each other by an emergent process. The aim is to examine how agent-based simulations created through general mechanisms derived and operationalized from theories and findings in psychology (see Sect. 2.1) can achieve the emergence of interpersonal synchrony. These interpersonal synchrony patterns will be evaluated against the principles of the In-Sync model and other theories of interpersonal coordination, as discussed in more detail in Sect. 2.2. The simulations are based on agent models where the internal agent processes are, in addition to the interactions between the agents, also modeled in some detail. To achieve this, we use a network-oriented agent modeling approach, as previously presented in [37, 38]. In this approach, the internal agent processes are modeled by a dynamic interplay of mental states based on general psychological (and neural) mechanisms. Section 3 presents the multi-agent model in terms of its scientific background and architecture. Section 4 describes the simulation methods, including parameter specifications. Section 5 presents the results of the performed social simulations, followed by concluding remarks in Sect. 6.

2 Psychological Background

2.1 General Psychological Mechanisms Used to Design the Agent Models

When individuals prepare to execute a certain action, like a movement, they assess what the effect of this action will be as part of their decision-making process. According to Damasio [2, 3], through a prediction loop such internal simulations generate an internal sensory representation of the likely outcome of an action. In other words, mental predictions of actions are done before these actions are actually executed; these predictions are triggered by an action preparation which can be activated via a stimulus-response effect or based on a similar action observed in other individuals [6, 7, 11]. In the latter case, mirror neurons are a relevant general mechanism that have received extensive empirical support from patient, brain stimulation and brain imaging studies [12]. Mirror neurons are neurons that would fire both when individuals prepare for their own action or body change to perform and when individuals observe a corresponding action by somebody else [13, 31]. Incoming connections (from sensory representation states) to mirror neurons (modeled as preparation states) are called mirroring links in the current paper. The preparation of the action by mirror neurons serves as a starting point for the internal simulation of the prediction loop. The twin concepts of internal simulations and mirror neurons provide a neurobiological explanation for the attunement of actions and emotions [13]. The precise role of mirror neurons in human behavior is still being investigated. Nevertheless, the notions of internal simulations and mirroring serve as usable and operationalizable constructs for a simulation model on interpersonal synchrony.

2.2 Emerging Synchrony Among Individuals

Of the three interpersonal synchrony – movement, physiological/affective and language synchrony - types that we consider here, movement synchrony is probably the most well-documented. Controlled experiments have shown that people naturally synchronize their movements, such as in finger-tapping paradigms [29]. More generally, people display a consistent tendency to synchronize their movements with familiar and unfamiliar others, in both structured and unstructured environments [5, 30, 42].

Physical experiences like movements have been argued to serve as grounding or scaffolding for higher-order mental processes [1, 14, 22, 43]. For example, emotional language comprehension has been shown to emerge faster when people's (facial) movements are congruent with the emotions from the text comprehension task [9]. Synchrony in language (also known as 'linguistic alignment', or 'accommodation') has also been reported to occur at several levels of representation, ranging from low-level speech properties to syntactic structure [15, 25, 27], and accommodation in speech is also well-documented.

Finally, a third type of interpersonal synchrony occurs for physiological responses. Physiological synchrony is shown to be important throughout development: Human infants in the uterus already adapt their physiological responses to their mother's [16, 41], and physiological synchrony between children and their caretaker during childhood prepares children to individually regulate their emotions [5]. Additionally, physiological synchrony emerges in close relationships between adults [23] and when unacquainted adults are involved in a collective ritual [17].

An influential account of affect is proposed by Russell [32] and states that physiological changes form the basis for core affect. Core affect is defined as 'a neurophysiological state consciously accessible as the simplest raw (nonreflective) feelings evident in moods and emotions'. Core affect is situated on two dimensions (valence and arousal) and fluctuates immediately after an event occurs to prepare people to act. Conscious emotions are enabled by core affect [32] and they arise when there is a conflict among lower-order processes (such as motor expressions and physiological responses). These conscious emotions at a higher-order level help to solve the insufficiency at the lower-order levels [8]. Verbal actions rely on language that can be generated once emotions are experienced in conscious awareness [8]. Once people put their feelings into words, this in turn can influence their emotional states [35]. Based on previous findings, we expect that the following patterns will be obtained in the agent simulations:

- Synchrony between people can be found in the form of comparable patterns over time.
- At the (intra-)individual level, movement will emerge first followed by conscious emotions (that are enabled by affect) to end with verbal actions.

- At the inter-individual level, movement synchrony will be followed by affective synchrony and language synchrony will emerge in the end.
- The different types of synchronies will be interdependent. Concretely, we expect that when the movements are disabled, the emergence of other types of synchrony will be complicated, as stated by the embodied cognition theories about synchrony.

3   The Two-Agent Model

3.1   General Approach of Agent Modeling

To model the emergence of interpersonal synchrony, two agents were designed with internal mental processes modeled as a dynamic interplay of mental states [36]. The structure of the two modeled agents is displayed in Fig. 1. The structure of the model is based on the general internal simulation and mirror neuron mechanisms outlined in Sect. 2.1 in order to test an emerging interplay of the different synchronies outlined in Sect. 2.2. These mechanisms are modeled by causal relations between mental states (e.g., the sensory representation of a stimulus, emotions, preparations). The mental states are represented by nodes with values that change over time (also simply called states) and the causal relations by connections between them, enabling interactive dynamics. In this way the mental states create an emergent mental process by which their activations dynamically change over time. These dynamical changes are affected by the input states and result in the output states, which in turn affect the input states of the agent itself and/or the other agent. Here the agent's input (sensing) states concern, for example, hearing the relevant verbal actions or seeing the relevant movements of the other agent. The output (execution) states concern the agents' actions and body states that are visible to the external world, including, for instance, the execution of a movement, the (facial) expression of affect and looking at the other agent. The interplay between internal (cognitive and affective) mental states involves, for example, the representations of the other agent's movement, the preparation of the agent's own movement, affect, and conscious emotion.

These causal networks are conceptualized by a labeled graph based on the following labels:

- A *connection weight* $\omega_{X,Y}$ is associated with each connection from a state X to state Y; this denotes the strength of that connection.
- A *combination function* $\mathbf{c}_Y$ for each state Y; this defines the aggregation of the impact from all incoming connections on that state.
- A *speed factor* η_Y for each state Y to time the effect of the impact in a state-specific manner.

Each of these labels contain specific parameter values that need to be tuned. As can be seen, each agent has the same 15 states, from which 7 internal (invisible for the outside world; colored white), 3 input and 5 external states. A brief explanation of all the states of agent A is provided in Table 1 and all states of two agents A and B are presented in Table A1 from the 23-page Appendix (https://www.researchgate.net/publication/349694211). Furthermore, the role matrices used in our MATLAB software environment (as described in [37] and [38], Ch 9) for the different experiments are also available in this Appendix (part G).

3.2 Conceptual Representations for the Agent Model

First, agents A and B can receive input from a stimulus $world^{sti}$ for some predefined time periods, meaning the activation of $world^{sti}$ alternates between 0 (*sti* not present) and 1 (*sti* present), with *sti* being an instance of a stimulus. The model structure of all agents is the same. Therefore, for the sake of simplicity, we focus in the current paper on the model of an agent A with respect to a single other agent B. Within the presented scenario, this external stimulus only influences A by a causal relation to the sensory representation rep_A^{sti} of this stimulus which in turn directly triggers the agent's three internal preparation states: $prep_A^{mov}$, $affect_A^{aff}$ and $prep_{A,B}^{ver}$, with *mov*, *aff* and *ver* being an instance of movement, affective response and a verbal action of agent A, respectively. Note that $prep_{A,B}^{ver}$ has an A, B subscript as this state denotes the preparation of only those verbal actions from agent A to B. The agent model also includes a sensory representation state for the verbal actions ver' ($rep_A^{ver'}$) and the movements mov' of any **other** agent ($rep_A^{mov'}$), with the prime symbol $'$ indicating that the behavior comes from the other agent B (without prime means that it comes from agent A). Each of these two sensory representation states is affected by the agent's three input states: hearing the verbal cues ver' ($hear_{A,B}^{ver'}$), seeing the affective expressions aff' ($see_{A,B}^{aff'}$) and seeing the movements mov' ($see_{A,B}^{mov'}$) of any **other** agent.

As mov' is assumed to be a movement similar to *mov*, $rep_A^{mov'}$ is directly connected with $prep_A^{mov}$, $affect_A^{aff}$ and $prep_{A,B}^{ver}$ and these (reciprocal) causal links show how the sensory representation of lower movement processes serve as a base for (higher) internal action preparations and the connections from each preparation state to $rep_A^{mov'}$ in turn reflect the feedback from the higher-order to the lower-order processes. Furthermore, $rep_A^{mov'}$ directly influences the gaze direction of the agent ($look_{A,B}$), because the sensory representation of the other agent's movement mov' can enhance the agent's visual focus. State $rep_A^{ver'}$ causally affects $affect_A^{aff}$ and $prep_{A,B}^{ver}$, but not the preparation state for movement because the latter is a lower-order process. The execution of $listen_{A,B}$ is also directly triggered by $rep_A^{ver'}$ because the sensory representation of the other agent's verbal action can alert the agent to listen more focused. The mental processes, starting from the representation states, ultimately lead to both conscious emotions (internal state $emotion_A^{aff}$) and executed actions in the physical world ($look_{A,B}$, $listen_{A,B}$, $move_A^{mov}$, $exp\_affect_A^{aff}$, $talk_{A,B}^{ver}$).

Regarding the preparation states, $prep_A^{mov}$ influences both the actual execution of the movement $move_A^{mov}$ and its representation $rep_A^{mov'}$, thereby highlighting the dynamic interplay of one's representation of mov' and one's own execution mov. The state $affect_A^{aff}$ directly influences $rep_A^{mov'}$, the expression of the affective response aff ($exp\_affect_A^{aff}$) and the conscious $emotion_A^{aff}$ of aff. The fact that the sensory representation of ver' does not get feedback from $affect_A^{aff}$ reflects the higher-order process of language compared to the lower-level affective changes. State $prep_{A,B}^{ver}$ has an immediate effect on $rep_A^{mov'}$,

$\text{rep}_A^{ver'}$ and the execution of the verbal action $\text{talk}_{A,B}^{ver}$. State $\text{talk}_{A,B}^{ver}$ in turn triggers emotion$_A^{aff}$ which in turn directly affects $\text{prep}_{A,B}^{ver}$. This feedback loop reflects the need of conscious emotions to initiate verbal actions *ver* and at the meantime how these verbal actions *ver* themselves further shape the conscious emotions of the affective response *aff*.

The Coupling Between the Sensing and Execution States

In a situation with multiple agents, we can connect the execution states of any agent A to the sensory states of any agent B. Specifically, each of agent A's sensing states receives two input connections, one from their own execution state and one from an execution state of agent B. Specifically, $\text{hear}_{A,B}^{ver'}$ gets input from $\text{listen}_{A,B}$ because listening is required to receive auditory cues and from the execution $\text{talk}_{B,A}^{ver'}$ of the verbal action *ver'* of agent B. Both $\text{see}_{A,B}^{aff'}$ and $\text{see}_{A,B}^{mov'}$ are activated by $\text{look}_{A,B}$ to capture the need of looking at agent B to get visual cues from this agent. Regarding the input connections from Agent B, the expression $\text{exp\_affect}_B^{aff'}$ of the affective response for *aff'* is directly linked to state $\text{see}_{A,B}^{aff'}$ for seeing *aff'* and similarly the execution state $\text{move}_B^{mov'}$ of the movement *mov'* is directly linked to $\text{see}_{A,B}^{mov'}$.

General Mechanisms

In line with the general psychological mechanisms outlined in Sect. 2.1, in addition to stimulus-response links, each agent contains prediction loops and mirroring links. Both direct and indirect effects are predicted through the prediction loops. The prediction loops from prep_A^{mov} to $\text{rep}_A^{mov'}$ and from $\text{prep}_{A,B}^{ver}$ to $\text{rep}_A^{ver'}$ consist of the prediction of direct effects (i.e., what the effect of the execution of a certain action will be on the sensory representation of this action). The indirect effects (i.e., the effect of a preparation of a certain action on the representation of another action) regard the prediction loops from $\text{prep}_{A,B}^{ver}$ to $\text{rep}_A^{mov'}$ and from affect_A^{aff} to $\text{rep}_A^{mov'}$. Concerning the mirroring links, the connection from $\text{rep}_A^{mov'}$ to prep_A^{mov} mirrors the action movement and the connection from $\text{rep}_A^{ver'}$ to $\text{prep}_{A,B}^{ver}$ mirrors the verbal action of another agent. In principle the connection from $\text{see}_{A,B}^{aff'}$ to affect_A^{aff} through both $\text{rep}_A^{mov'}$ and $\text{rep}_A^{ver'}$ can also be interpreted as a mirroring path, because every sensory representation is a) influenced by $\text{see}_{A,B}^{aff'}$ and b) internally influences affect_A^{aff} through the representation states of both the verbal action ($\text{rep}_A^{ver'}$) and the movement ($\text{rep}_A^{mov'}$). It is argueable that the model could also in addition contain a $\text{rep}_A^{aff'}$, however, we have decided to not include this additional state for reasons of simplicity. There were already multiple pathways from $\text{see}_{A,B}^{aff'}$ to affect_A^{aff} itself.

Connection Weights

All the connection weight $\omega_{X,Y}$ values were fixed on the value 1, except the $\omega_{X,Y}$ of all incoming connections to affect_A^{aff} and $\text{affect}_B^{aff'}$. The incoming connections to these affect states from respectively $\text{rep}_A^{mov'}$ and rep_B^{mov} were set to 2 and all the other connections were set to 0.5. In this way, the less complex sensorimotor processes serve as a foundation or 'grounding' [1] for the affective responses. Furthermore, the connection weight $\omega_{world^{sti},\, rep_B^{sti}}$ is set to 0 because agent B did not receive a *sti*.

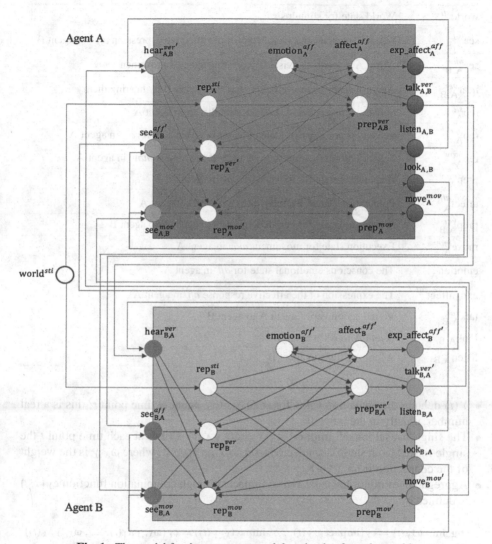

Fig. 1. The model for the two agents and the stimulus from the world.

3.3 Numerical Representations for the Agent Model

We used the software environment described in [37] and [38], Ch 9. In this software environment, the conceptual representations of the multi-agent model are mapped onto their associated numerical representations as follows:

Table 1. The description of all the states of agent A

State	Explanation
$world^{sti}$	World state for stimulus sti
$see_{A,B}^{aff'}$	Agent A receives the visual cues of the affective expression aff' of agent B
$see_{A,B}^{mov'}$	Agent A receives the visual cues of the agent B movement mov'
$hear_{A,B}^{ver'}$	Agent A receives the verbal cues ver' of agent B by hearing them
rep_A^{sti}	Sensory representation state for stimulus sti in agent A
$rep_A^{ver'}$	Sensory representation state of agent B verbal action ver' in agent A
$rep_A^{mov'}$	Sensory representation state of agent B movement mov' in agent A
$prep_A^{mov}$	Preparation state for movement mov in agent A
$affect_A^{aff}$	Preparation state for affective response aff in agent A
$prep_{A,B}^{ver}$	Preparation state for verbal action ver of agent A to agent B
$move_A^{mov}$	Execution state for movement mov in agent A
$emotion_A^{aff}$	The conscious emotional state for aff in agent A
$exp\_affect_A^{aff}$	The expression of the affective response aff in agent A
$talk_{A,B}^{ver}$	Verbal action ver of agent A to agent B
$look_{A,B}$	Agent A looks at agent B
$listen_{A,B}$	Agent A listens to agent B

- $Y(t)$ denotes the activation value for state Y of an agent at time point t; this is a real number, usually in the range [0, 1].
- The single causal impact $\mathbf{impact}_{X,Y}(t) = \omega_{X,Y}X(t)$ defines at each time point t the single impact from state X connected to state Y on state Y, where $\omega_{X,Y}$ is the weight of the connection from X to Y.
- Aggregating of multiple single causal impacts through combination function $\mathbf{c}_Y(\ldots)$ is defined by

$$\mathbf{aggimpact}_Y(t) = \mathbf{c}_Y\big(\mathbf{impact}_{X_1,Y}(t), \ldots, \mathbf{impact}_{X_k,Y}(t)\big) = \mathbf{c}_Y\big(\omega_{X_1,Y}X_1(t), \ldots, \omega_{X_k,Y}X_k(t)\big)$$

for the states $X_1, \ldots, X_k$ from which Y has incoming connections.
- The speed factor η_Y determines how the effect of $\mathbf{aggimpact}_Y(t)$ on state Y is exerted gradually over time:

$$Y(t + \Delta t) = Y(t) + \eta_Y\big[\mathbf{aggimpact}_Y(t) - Y(t)\big]\Delta t$$

- This leads to the following difference or differential equation for Y:
$Y(t + \Delta t) = Y(t) + \eta_Y\big[\mathbf{c}_Y\big(\omega_{X_1,Y}X_1(t), \ldots, \omega_{X_k,Y}X_k(t)\big) - Y(t)\big]\Delta t$, or
$\frac{dY(t)}{dt} = \eta_Y\big[\mathbf{c}_Y\big(\omega_{X_1,Y}X_1(t), \ldots, \omega_{X_k,Y}X_k(t)\big) - Y(t)\big]$

All agent states use the advanced logistic sum combination function $c_Y(\ldots)$, whereas the world state for stimulus *sti* uses the step-modulo combination function $c_Y(\ldots)$; see Table 2.

Table 2. The two combination functions used

Name	Formula	Parameters
Advanced logistic sum combination function $\mathbf{alogistic}_{\sigma,\tau}(V_1,\ldots,V_k)$	$\left[\dfrac{1}{1+e^{-\sigma(V_1+\cdots+V_k-\tau)}} - \dfrac{1}{1+e^{\sigma\tau}}\right](1+e^{-\sigma\tau})$	Steepness σ Excitability threshold τ
Step-mod function $\mathbf{stepmod}_{\rho,\delta}(V_1,\ldots,V_k)$	for time t if $mod(t,\rho) < \delta$ then $x = 0$, else 1	Repeated time interval ρ Duration of value 0 δ

4 Simulation Method for the Agents

We will present three scenarios. All initial state values were set to 0 in all simulations. Regarding the first/main simulation, as specified with the input parameters of the step-modulo combination function (see Table 3), agent A is exposed to an external stimulus *sti* for 150 time units every time after 150 time units without stimulation. This process (a total of 300 time units) is repeated until the end of the simulations. We deliberately do not further specify stimulus *sti* because there are numerous situations that can provoke interpersonal synchrony. Such repeated stimuli may concretely regard, for instance, daily life events that one person shares with another person, a series of therapy sessions or a dance choreography, meaning these agent simulations might have a wide variety of applications. The activation level of *sti* can vary over specific applications, however, for the sake of simplicity, we have decided to use activation level 1 over all simulations. The (length of the) stimulus *sti* intervals for this main social simulation were selected such that, as can be seen in Fig. 2 and Fig. B1-4 from the Appendix, (most of) the mental states ended in their equilibrium phase for both the stimulus *sti* present and absent periods. In Fig. 2 and the Appendix Fig. B1-4 and C1-4 is it shown that emerging limit cycle behavior occurs right from the start.

The characteristics of the two agents have been set according to the homeostatic regulation of neuronal excitability principle, which refers to the adaptation of neurons' internal properties to control a desired activation level; e.g., [44]. More specifically, as agent B (the agent not directly receiving the stimulus) gets less incoming activation than agent A, we have mimicked this principle by putting some of the excitability threshold and steepness values from the advanced logistic sum combination function of agent B lower than for agent A. The speed factors of almost all states equaled 0.5. The speed factor of the stimulus was set to 2 to ensure the fast appearance and disappearance of the stimulus. In contrast, the speed factors of the looking direction and the focus of listening were set to 0.2 (possible scale range: 0 to 1, with higher speed factors indicating that the specific state will change quicker) for both agents because in the real world these actions often do not rapidly change.

The second simulation consists of shorter stimulus and non-stimulus intervals (each of them lasting 10 time units instead of 150), and this is the only difference from the main simulation. This is a representative example for the cases where no equilibria are reached within the stimulus and non-stimulus periods. The third simulation is exactly the same as the main simulation except that the states related to movement were disabled in both agents (see Appendix, part H). The aim of this third simulation was to test whether synchrony can emerge without movement.

Table 3. The values for the main characteristics of the model: speed factors η and combination function parameters σ and τ for each agent state and combination function parameters ρ and δ for the stimulus *sti*

State	η	σ	τ	State	η	σ	τ
$see_{A,B}^{aff'}$	0.5	1	0.4	$see_{B,A}^{aff}$	0.5	1	0.4
$see_{A,B}^{mov'}$	0.5	1	0.4	$see_{B,A}^{mov}$	0.5	1	0.4
$hear_{A,B}^{ver'}$	0.5	1	0.4	$hear_{B,A}^{ver}$	0.5	1	0.4
rep_A^{sti}	0.5	20	0.6	rep_B^{sti}	0.5	20	0.6
$rep_A^{ver'}$	0.5	1	0.4	rep_B^{ver}	0.5	1	0.4
$rep_A^{mov'}$	0.5	1	3	rep_B^{mov}	0.5	1	2
$prep_A^{mov}$	0.5	4	0.8	$prep_B^{mov'}$	0.5	2	0.3
$affect_A^{aff}$	0.5	5	0.8	$affect_B^{aff'}$	0.5	2	0.6
$prep_{A,B}^{ver}$	0.5	1	3.5	$prep_{B,A}^{ver'}$	0.5	1	2.5
$move_A^{mov}$	0.5	4	0.3	$move_B^{mov'}$	0.5	4	0.1
$emotion_A^{aff}$	0.5	2	0.3	$emotion_B^{aff'}$	0.5	2	0.1
$exp\_affect_A^{aff}$	0.5	2	0.4	$exp\_affect_B^{aff'}$	0.5	2	0.4
$talk_{A,B}^{ver}$	0.5	4	0.3	$talk_{B,A}^{ver'}$	0.5	4	0.3
$look_{A,B}$	0.2	1	0.3	$look_{B,A}$	0.2	1	0.5
$listen_{A,B}$	0.2	2	0.3	$listen_{B,A}$	0.2	1	0.4
$world^{sti}$	2	ρ 300	δ 150				

5   Analysis of the Two-Agent Model: Main Simulation

To validate the two-agent model, we derived some testable predictions from the literature (as discussed in Sect. 2). First, the occurrence of a limit cycle. Synchrony is quantified as the same states of agent A and B that exhibit comparable patterns over time. Therefore, we focus for each agent on corresponding actions. Equivalent states of agent A (solid lines) and B (dashed lines) are colored the same in all figures. As shown in Fig. 2, Fig. B1-4 and Fig. C1-4 from the Appendix regarding the main simulation, all the states of both agent A and B are activated after the stimulus *sti* is presented to agent A and deactivated when *sti* is no longer present, resulting in a limit cycle for the model.

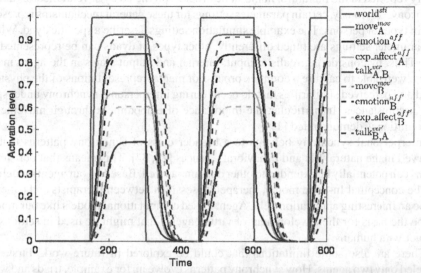

Fig. 2. Activation levels over 800 time units (with 150 non-stimulus time units alternated with 150 stimulus time units) for the execution states of the two agents. Corresponding states of agent A (solid lines) and B (dashed lines) are indicated in the same color, whereas the stimulus *sti* is indicated in yellow. (Color figure online)

This finding demonstrates that emergent synchrony patterns between agents can originate through communication/interaction when only one agent actually receives a stimulus *sti*. Note that such synchrony patterns would not be able to emerge when agent B cannot receive sensing information from agent A as an input (i.e., see or hear agent A). These emergent synchrony patterns remain consistent over time, indicated by the repetitive (equally high) peaks of each of two agents' states across the stimulus *sti* episodes. Furthermore, as can be seen in Fig. 2 and Fig. B1-4 from the Appendix, each of the state activations of agent A precedes activation of the equivalent state of agent B, except the input and representation states. The reasoning behind the latter is that the input states, and thereby the representation states that are directly dependent on the input states, of agent A require input from the output states of agent B and thus cannot precede these states of agent B in terms of activation. The analysis of the simulation with shorter stimulus and non-stimulus intervals, a more extensive evaluation of the sequence of the different types of synchrony and the simulation without movement can be retrieved from the Appendix, part H.

6 Discussion

Our agent models demonstrate the emergence of movement, expression of affective response, and language synchrony in two agents. Moreover, conscious emotional synchrony occurred as well. The social simulations based on the described general psychological mechanisms succeeded in reproducing emerging synchrony patterns that are widely reported in the literature, in the same order as predicted by several theories about synchrony. Obviously, certain parameter settings for these general mechanisms represent certain types of persons. The example simulation settings describe a specific dyad. When the parameter settings are tuned differently, other types of dyads can be represented as well. Thus, by considering realistic input, internal and output states in the agent models, we were able to capture a complex process of mental representations of the physical world and perceived similarities that do occur during interpersonal synchrony under specific circumstances. In particular, the importance of embodiment through movements for cognition is demonstrated [1].

Interpersonal synchrony belongs to a broader class of synchrony patterns that is observed in the natural life and behavioral sciences [28, 34]. This means that our simulations can potentially be extended to other domains as well. Based on our agent modeling and the conceptual In-Sync model, therapeutic sessions between therapists and patients can be an interesting application field. Agent-based computational models like our model can be the basis for the development of virtual agents that might be used in settings to interact with humans.

There are also some limitations that could be explored in future work. First, we modeled only two agents. How synchrony patterns evolve in, for example, triads and with different stimulus episodes across agents are potential future simulations. Second, future work should verify whether the same synchrony patterns in the agents hold on empirical data. Third, the current agents are non-adaptive: for example, the excitability thresholds are fixed over time. Adaptive agents might be able to automatically tune their synchrony behavior in varying situations, thereby maintaining their equilibria states in even more unpredictable environments. Fourth, the internal states of our agent models could always be extended, for example by including more specific states. A typical example would be to include a representation state of the affective expression of other agents or to separate the representation states for one's own movements and the movements of other agents. Fifth, we did not include some anticipation theories from psychology in our agent models. Based on some finger tapping experiments [40], it would also be possible that the follower (in our case agent B) anticipates on the leader (agent A) and thereby becomes effectively the leader in synchrony. Sixth, in the future, variable stimulus intervals and/or levels might be incorporated to explore how the emerging synchrony and common ground evolve. Finally, future work is needed in which more extensive analysis on the interplay between limit cycles, equilibria and synchronization is conducted.

References

1. Barsalou, L.W.: Grounded cognition. Ann. Rev. Psychol. **59**, 617–645 (2008)
2. Damasio, A.R.: Descartes' Error: Emotion, Reason, and the Human Brain. Penguin, London (1994)
3. Damasio, A.R.: The Feeling of What Happens: Body and Emotion in the Making of Consciousness, Harvest edn. Harcourt, San Diego (1999)
4. Dumas, G., Nadel, J., Soussignan, R., Martinerie, J., Garnero, L.: Inter-brain synchronization during social interaction. PLoS ONE **5**(8), e12166 (2010)
5. Feldman, R.: Parent–infant synchrony: biological foundations and developmental outcomes. Curr. Dir. Psychol. Sci. **16**, 340–345 (2007)
6. Gallese, V., Goldman, A.: Mirror neurons and the simulation theory of mindreading. Trends Cogn. Sci. **2**, 493–501 (1998)
7. Goldman, A.I.: Simulating Minds: The Philosophy, Psychology, and Neuroscience of Mindreading. Oxford University Press, New York (2006)
8. Grandjean, D., Sander, D., Scherer, K.R.: Conscious emotional experience emerges as a function of multilevel, appraisal-driven response synchronization. Conscious. Cogn. **17**(2), 484–495 (2008)
9. Havas, D.A., Glenberg, A.M., Rinck, M.: Emotion simulation during language comprehension. Psychon. Bull. Rev. **14**(3), 436–441 (2007). https://doi.org/10.3758/BF03194085
10. Hove, M.J., Risen, J.L.: It's all in the timing: interpersonal synchrony increases affiliation. Soc. Cogn. **27**(6), 949–960 (2009)
11. Hesslow, G.: Conscious thought as simulation of behaviour and perception. Trends Cogn. Sci. **6**, 242–247 (2002)
12. Heyes, C., Catmur, C.: What happened to mirror neurons? Perspect. Psychol. Sci. (2021). Article number: e17456916219906138
13. Iacoboni, M.: Mirroring People: The New Science of How We Connect with Others. Farrar, Straus & Giroux, New York (2008)
14. IJzerman, H., Koole, S.L.: From perceptual rags to metaphoric riches: bodily, social, and cultural constraints on sociocognitive metaphors: comment on Landau, Meier, and Keefer (2010). Psychol. Bull. **137**, 355–361 (2011). https://doi.org/10.1037/a0022373
15. Ireland, M.E., Pennebaker, J.W.: Language style matching in writing: synchrony in essays, correspondence, and poetry. J. Pers. Soc. Psychol. **99**, 549–571 (2010). https://doi.org/10.1037/a0020386
16. Ivanov, P.C., Ma, Q.D.Y., Bartsch, R.P.: Maternal–fetal heartbeat phase synchronization. Proc. Natl. Acad. Sci. **106**(33), 13641–13642 (2009)
17. Konvalinka, I., et al.: Synchronized arousal between performers and related spectators in a fire-walking ritual. Proc. Natl. Acad. Sci. **108**(20), 8514–8519 (2011)
18. Koole, S.L., Tschacher, W.: Synchrony in psychotherapy: a review and an integrative framework for the therapeutic alliance. Front. Psychol. **7**, e862 (2016)
19. Koole, S.L., Tschacher, W., Butler, E., Dikker, S., Wilderjans, T.F.: In sync with your shrink. In: Forgas, J.P., Crano, W.D., Fiedler, K. (eds.) Applications of Social Psychology, pp. 161–184. Taylor and Francis, Milton Park (2020)
20. Miles, L.K., Lumsden, J., Richardson, M.J., Macrae, C.N.: Do birds of a feather move together? Group membership and behavioral synchrony. Exp. Brain Res. **211**(3–4), 495–503 (2011). https://doi.org/10.1007/s00221-011-2641-z
21. Nguyen, T., Abney, D.H., Salamander, D., Bertenthal, B., Hoehl, S.: Social touch is associated with neural but not physiological synchrony in naturalistic mother-infant interactions. BioRxiv (2021)

22. Niedenthal, P.M.: Embodying emotion. Science **316**, 1002–1005 (2007)
23. Palumbo, R.V., et al.: Interpersonal autonomic physiology: a systematic review of the literature. Pers. Soc. Psychol. Rev. **21**(2), 99–141 (2017)
24. Pan, Y., Novembre, G., Song, B., Zhu, Y., Hu, Y.: Dual brain stimulation enhances interpersonal learning through spontaneous movement synchrony. Soc. Cogn. Affect. Neurosci. **16**(1–2), 210–221 (2021)
25. Pickering, M.J., Garrod, S.: Toward a mechanistic psychology of dialogue. Behav. Brain Sci. **27**, 169–190 (2004). https://doi.org/10.1017/S0140525X04000056
26. Pickering, M.J., Garrod, S.: Alignment as the basis for successful communication. Res. Lang. Comput. **4**(2–3), 203–228 (2006). https://doi.org/10.1007/s11168-006-9004-0
27. Pickering, M.J., Garrod, S.: Understanding Dialogue: Language Use and Social Interaction. Cambridge University Press, Cambridge (2021)
28. Pikovsky, A., Rosenblum, M., Kurths, J.: Synchronization: A Universal Concept in Nonlinear Sciences. Cambridge University Press, New York (2003)
29. Repp, B.H., Su, Y.-H.: Sensorimotor synchronization: a review of recent research (2006–2012). Psychon. Bull. Rev. **20**(3), 403–452 (2013). https://doi.org/10.3758/s13423-012-0371-2
30. Richardson, M.J., Marsh, K.L., Isenhower, R.W., Goodman, J.R.L., Schmidt, R.C.: Rocking together: dynamics of intentional and unintentional interpersonal coordination. Hum. Mov. Sci. **26**(6), 867–891 (2007)
31. Rizzolatti, G., Sinigaglia, C.: Mirrors in the Brain: How Our Minds Share Actions and Emotions. Oxford University Press, Oxford (2008)
32. Russell, J.A.: Core affect and the psychological construction of emotion. Psychol. Rev. **110**(1), 145 (2003)
33. Shamay-Tsoory, S.G., Saporta, N., Marton-Alper, I.Z., Gvirts, H.Z.: Herding brains: a core neural mechanism for social alignment. Trends Cogn. Sci. **23**, 174–186 (2019)
34. Strogatz, S.: Sync: The Emerging Science of Spontaneous Order. Hyperion Books, New York (2003)
35. Torre, J.B., Lieberman, M.D.: Putting feelings into words: affect labeling as implicit emotion regulation. Emot. Rev. **10**(2), 116–124 (2018)
36. Treur, J.: Network-Oriented Modeling: Addressing Complexity of Cognitive, Affective and Social Interactions. Springer, Cham (2016). https://doi.org/10.1007/978-3-319-45213-5
37. Treur, J.: A modeling environment for reified temporal-causal networks: modeling plasticity and metaplasticity in cognitive agent models. In: Baldoni, M., Dastani, M., Liao, B., Sakurai, Y., Zalila Wenkstern, R. (eds.) PRIMA 2019. LNCS (LNAI), vol. 11873, pp. 487–495. Springer, Cham (2019). https://doi.org/10.1007/978-3-030-33792-6_33
38. Treur, J.: Network-Oriented Modeling for Adaptive Networks: Designing Higher-Order Adaptive Biological, Mental and Social Network Models. Springer, Cham (2020). https://doi.org/10.1007/978-3-030-31445-3
39. Valdesolo, P., DeSteno, D.: Synchrony and the social tuning of compassion. Emotion **11**(2), 262–266 (2011)
40. Van Der Steen, M.C., Keller, P.E.: The ADaptation and Anticipation Model (ADAM) of sensorimotor synchronization. Front. Hum. Neurosci. **7**, e253 (2013)
41. Van Leeuwen, P., et al.: Influence of paced maternal breathing on fetal–maternal heart rate coordination. Proc. Natl. Acad. Sci. **106**(33), 13661–13666 (2009)
42. van Ulzen, N.R., Lamoth, C.J.C., Daffertshofer, A., Semin, G.R., Beek, P.J.: Characteristics of instructed and uninstructed interpersonal coordination while walking side-by-side. Neurosci. Lett. **432**(2), 88–93 (2008)
43. Williams, L.E., Huang, J.Y., Bargh, J.A.: The scaffolded mind: Higher mental processes are grounded in early experience of the physical world. Eur. J. Soc. Psychol. **39**(7), 1257–1267 (2009)

44. Williams, A.H., O'Leary, T., Marder, E.: Homeostatic regulation of neuronal excitability. Scholarpedia **8**, 1656 (2013)
45. Wiltermuth, S.S., Heath, C.: Synchrony and cooperation. Psychol. Sci. **20**(1), 1–5 (2009)

Multi-agent Simulation for AI Behaviour Discovery in Operations Research

Michael Papasimeon[✉][iD] and Lyndon Benke[iD]

Defence Science and Technology Group, 506 Lorimer Street,
Fishermans Bend, VIC 3207, Australia
{michael.papasimeon,lyndon.benke}@dst.defence.gov.au

Abstract. We describe ACEO, a lightweight platform for evaluating the suitability and viability of AI methods for behaviour discovery in multi-agent simulations. Specifically, ACEO was designed to explore AI methods for multi-agent simulations used in operations research studies related to new technologies such as autonomous aircraft. Simulation environments used in production are often high-fidelity, complex, require significant domain knowledge and as a result have high R&D costs. Minimal and lightweight simulation environments can help researchers and engineers evaluate the viability of new AI technologies for behaviour discovery in a more agile and potentially cost effective manner. In this paper we describe the motivation for the development of ACEO. We provide a technical overview of the system architecture, describe a case study of behaviour discovery in the aerospace domain, and provide a qualitative evaluation of the system. The evaluation includes a brief description of collaborative research projects with academic partners, exploring different AI behaviour discovery methods.

1 Introduction

In this paper we provide an overview of ACEO, a lightweight multi-agent-based simulation (MABS) environment designed for evaluating AI behaviour discovery methods for operations research studies. In operations research and analysis, multi-agent simulations have a long track record of being used to evaluate technologies for acquisition and their subsequent employment. In the aerospace domain, multi-agent simulations have been used to model, simulate and ultimately compare and assess aircraft to support acquisition programs and to help evaluate how they may be operated at both a tactical and strategic level. In large engineering projects, these constructive simulation environments allow large organisations in government and industry to reduce cost and risk on complex projects.

In many of these simulations, agent behavioural models have been used to represent the decision making of both human and autonomous systems. For example, a significant body of work exists around using agent models to represent pilot decision making in constructive simulations of air operations [5,8,18,25]. Typically, agent oriented software engineering (AOSE) techniques are used to

© Springer Nature Switzerland AG 2022
K. H. Van Dam and N. Verstaevel (Eds.): MABS 2021, LNAI 13128, pp. 72–85, 2022.
https://doi.org/10.1007/978-3-030-94548-0_6

elicit domain knowledge [4] and to then handcraft agent behaviour models using technologies such as finite state machines, behaviour trees, or more sophisticated approaches such as the belief-desire-intention (BDI) model of agent reasoning. However, one of the limitations of using traditional AOSE techniques is that the domain knowledge elicited and ultimately programmed in agent code represents current operational practices for existing technologies. The introduction of new technologies such as autonomous aircraft (also commonly known as UAV; unmanned air vehicles) poses a challenge for the development of agent behavioural models, as they are unlikely to be operated in the same way that traditional aircraft are operated.

Hence, there is a requirement to augment traditional AOSE techniques with exploratory AI methods from fields such as machine learning, evolutionary algorithms and automated planning. The long term goal is to discover novel tactics, strategies and concepts of operations (CONOPS) that current domain experts may otherwise not have considered [24]. We use the term *behaviour discovery* to include all of these methods and their application.

One of the challenges in evaluating new exploratory AI methods for their viability for behaviour discovery, is the complexity of production simulation environments. Production simulators are often complex, requiring significant software engineering and domain expertise to deploy effectively, and typically involve the interplay of many high-fidelity computational models. The added complexity of deployment on high performance computing clusters can make it cost prohibitive (in schedule and resources) to use one of these environments to evaluate the viability of an exploratory AI algorithm. Often there are additional complications relating to intellectual property and security that make academic collaboration difficult.

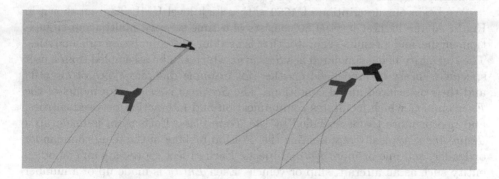

Fig. 1. 3D visualisation of autonomous aircraft simulated in `ACE0`

In this paper we propose using a lighter weight, lower fidelity MABS for evaluating exploratory AI methods that does not incur the overhead of a production environment. We present `ACE0` as one such lighter weight MABS, and describe our experience to date in evaluating exploratory AI methods in the aerospace domain.

The remainder of the paper provides a high level system overview of the ACEO MABS, followed by a case study of its application in the aerospace tactics domain, with an evaluation of some of the exploratory AI methods that have been investigated to date. We conclude by discussing some of the future challenges for agent behaviour discovery with multi-agent simulation.

Our contributions in this paper are threefold; (a) we pose the problem of agent behaviour discovery as future challenge for the fields of both multi-agent simulation and agent oriented software engineering; (b) we present ACEO as a reference MABS for conducting exploratory AI analysis in a lightweight environment; and (c) we outline a series of lessons and challenges for agent behaviour discovery arising from our experience with ACEO in the aerospace domain.

2   System Overview

In this section we provide a high level overview of ACEO and its associated components. As mentioned in Sect. 1, ACEO was developed as a research simulator to reduce the costs of exploring AI algorithms in a production simulation environment. In the air combat operations analysis domain, lightweight research simulators are not uncommon, with LWAC [26] and AFGYM [28] being recent examples. While ACEO does have a focus on the aerospace domain, the architecture is generic and can be extended to model naval and ground entities. Furthermore, the architecture supports the grouping of entities into teams, and allows agents to undertake command and control of both individual entities and teams of entities. This allows for the modelling and representation of joint (air, maritime and land) operations. The complexities of team modelling are outside the scope of this paper and hence the focus will be on exploratory AI methods for multiple agents outside of a team structure.

We begin our description of ACEO with a high level UML diagram shown in Fig. 2. At the highest level ACEO consists of a time-stepped multi-agent simulation engine, and a results generator that is used for post simulation run analytics. The top entity being simulated is a *Scenario*, which can be assembled from a user specified library of predefined entities (for example different types of aircraft) and their associated initial conditions. The *Scenario* consists of a model of the *Environment* which facilitates communication and interaction between entities, and one or more teams specified by the *Team* class. Each team is made up a *Team Agent*, typically representing the decision making of the team commander or leader, and one or more *Entity* objects. Each object represents an embodied entity such as an aircraft, ship or vehicle. Each *Entity* is made up of a number of computational components. These include sensor and weapon models, and a dynamics model that represents how the entity moves through the physical environment. The control system is a separate model that can take high level commands from an agent and translate them into lower level commands that are understood by the dynamics model. Finally, the agent model represents the decision making model for the entity, taking as input the entire entity state (dynamics, sensors, weapons etc.) and generating commands for all these components. The *Agent* represents the decision making component of the entity,

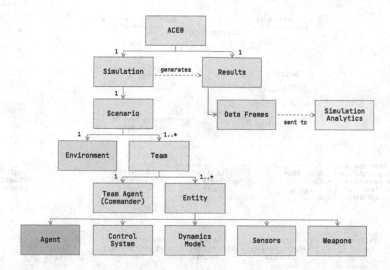

Fig. 2. High level static design architecture of the ACE0 MABS.

which may be a model of a human decision making or the reasoning component of an autonomous system.

When representing an autonomous aircraft, the pilot agent can reason about higher level decision making, and generate higher level actions (such as flying to a waypoint or changing heading). The flight control system (FCS) model has the responsibility for translating these into low level aircraft roll, pitch and throttle commands which are understood by the flight dynamics model. As will be discussed later, selecting a suitable level of action abstraction has a significant effect on the suitability and viability of exploratory AI algorithms for behaviour discovery.

The ability to reason about behaviour at different levels of abstraction is key to evaluating different exploratory algorithms for behaviour discovery. This is critical for client driven operations analysis studies where the level of abstraction selected for the state and action spaces has a significant effect on how the results of the study can be presented and explained. One can imagine that a study investigating behaviour algorithms for a control system would use lower level representations of system state and action when compared to studies which focus on behaviour discovery at the tactical, operational or strategic level.

To address this requirement, ACE0 supports a spectrum of abstraction levels for behaviour discovery. This is demonstrated in Fig. 3. In the top half of Fig. 3 we see the common $\langle Agent, Action, Environment, State \rangle$ reasoning loop. However, the abstraction level for agent action and environment state varies depending on the type of agent being used. ACE0 provides examples of three levels of agent abstraction, including low-level implementations using goal-based agents, intermediate levels using finite state machines (FSMs), and higher levels where behaviours are assembled into reusable behaviour trees [3,14]. This allows

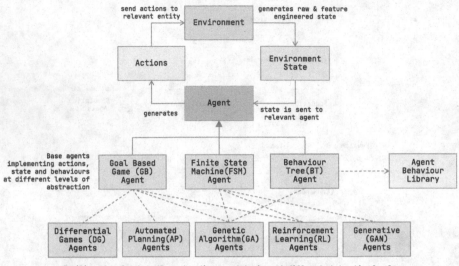

Fig. 3. A spectrum of behaviour abstractions (with respect to agent actions, behaviours and state space representations) are supported in ACEO.

the evaluation of an exploratory AI algorithm at different levels of abstraction. Figure 3 shows examples of agents integrated into ACEO using different approaches. In some cases, such as for evolutionary algorithms, they were evaluated at all three of the levels of abstraction exposed by ACEO. Specific details in the context of a use case will be provided in the next section.

3   Case Study: Aerial Manoeuvring Domain

In this section we present a case study from the aerial manoeuvring domain, which involves one autonomous aircraft manoeuvring behind another while maintaining the position for a certain amount of time. We use this simple scenario as a case study (a) as a way of providing an initial evaluation of exploratory algorithms, (b) because it requires a relatively simple explanation in terms of domain knowledge, (c) it can be implemented at multiple levels of action abstraction, and (d) it can be easily implemented using well known behaviour specification methods such as finite state machines or behaviour trees, providing standardised baselines. This type of manoeuvre is called a *Stern Conversion Intercept* [23] and can be employed operationally for a number of reasons including formation flying, aerial refuelling, visual identification or in the case of air combat situations, weapons employment. A schematic of this manoeuvre can be seeing in Fig. 4a.

While it is possible to provide raw environmental state information to various exploratory algorithms (such as the position and orientation of both aircraft), we can consider a smaller subset of features if we consider the relative orientation of the two aircraft. Consider two aircraft (denoted *blue* and *red*) flying relative to each other at separation distance R. We can define their relative orientation through a number of angles as shown in Fig. 4b. From the perspective of the *blue* aircraft, the *red* aircraft is at an antenna train angle ATA_{BR} relative to the *blue's* aircraft's velocity vector $\vec{V}_B$. The *blue* aircraft is also at an aspect angle of AA_{BR} relative to the *red* aircraft's tail (the anti-parallel of the *red* velocity vector $\vec{V}_R$). From the perspective of the *blue* aircraft, we can define any situation[1] using four features; ATA, AA, R and the difference in velocity ΔV.

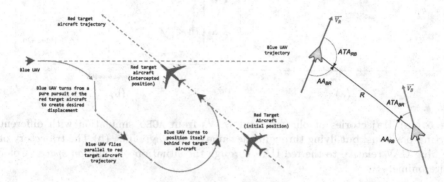

Fig. 4. (Left) Schematic of a stern conversion intercept. (Right) Relative Orientation: $AA_{RB} + ATA_{BR} = AA_{BR} + ATA_{RB} = \pi$ where $ATA \in (-\pi, \pi)$ and $AA \in (-\pi, \pi)$.

Given a random starting position and orientation, the initial goal of the blue aircraft is to manoeuvre itself behind the red aircraft's tail such that $ATA = 0$ and $AA = 0$. There may be additional constraints on range and velocity differential given the nature of the blue aircraft's mission. In order to achieve the goal we need to find a policy, behaviour or tactic that satisfies these conditions either as a single manoeuvre or a sequence of manoeuvres. By plotting the absolute value of the aspect angle $|AA|$ against the absolute value of the $|ATA|$, we can plot the trajectory of the blue aircraft through *orientation space* as demonstrated by Park [19]. This allows us to classify the angular situation at any given time into broad categories such as *Offensive*, *Defensive*, *Neutral* and *Head-On*. An example of such a trajectory can be see in Fig. 5(b).

We can use the angular situation information together with other parameters to allow us to score and assess how well the blue *UAV* is doing relative to the *red* UAV. By defining a number of scoring functions we can compare the performance of different AI aerial manoeuvring algorithms. We define three scoring functions S_1, S_2 and S_3; some from existing approaches in the literature and some adapted from operational metrics.

---

[1] This is a simplified view of the situation, as one can consider higher order features such as turn rates and other time derivatives of the basic state space variables.

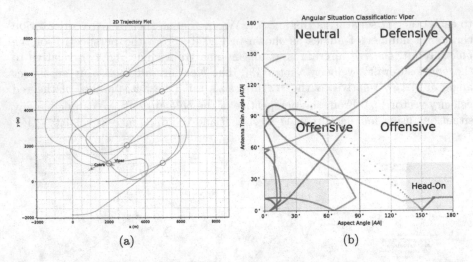

Fig. 5. (a) Trajectories of blue and red UAVs from ACEO simulation with different starting positions, but flying throught the same set of waypoints. (b) The trajectory of the blue UAV relative to the red UAV through the situation *orientation space*. (Color figure online)

We denote the first scoring function S_1 as the *Offensive Quadrant* score as it provides a score of +1 if the blue UAV is located in the bottom left quadrant of the angular situation chart shown in Fig. 5(b).

$$S_1 = \begin{cases} 1, & |AA| \leq \frac{\pi}{2} \text{ and } |ATA| \leq \frac{\pi}{2} \\ 0, & \text{otherwise} \end{cases} \tag{1}$$

The second scoring function consists of an angular and a range component. The score for the intercepting UAV is maximised when the $ATA = 0$, $AA = 0$ and the range between the two UAVs is $R = R_d$, where R_d is the desired range and will be mission dependent. The hyperparameter k modulates the relative effect of the range component on the overall score. The angular component of the score has been used widely [1,2], but the range dependence was introduced by McGrew [17] and hence we refer to S_2 as the *McGrew Score*.

$$S_2 = \frac{1}{2} \left[\left(1 - \frac{AA}{\pi}\right) + \left(1 - \frac{ATA}{\pi}\right) \right] exp\left(\frac{-|R - R_d|}{\pi k}\right) \tag{2}$$

The third scoring function is constructed from Shaw's description [23] based on the conditions required for a rear quarter weapon employment against a hostile aircraft. The conditions that must be met for a period of time include constraints on the aspect and antenna train angles ($|AA| \leq 60°$ and $|ATA| \leq 30°$), a range between the minimum and maximum range of the weapon system, and a difference in speed less than a nominated minimum. This is a strict set of constraints that need to be met and in the terminology of reinforcement learning may be considered a sparse reward. We designate this as the *Shaw Score* and define it as follows.

$$S_3 = \begin{cases} 1, & |AA| \leq \frac{\pi}{3}, |ATA| \leq \frac{\pi}{6}, R_{min} \leq R \leq R_{max}, \Delta v \leq v_{min} \\ 0, & \text{otherwise} \end{cases} \quad (3)$$

While these scoring functions are not the only ones that can be considered, having a variety of ways of evaluating the performance of an AI algorithm or approach is important as different approaches will perform differently against different metrics. The scoring functions in practice serve two purposes. First, they are domain-specific operational metrics that allow one AI algorithm to be compared to another. Second, they can be used within an AI algorithm either in their current form or in a modified form to find a solution. For example, they may take the form of a reward function in reinforcement learning, or a fitness function in an evolutionary algorithm.

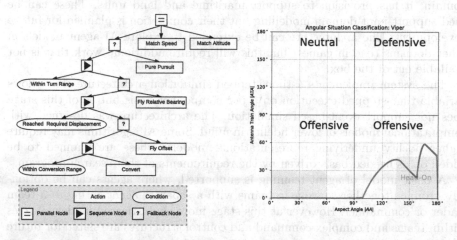

Fig. 6. (Left) Implementation of the *Stern Conversion Intercept* as a Behaviour Tree in ACE0. Higher-level behaviours such as *PurePursuit* become available as first order actions to exploratory AI algorithms. (Right) Trajectory of a blue aircraft in orientation space successfully performing a *Stern Conversion Intercept*.

The scoring functions were implemented in ACE0 together with a number of baseline handcrafted agents using approaches such as finite state machines and behaviour trees. The environment state space was implemented at multiple levels including both raw state space information (such as the positions, orientations and velocities of each aircraft), as well as engineered features as described previously. The action space was also implemented in a number of ways. Traditional approaches to action space representation in these types of simulations are quite low-level; for example $\langle TurnLeft, TurnRight, SpeedUp, SlowDown \rangle$.

By implementing baseline behaviours as finite state machines and behaviour trees, the possibility for high-level action spaces becomes available to the algorithms being considered. For example, the behaviour nodes shown in the hand-engineered behaviour tree in Fig. 6 become available to exploratory algorithms for reasoning at higher levels of abstraction.

4   Evaluation

We provide a qualitative evaluation of the ACEO MABS focusing on limitations, the user experience of AI researchers and software engineers and we briefly describe four research projects in which ACEO was used to evaluate AI behaviour discovery methods in collaboraiton with university partners.

4.1   Multi-agent-Based-Simulation Architecture Limitations

While ACEO was specifically designed for exploring AI problems in the aerospace domain, it has provision to support maritime and land units. These can be used support joint domain modelling but their completion is planned for future development. The architecture can be extended to explore AI agent models in other domains (e.g. in games) but this will require additional work that is not available out of the box.

The system implements a time-stepped simulation architecture that allows variable time-stepped execution on a per component basis but as of this stage does not support event-based simulation. The architecture was designed with computational models of lower fidelity in mind. Some AI algorithms may require higher fidelity underlying representational models. These are planned to be added on as needed basis driven by the requirements of the research program.

A basic model of agent teaming is supported, where agents can be optionally grouped together to work in teams with a separate agent acting as a team leader or commander. However at this stage more sophisticated models of roles within teams and complex command and control structures are slated for future releases.

4.2   User Evaluation

The ACEO environment was developed for users with software development experience in either computer science or software engineering with a background in artificial intelligence and/or multi-agent systems but not necessarily with any prior knowledge about the aerospace operations domain.

A key driver was to enable researchers to learn both the simulation environment and the domain relatively quickly so that they could focus their efforts in their specific area of agent decision making expertise. To do this, a series of interactive computational tutorials in the form of JupyterLab notebooks [9,20] were developed. The notebooks not only formed the core documentation for ACEO but also allowed researchers to experiment with parameters and agent behavioural

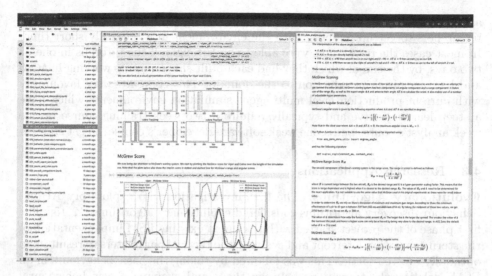

Fig. 7. Screenshot of interactive ACEO tutorials in the form of computational Jupyter-Lab notebooks.

models and observe the results in real-time. Figure 7 shows a screenshot of the tutorial interface. The researchers were also provided with a copy of XCombat a 3D animation tool for visualising the trajectories of the aircraft flown by the pilot agents (see Fig. 1).

Over twenty notebooks were developed covering a spectrum of topics ranging from installation, to explaining the architecture, details about the aerospace domain, explaining the agent percept and action interfaces, metrics and measures of effectiveness for evaluating, data processing, analysis and visualisation. Notebooks were also used as a step by step guide on rapidly developing pilot agent models using either finite state machines (FSMs) or Behaviour Trees (BTs), that could be deployed immediately and run within the JupyterLab notebook environment.

The tutorials start with describing how to develop a pilot agent to control the simulated aircraft using lower level actions such as turning, climbing, descending and changing speed. These basic building blocks are then used to develop more sophisticated maneuvers, initially as an individual aircraft, then relative to another adversarial aircraft and finally developing more complex tactics for multiple aircraft working together as team. These examples are followed by tutorials on the calculation of metrics for evaluating agent performance as well as data analysis and visualisation for explaining agent behaviour.

To date, over twenty five researchers from six institutions (four universities, a public R&D lab and a software development company) have used ACEO to develop agents for behaviour discovery as will be described in Sect. 4.3. This has included researchers and engineers with a range of expertise including professors, lecturers, post-doctoral researchers, software engineers and PhD, masters and undergraduate students. By all accounts the combination of the tutorials as well as ongoing support and collaboration from the development team allowed the researchers to get up to speed with the environment in a relatively short time. In most cases the researchers were able to go through all the tutorials in one or two days, by the end of which they had each built simple agents working in ACEO and had an initial introduction to the domain. This compares very favourably with current production level multi-agent simulation environments which have a steep learning curve and typically require a two week training course (a one week analyst's course and a one week software developer's course) to get started.

4.3   Research Applications

Evolutionary Algorithms. The first investigation into exploratory AI and behaviour discovery algorithms considered evolutionary algorithms [12,15]. The first phase of the project started with taking an existing FSM implementation of the stern conversion intercept and evolving the tactical parameters to result in an optimally evolved tactic. This was followed by taking the basic behaviours in an FSM, deleting the transitions between them and evolving a new behavioural agent with evolved state transitions. The third phase involved breaking the behaviours down even further and looking at evolving behaviours from the low level commands available to the UAV. More complex behaviours in the form of behaviour trees (BTs) were explored in the fourth and fifth stages of the project. The research investigated the effect of evolving tactical behaviours for complex behaviour trees and using a library of conditions and behaviours, and then using genetic programming methods to generate new behaviour trees [16]. Developing a viable cost function was a primary challenge in all the evolutionary algorithm research undertaken.

Automated Planning. The second project investigated the application of automated planning using width-based search techniques [13] to develop an agent capable of executing a stern conversion manoeuvre. In order to generate a plan for the *blue* aircraft one must be able to predict the state of the simulation (for blue and red) at a finite horizon. Since classical planning is a model-based approach, a model of the dynamics of the system was required. As such this work involved a novel combination of hybrid planning with optimal control [21,22] (specifically model predictive control) that resulted in a high-performing pilot agent capable of manoeuvring the *blue* UAV to achieve the goal. As a follow-on from this research project, ACEO was used to investigate behaviour recognition using planning, building on the methods developed by Vered [27].

Generative Adversarial Networks. The third project involved exploring the feasibility of Generative Adversarial Networks (GANs) for behaviour generation in ACEO. The aim of this work was to generate new tactical behaviour based on examples of existing *successful* behaviours or tactics. The initial focus in this project was to consider behaviours (or plans) as sequences of goal-directed actions. As such, a generalised technique to generate goal-optimised sequences could be used not only for tactical behaviour but also other sequences (such as text generation [7]). While the research here is still in progress, further details can be found in the work on OptiGAN [6] that uses trajectory data from ACEO, with a combination of a GAN and a reinforcement learning (RL) approach to generate sequences of actions to achieve the goal of a stern conversion manoeuvre.

Reinforcement Learning. The fourth project (currently in progress) is focused on generating pilot tactical behaviour (i.e. policies) using reinforcement learning. The project has two distinct parts. The first part is to look at traditional reinforcement learning techniques with a view to exploring multi-objective reinforcement learning (MORL) using ACEO. Preliminary results have investigated reward structures [10] and supervised policy learning [11].

The longer term plan is to explore deep reinforcement learning in ACEO. Specific research questions of interest include exploring state space representations, continuous action spaces, reward shaping and more importantly, multi-agent and team based reinforcement learning to discover and learn new tactical behaviours for teams of autonomous aircraft.

5 Conclusions

The ACEO MABS has undergone an initial round of evaluation in four separate academic research groups with specialties in different sub-fields of artificial intelligence. The outcomes from these initial studies are currently being evaluated for consideration to transition into a large scale simulation environment. ACEO is intended as a lightweight environment for AI algorithm evaluation, and as a result may not capture all of the nuances that arise in a large-scale deployed simulation environment. A number of challenges arise when developing an environment such as this. The first is maintaining a balance between simplicity and the complexity present in a production simulation environment. The second is one of scale; while some behaviour discovery approaches might be viable in a simpler environment, the extended computation time required by a more complex environment might make the approach unviable for practical use.

The results from the previously described research projects provide a baseline for considering which AI techniques should be transitioned from research into development for production-level simulation environments. In addition to assessing the suitability and viability of a specific method for operations analysis studies, the experience also allows the operations researchers to scope resource requirements in terms of budget, schedule and staffing (i.e. AI and software engineering expertise required for deployment).

A number a future challenges remain. First, a deeper understanding must be developed of the suitable levels of abstraction for state space, action space and cost/reward representation. Second, in a future where algorithms can discover new tactical behaviour, how do we measure both the novelty and robustness of the discovered behaviour? Finally, we need to consider how exploratory AI methods can be integrated into existing techniques and methods in agent-oriented software engineering.

References

1. Austin, F., Carbone, G., Lewis, M.: Automated maneuvering decisions for air-to-air combat. In: In Proceedings of the Military Computing Conference. Anaheim, California, May 1987
2. Burgin, G.H., Sidor, L.B.: Rule-Based Air Combat Simulation. Technical Report, Contractor Report 4160, National Aeronautics and Space Administration (NASA) (1988)
3. Colledanchise, M., Ögren, P.: How behavior trees modularize hybrid control systems and generalize sequential behavior compositions, the subsumption architecture, and decision trees. IEEE Trans. Rob. **33**(2), 372–389 (2017). https://doi.org/10.1109/TRO.2016.2633567
4. Evertsz, R., Thangarajah, J., Papasimeon, M.: The conceptual modelling of dynamic teams for autonomous systems. In: Mayr, H.C., Guizzardi, G., Ma, H., Pastor, O. (eds.) ER 2017. LNCS, vol. 10650, pp. 311–324. Springer, Cham (2017). https://doi.org/10.1007/978-3-319-69904-2_25
5. Heinze, C., Papasimeon, M., Goss, S., Cross, M., Connell, R.: Simulating fighter pilots. In: Pěchouček, M., Thompson, S.G., Voos, H. (eds.) Defence Industry Applications of Autonomous Agents and Multi-Agent Systems. WSSAT, pp. 113–130. Birkhäuser Basel, Basel (2008). http://dx.doi.org/10.1007/978-3-7643-8571-2_7
6. Hossam, M., Le, T., Huynh, V., Papasimeon, M., Phung, D.Q.: OptiGAN: generative adversarial networks for goal optimized sequence generation. In: International Joint Conference on Neural Networks (IJCNN). Glasgow, Scotland, UK, July 2020
7. Hossam, M., Le, T., Papasimeon, M., Huynh, V., Phung, D.: Text generation with deep variational GAN. In: NeurIPS 3rd Workshop on Bayesian Deep Learning. Montreal, Canada, December 2018. http://bayesiandeeplearning.org/2018/papers/157.pdf
8. Jones, R.M., Wray, R., van Lent, M., Laird, J.E.: Planning in the Tactical Air Domain. Technical Report, aAAI Technical Report FS-94-01, AAAI (1994)
9. Kluyver, T., et al.: Jupyter Notebooks - a publishing format for reproducible computational workflows. In: Positioning and Power in Academic Publishing: Players, Agents and Agendas, pp. 87–90. IOS Press (2016). https://doi.org/10.3233/978-1-61499-649-1-87
10. Kurniawan, B., Vamplew, P., Papasimeon, M., Dazeley, R., Foale, C.: An empirical study of reward structures for actor-critic reinforcement learning in air combat manoeuvring simulation. In: Liu, J., Bailey, J. (eds.) AI 2019. LNCS (LNAI), vol. 11919, pp. 54–65. Springer, Cham (2019). https://doi.org/10.1007/978-3-030-35288-2_5
11. Kurniawan, B., Vamplew, P., Papasimeon, M., Dazeley, R., Foale, C.: Discrete-to-Deep supervised policy learning: an effective training method for neural reinforcement learning. In: ALA 2020: Adaptive Learning Agents Workshop at AAMAS 2020. Auckland, New Zealand (2020)
12. Lam, C.P., Masek, M., Kelly, L., Papasimeon, M., Benke, L.: A simheuristic approach for evolving agent behaviour in the exploration for novel combat tactics. Oper. Res. Perspect. **6**, 100123 (2019). https://doi.org/10.1016/j.orp.2019.100123
13. Lipovetzky, N., Geffner, H.: Width and serialization of classical planning problems. In: ECAI, pp. 540–545 (2012)
14. Martzinotto, A., Colledanchise, M., Smith, C., Ögren, P.: Towards a unified behavior trees framework for robot control. In: In proceedings of 2014 IEEE International Conference on Robotics and Automation (ICRA 2014), pp. 5420–5427 (2014). https://doi.org/10.1109/icra.2014.6907656

15. Masek, M., Lam, C.P., Benke, L., Kelly, L., Papasimeon, M.: Discovering emergent agent behaviour with evolutionary finite state machines. In: Miller, T., Oren, N., Sakurai, Y., Noda, I., Savarimuthu, B.T.R., Cao Son, T. (eds.) PRIMA 2018. LNCS (LNAI), vol. 11224, pp. 19–34. Springer, Cham (2018). https://doi.org/10.1007/978-3-030-03098-8_2
16. Masek, M., Lam, C.P., Kelly, L., Benke, L., Papasimeon, M.: A genetic programming framework for novel behaviour discovery in air combat scenarios. In: Ernst, A.T., Dunstall, S., García-Flores, R., Grobler, M., Marlow, D. (eds.) Data and Decision Sciences in Action 2. LNMIE, pp. 263–277. Springer, Cham (2021). https://doi.org/10.1007/978-3-030-60135-5_19
17. McGrew, J.S., How, J.P.: Air combat strategy using approximate dynamic programming. J. Guidance Control Dyn. 33, 1641–1654 (2010)
18. Papasimeon, M., Pearce, A., Goss, S.: The human agent virtual environment. In: Proceedings of the 6th International Joint Conference on Autonomous Agents and Multiagent Systems. AAMAS 2007. Association for Computing Machinery, New York, NY, USA (2007). https://doi.org/10.1145/1329125.1329463
19. Park, H., Lee, B.Y., Tahk, M.J., Yoo, D.W.: Differential game based air combat maneuver generation using scoring function matrix. Int. J. Aeronaut. Space Sci. 17(2), 204–213 (2016)
20. Pérez, F., Granger, B.E.: IPython: a system for interactive scientific computing. Comput. Sci. Eng. 9(3), 21–29 (2007)
21. Ramirez, M., Papasimeon, M., Benke, L., Lipovetzky, N., Miller, T., Pearce, A.R.: Real-Time UAV maneuvering via automated planning in simulations. In: 26th International Joint Conference on Artificial Intelligence (IJCAI), pp. 5243–5245. Melbourne, Australia, August 2017
22. Ramirez, M., et al.: Integrated hybrid planning and programmed control for real time UAV maneuvering. In: 17th Int. Conference on Autonomous Agents and Multiagent Systems (AAMAS), pp. 1318–1326. Stockholm, Sweden, July 2018
23. Shaw, R.L.: Fighter Combat: Tactics and Maneuvering. Naval Institute Press, Annapolis (1985)
24. Smith, R., Dike, B., Ravichandran, B., El-Fallah, A., Mehra, K.: Discovering novel fighter combat maneuvers: simulating test pilot creativity. In: Bentley, P.J., Corne, D.W. (eds.) Creative Evolutionary Systems, p. 467 - VIII. The Morgan Kaufmann Series in Artificial Intelligence, Morgan Kaufmann, San Francisco (2002). https://doi.org/10.1016/B978-155860673-9/50059-8
25. Tidhar, G., Heinze, C., Selvestrel, M.: Flying together: modelling air mission teams. Appl. Intell. 8(3), 195–218 (1998)
26. Toubman, A.: Calculated Moves: Generating Air Combat Behaviour. Ph.D. thesis, Leiden University, The Netherlands (2020)
27. Vered, M., Kaminka, G.A.: Heuristic online goal recognition in continuous domains. In: Proceedings of the 26th International Joint Conference on Artificial Intelligence (IJCAI-17), pp. 4447–4454. Melbourne, Australia (2017)
28. Zhang, L.A., et al.: Air Dominance Through Machine Learning: A Preliminary Exploration of Artificial Intelligence-Assisted Mission Planning. Technical Report, RR4311, RAND Corporation, Santa Monica, CA, USA (2020). https://www.rand.org/pubs/research_reports/RR4311.html

Using Agent-Based Modelling to Understand Advantageous Behaviours Against COVID-19 Transmission in the Built Environment

Arnaud Grignard[1]([✉]), Tri Nguyen-Huu[2], Patrick Taillandier[3], Luis Alonso[1], Nicolas Ayoub[1], Markus Elkatsha[1], Gamaliel Palomo[4], Monica Gomez[5], Mario Siller[4], Mayra Gamboa[5], Carlos Ivan Moreno[5], and Kent Larson[1]

[1] MIT Media Lab, City Science, Cambridge, USA
agrignar@media.mit.edu
[2] Sorbonne University, IRD, UMMISCO, Paris, France
[3] INRAE, Paris, France
[4] Cinvestav, Mexico City, Mexico
[5] UdeG, Guadalajara, Mexico

Abstract. The global Covid-19 pandemic has raised many questions about how we occupy and move in the built environment. Interior environments have been increasingly discussed in numerous studies highlighting how interior spaces play a key role in the spread of pandemics. One societal challenge is to find short-term strategies to reopen indoor venues. Most current approaches focus on an individual's behavior (maintaining social distance, wearing face masks, and washing their hands) and government policies (confinement, curfew, quarantine, etc.). However, few studies have been conducted to understand a building's interior where most transmission takes place. How will the utilization of existing interior spaces be improved above and beyond universally applied criteria, while minimizing the risk of disease transmission? This article presents an agent-based model that examines disease transmission risks in various "interior types" in combination with user behaviors and their mobility, as well as three types of transmission vectors (direct, airborne and via surfaces). The model also integrates numerous policy interventions, including wearing masks, hand washing, and the possibility of easily modifying the organization of spaces. Different studies at various scales were conducted both on the University of Guadalajara (UdeG) campus as well as at the MIT Media Lab to illustrate the application of this model.

1 Introduction

The Covid-19 pandemic has caused great disruption in higher education institutions. Institutional coordination challenges dramatically increased when considering the process of reintroducing in person learning both during and post pandemic. In this context, setting up experiments with real people to test different interventions poses too high a risk for participants. To overcome this

© Springer Nature Switzerland AG 2022
K. H. Van Dam and N. Verstaevel (Eds.): MABS 2021, LNAI 13128, pp. 86–98, 2022.
https://doi.org/10.1007/978-3-030-94548-0_7

challenge, computer models can be used as a tool to explore different strategies in a virtual environment, so called in silico, before implementation [1]. Strategies for mitigating an influenza pandemic are well known and have been tested in silico [2]. Traditional approaches, based on compartmentalized epidemiological models, can be found as well as other approaches like this individual example [3]. These approaches have provided promising results at the scale of an entire country but they are not sufficient to assess risk at the scale of interiors as this approach cannot embed the actual dynamic of local interaction [4]. Our approach studies the dynamics of the infection risk at the building level and offers an increased understanding of the impact of a localized intervention in both time and space.

This context is particularly well suited for agent-based modeling (ABM) [5]. With this approach, the profiles of users as well as characteristics of the built environment can be considered. The characteristics can include the interactions among occupants as well as the interactions between the occupants and their environment where they are operating. ABM enables rapid comparisons of different interventions and evaluation of their respective influence on the dynamics of the disease in order to determine an optimized combination of strategies such as the one developed by [6].

The model, developed using the GAMA Platform [7], explores successive simulations showing the effects of different interventions on the risk of infection inside of a specific space (e.g. classrooms, building, campus) for a given population (student, teachers, etc.). It is based on scientific observations and statements and policies from global experts (e.g. OECD [8] and (WHO) [9]) regarding health measures applied to school contexts. It allows rapid comparisons between interventions to assess their influence and efficacy on disease transmission to support the optimizations of combined strategies. Finally, this tool has been conceived as an interactive platform where decision makers can test and evaluate different policies that can be easily replicated on other spaces and potentially with other types of diseases.

The article is organized as follows. Section 2 presents in detail the implementation of the model. Section 3 compares different interventions and illustrates the use case of the different campuses of the University of Guadalajara. We finally conclude in Sect. 4 on the perspective and limitations of such an approach.

2   Model

2.1   Overview of the Model

To evaluate and minimize the risk of infection for the users of the built environment, we created a model that estimates each person's potential exposure to the virus in each location considered. The experiment consisted of people involved in daily activities in a given space, some of whom were assumed to be infected. We estimated the viral load to which non-infected individuals can be exposed throughout a day. We thus considered that exposure is a function of concentration and time. Three transmission vectors were assumed (droplets, fomites, and aerosols) and taken in account as shown in Fig. 1. This approach gives the possibility not only to identify the risk of infection at the individual level but also at a macro level. The model then allows for the comparison of the mitigation efficiency of different interventions or policies.

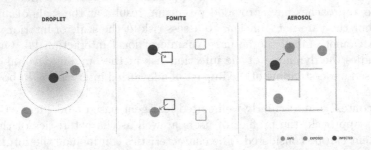

Fig. 1. Illustration of the three different modes of transmission of the virus. (a) droplets transmission: an infected person transmits a viral load to other humans at a given range. (b) Fomites transmission: an infected person transmits a viral load to a surface by contact. The surface then transmits a viral load to the people who touch it. (c) Aerosols transmission: light particles transmit an airborne viral load to people in the same room. Circles represent people and squares represent objects. Red: infectious, orange: exposed to the virus, green: safe. (Color figure online)

2.2   Description of the Model Entities

People. In our study, agents representing individual *people* have individual behaviors that are determined according to personal characteristics such as agenda, age, occupation etc. Daily generic agendas can be easily modified or extended. They describe activities such as working in an office, entering a room, going to a workstation, eating out, going home, etc., which are events occuring at specific moments. Agendas are created using an ad hoc generator: a set of scenario-dependant activities (with their target location and start time) for each agent. The choice of activities can be refined thanks to behavioral data extracted from questionnaires and interviews. Some activities lead to specific agent behaviors: for example, an agent working at the library may move to pick up a book or to talk with a colleague. In the same way, a queue system can optionally be used: if a queue policy is chosen, agents wishing to enter a room will have to queue to enter it (queue respecting a certain physical distance defined in parameter if possible). Agents have a fixed epidemiological status as *infected, susceptible*. Susceptible agents also have a *cumulated_viral_load* attribute which is a list of three elements representing the viral load received by droplets, fomites and aerosols transmission.

Space. The spatial environment consists of a collection of spatial entities *Room* in which *People* can perform different kind of activities. Rooms are made of a list of entrances and places such as desks and/or chairs. Aerosol particles can spread the virus within a room. Each **Room** has a *viral_load* attribute that represents the virus concentration in the air and which is increased by the respiration of infected **people** and decreased by ventilation. Susceptible **People** receive a quantity of virus that is a function of that concentration (see Sect. 2.3). The viral concentration in each room is represented by a color gradient in order to easily identify risky areas.

2.3 Description of the Model Processes

Simulation Initialization. A simulation is initialized by creating a synthetic population of agents **people**, and agents **Room** from floor plan files (.dxf or .gis). A compatible file should specify at least the four following layers as closed polylines: Walls; Entrance; Offices or Meeting rooms. Optional layers include Furniture, Chair, Sanitation and Toilets. The virtual pedestrian network is built by defining the walking zone, then applying a Delaunay triangulation to it to calculate the skeleton of the virtual pedestrian network. Other parameters are loaded from data files or can be directly modified to trigger different interventions. The number of generated people is set accordingly to the *density_scenario variable*. Based on a normal day activities, they are assigned schedules and targets such as work places that can be set by different methods:

- **data**: if the floor plan contains a layer describing the desk layout then each people has a desk assigned to him as a target;
- **distance**: people's targets are defined in order to respect a minimal distance between people (e.g. 2 m);
- **building occupancy**: the maximum number of people in a building is set by its capacity;
- **room occupancy**: the maximum number of people in a room is set by its capacity.

Epidemic Status Initialization. At the start of each simulation, a given amount of the people (*initial_nb_infected*) is set to the *infected* status, others are set to *susceptible*. Note that since the experiment duration is at the scale of the day, susceptible people do not have the time to turn infectious, thus the epidemiological status of agents remains unchanged during the whole simulation time. As a consequence, the risk of contamination is quantified by a person's viral load people.

Process Overview and Scheduling. Simulations run during a given duration expressed in hour by (*time_spent*). Different agenda scenarios can be chosen, by default a person who enters the building by one of the entrances (chosen randomly) then goes to his assigned *working place* for a given amount of time (*time_spent*) and exits by the same entrance as he entered. A more typical day would be when people enter the building in the morning, go out for lunch and go back to work. The agenda or activity can easily be modified to add activity such as going to get a coffee or to the restrooms. Regarding people agents mobility, we use the method developed in [10]: agents walk on a continuous space and follow a pre-constructed virtual pedestrian network. They calculate the shortest path and follow the succession of nodes as intermediate objectives. The agents avoid collisions with others by using a repulsion mechanism inspired by the social force model [11]. More details on pedestrian mobility can be found in [10,12].

2.4 Virus Propagation - Risk Prediction

It is now established that respiratory viruses are transmitted in three different ways. Firstly, the virus can be transmitted by large respiratory droplets which is a vector of transmission to nearby persons. Secondly airborne transmission due to smaller droplets (aerosols) which stay suspended in the air and can travel longer distances can also lead to infection [13,14]. Finally transmission can happen via a contaminated surface.

Droplets. Most of the respiratory virus transmission occurs from large infected droplets that can be produced either by coughing, sneezing or even breathing in close proximity to another person. As a consequence, social distancing is considered as an efficient protection measure. Droplets are involved in a person-to-person infection, which means that an infected person transmits a viral load to other persons next to him/her. If a susceptible person is at a distance below a given threshold, he/she will receive a viral load per time step given by

$$v_d^0 \Delta t \left(1 - e_{separator}\right)\left(1 - e_{mask}^{emission}\right)\left(1 - e_{mask}^{reception}\right),$$

where Δt is the time step duration and v_d^0 the viral load transmitted per unit of time by an infected person. The quantity of virus transmitted is reduced by prevention measures like separators, a mask worn by the infected person and a mask worn by the susceptible person, with respective efficiency $e_{separator}$, $e_{mask}^{emission}$ and $e_{mask}^{reception}$.

Aerosols. Studies have historically used a threshold of 5 μm to differentiate between large and small particles, but researchers are now suggesting that a threshold of 100 μm better differentiates aerodynamic behaviour of particles. Particles that would fall to the ground within 2 m are likely to be 60–100 μm in size. Investigators have also measured particle sizes of infectious aerosols and have shown that pathogens are most commonly found in small particle aerosols (<5 μm), which are airborne and breathable. Initially it was thought that airborne transmission of Covid-19 was unlikely, but growing evidence has highlighted that infectious microdroplets are small enough [13]. In the model, the concentration of virus in aerobic particles is considered for each room, and is increased due to the infected people's respiration and talking. At each time step, each infected person transmits a viral load that can be reduced by wearing masks. The viral load in the air is updated according to the formula

$$v_{air} := v_{air} + cV_{breath}(1 - e_{mask}^{emission})\Delta t$$

for each infected person, where V_{breath} is volume of air inspired/expired per unit of time, and c the viral concentration in the air expired.

The viral load in the air decays because of ventilation. After a time Δt, the viral load in the air is updated according to the formula

$$v_{air} := v_{air}(1 - d_{air})^{\Delta t}$$

where d_{air} is the decay rate per unit of time due to ventilation.

People get infected by breathing the air. The amount of viral load ingested by breathing decreases with masks. It is given by

$$(1 - e_{mask}^{reception})v_{air}\left(1 - \left(1 - \frac{V_{breath}}{V}\right)^{\Delta t}\right)$$

where V is the volume of the room. The same quantity of viral load is removed from the room's air.

Fomites. Latest research suggests that fomites are not a major route of transmission. However, even if attempts to culture the virus on surfaces were unsuccessful, Covid-19 can persist for days on inanimate surfaces. Surface agents has a viral load attribute which increases by interaction with infected individuals, decreases when transmitting the virus to a susceptible individual by contact, and decays at a given rate. Contamination of a surface per cycle and per infected person is given by

$$v_{surface} := v_{surface} + v_f^0 \Delta t (1 - e_{mask}^{emission})$$

where v_f^0 is the viral load transmitted by an infected person per unit of time. Decay per time step is given by

$$v_{surface} := v_{surface}(1 - d)^{\Delta t}$$

where d is the decay rate per unit of time. When in contact with a susceptible person during a time Δt, the viral load on the surface decreases and is updated according to the following formula:

$$v_{surface} := v_{surface}(1 - r)^{\Delta t}$$

where $r \in [0,1]$ is the proportion of virus transmitted to the person per unit of time. The actual viral load that is ingested through hand-to-mouth after touching an infected surface is decreased by wearing a mask. The amount of viral load ingested is then

$$v_{surface}T_{HtM}\left(1 - e_{mask}^{reception}\right)\left(1 - (1 - r)^{\Delta t}\right)$$

where T_{HtM} is the proportion of virus transmitted from the hand to the mouth.

2.5   Parameters

Some parameters are set based on values found in the literature, while others are estimated. Values are shown in Table 1. We normalize the viral load transmitted via droplets to 1, and estimate the other viral loads relatively. It is suggested in [15] that the mask efficiency is high (above 70%). Masks prove to be a good protection while worn by emitters and receivers, and they also reduce transmission via fomites. The proportion of the droplets which evaporate to aerosols is not well known. The proportion of small aerosols is larger, but the viral load per particle is smaller [16]. The proportion of contamination through aerosol is unclear. As a consequence, we choose to set parameter c in order to emit an equivalent viral load to the droplets. Fomite parameters are estimated bearing in mind that the transmission is supposed to be very low [15]. The decay rate on surface is estimated based on experiments on plastic in [17]. Ventilation parameter is set in order to renew 98% of the air of a room in 10 h (natural ventilation) or 1 h (forced ventilation).

Table 1. Parameters used in the model. Variable with no reference have been estimated.

Variable	Definition	Value	Source
v_d^0	Viral load transmitted per unit of time (droplets)	$1\,s^{-1}$	Set as a reference
v_f^0	Viral load transmitted per unit of time on surfaces	$0.25\,s^{-1}$	Estimated
V_{breath}	Air volume inspired or expired	$8\,L.mn^{-1}$	[15]
c	Viral concentration in breath	$10\,L^{-1}.mn^{-1}$	[15, 16]
T_{HtM}	Transfer rate from hand to mouth	30%	Estimated
r	Virus transfer rate from surface to hand when	$0.01\,s^{-1}$	Estimated
d_{air}	Virus load decay rate: by natural ventilation	10^{-4}	Estimated
	by forced ventilation	10^{-3}	Estimated
d	Virus load decay rate on surface	3.10^{-5}	[17]
$e_{mask}^{emission}$	Mask efficiency: percentage of the viral load emission being blocked	70%	[15]
$e_{mask}^{reception}$	Mask efficiency: percentage of the viral load reception being blocked	70%	[15]
$e_{separator}$	Separator efficiency: percentage of particles blocked	90%	Estimated

2.6 Outputs

We illustrate the possibilities of the proposed model on a specific case study (one floor of the MIT Media Lab) in order to compare the impact of separated interventions against a reference scenario without any interventions (Fig. 2). The outputs provide global indicators about the population and a more detailed visualisation of the status of each individual to allow comparison of different kinds of interventions. Global indicators consist of time series representing the temporal evolution of the viral load to which people have been exposed to for each type of contamination, and a histogram representing the distribution of the population into three levels of risk (low, medium and high) to which each individual has been exposed. Simulations also provide an animated spatial visualisation of the building (floor plan) with the location and epidemiological status of people (infected, or low/medium/high risk).

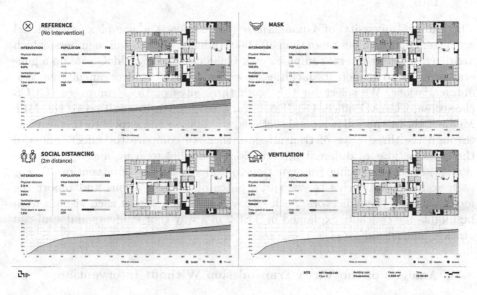

Fig. 2. Comparison of the three interventions with the reference scenario, for the MIT Media Lab building. 1) no intervention, 2) use of masks, 3) social distancing and lowering the density, and 4) replacing the natural ventilation by air conditioning.

3 Results

3.1 Stochasticity Sensitivity Analysis

We first analyze the impact of the randomness of the simulations on the three types of transmissions. The main objective is to find a threshold number of replicates beyond which the mean values of such indicators are sufficiently accurate. To do this, we compare the output of these three indicators between replicates of the simulation. We undertake this exploration on a typical example of use of the model (one floor of the MIT Media Lab) with no specific intervention. We perform 100 replicates of such a simulation and compare the variability of the results with different number of replicates. We observe that with a low number of replicates the standard error is very high. With 20 replicates, the standard error is low for the droplet transmission but remains high for the two other transmission types. With 50 replicates, the difference is very slight for all indicators. Increasing the number of replicates further beyond 50 does not have a great impact on the aggregate trend of the simulation results. For the study of the scenario presented in the following section, we decide to set the number of replicates at 50 in order to minimize the required computation time while maintaining a good statistical accuracy.

3.2   Use Cases: University of Guadalajara (UdeG) and MIT Media Lab

The public University of Guadalajara (UdeG) leads a complex educational ecosystem that includes more than 300.000 students, 16.000 staff members, which are distributed on several campuses over Guadalajara City. UdeG sets up a general protocol to reopen its facilities based on international organizations' recommendations. We select for this work three sites of UdG campuses (CUCS classroom, CUAAD office, CUCEA library, see Fig. 3), in addition to the MIT Media Lab. In the following subsections, we analyse the exposure to the virus through the three ways of transmission, then we compare the effectiveness of the combinations of different interventions including wearing masks (intervention 1), social distancing (intervention 2) and ventilation (intervention 3). For each scenario and each site, we run a batch of 50 replications and report the mean values of the indicators. Such scenarios are built so that each visualization highlights the concepts explained in Sect. 2 in a way that students and staff can quickly understand.

3.3   Analysis of the Virus Transmission Without Intervention

For all use cases, transmission by droplets appears to be the most effective way, while fomites is the least effective. Without any intervention, people are at high risk when in the same room as an infected person, even if the room size is large, highlighting a high transmission rate despite a relatively modest contribution in the viral load. Scarce presence of people at high risk in rooms without infected people suggests that they were exposed at close range to infected people when moving. It is confirmed by the fact that the viral load time series show a fast increase of droplet contamination at the beginning of the simulation and at the end, when people go to their desk or go away. Aerosols contamination starts later, since the quantity of virus in the air slowly increases with time.

As shown on Fig. 4, the configuration and usage of the buildings impacts the relative proportions of exposure to droplets, fomites and aerosols: large rooms like the library in CUCEA are less favourable to the transmission via aerosols.

3.4 Comparison of Different Combinations of Interventions

We study the impact of three interventions: 1) use of masks, 2) social distancing and lowering the density and 3) replacing the natural ventilation using air conditioning. Simulations outputs are presented in Fig. 2. The risk reduction is compared for the different combinations of interventions. The mean risk reductions for each combination are shown in Table 2.

It appears that the most efficient single intervention is the use of masks. Indeed, under the assumption that high filtering capability is provided and that they are used properly, they provide a protection against the three ways of contamination. Masks effectiveness is homogeneous among the different scenarios. In Fig. 2.1, wearing masks significantly decreases the exposure to the virus in

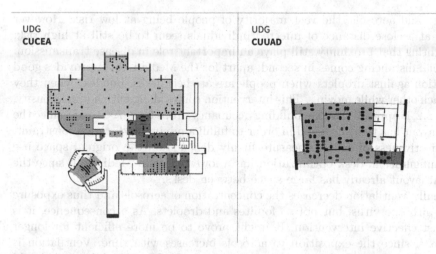

Fig. 3. The model has been experimented on three sites in the UdG university. The 3 sites have been chosen in order to cover different use cases. CUCS represents the first floor of a building made of 10 different classrooms and two meeting rooms. CUCEA is a mix between classrooms, meeting rooms and contains also a library used as a common area. CUAAD is made of meeting rooms and classrooms.

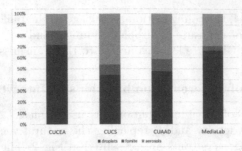

Fig. 4. Comparison of the exposure to the virus through the different vectors of transmission for the different UdG sites.

Table 2. Risk reduction measured as the percentage of drop in cumulative viral load relative to a scenario without any intervention, for different use cases and for all kinds of combinations of interventions (1: masks, 2: social distance and lower density, 3: ventilation).

Site	Interventions						
	1	2	3	1+2	1+3	2+3	1+2+3
CUCS	90.4%	47.7%	31.6%	95.2%	93.4%	78.2%	98.0%
CUAAD	90.4%	56.3%	27.3%	96.0%	93.1%	83.4%	98.5%
CUCEA	91.1%	65.5%	17.9%	97.0%	92.2%	76.3%	97.9%
Media Lab	90.3%	15,0%	14,0%	92,1%	92.2%	33.2%	94.3%

droplets and aerosols, the vast majority of people being at low risk. However people at a close distance of infected individuals seem to be still at high risk, highlighting that proximity still plays an important role in disease transmission.

Social distancing comes in second, apart for the Media Lab. It provides good protection against droplets when people are at their desks, but less when they pass each other while moving. This intervention comes along with a lower density. In Fig. 2.2, it appears that the building occupancy drops from 796 to 583 since the desks layout has to be changed in order to fulfill a minimum distance constraint. The effectiveness of such a measure highly depends on the original space use and configuration: desk optimization has a lower effect in Media Lab since the original layout already has large space between desks.

Finally, ventilation decreases the concentration of aerosols and thus exposure to the airborne virus, but not to fomites and droplets. As a consequence, it is the least effective intervention. It might prove to be more efficient for longer durations, since the exposition to aerosols increases with time. Ventilation is more efficient within buildings with small rooms (CUCS, CUAAD), and should be recommended accordingly. A combination of two interventions increases the protection, 1+2 and 1+3 being more efficient than 2+3. Combination 1+2+3 marginally increases the protection compared to 1+2 alone (less than 2.8%).

Complying with the CDC recommendation social distancing and improving ventilation comes at a cost that may be difficult to handle. If wearing a mask is cheap and easy to impose, ventilation may require work on buildings. Social distancing maybe the hardest to comply with, since a lower building occupancy may require that students partly attend classes from home. The logistics for such an intervention may also be a barrier. This study suggests that the most effective intervention is wearing masks. It can be complemented with others interventions, but since they marginally increase the effectiveness, they should be considered as secondary, and may be omitted in case their cost or logistic is too important.

4   Conclusion and Perspective

This model has been used to inform the academic community of UdeG about efficient ways to protect their community from the spread of Covid-19. Graphical and quantitative outputs have proven to be a good medium to illustrate the way the pandemic propagates and the efficiency of the different recommendations. Once the different simulation scenarios were analyzed and the most appropriate forecasts were developed for the use of the different spaces on campuses, the results were disseminated in an educational video and campaign, in order to educate people about the benefits of complying with the CDC recommendations. Further developments of the model will aim at providing not only a better prediction of the risk of contamination but also a more realistic agent behavior in order to take in account other dynamics. It is however, important to consider the results from this work with care, since there is still a major uncertainty on the relative importance of aerosols and droplets in the chain of contamination.

References

1. Walport, M., et al.: Computational modelling: technological futures (2018)
2. Ferguson, N.M., Cummings, D.A.T., Fraser, C., Cajka, J.C., Cooley, P.C., Burke, D.S.: Strategies for mitigating an influenza pandemic. Nature **442**(7101), 448–452 (2006)
3. Keeling, M.J., Rohani, P.: Modeling Infectious Diseases in Humans and Animals. Princeton University Press, Princeton (2011)
4. Ferguson, N.: Capturing human behaviour. Nature **446**(7137), 733 (2007)
5. Railsback, S.F., Grimm, V.: Agent-Based and Individual-Based Modeling: A Practical Introduction. Princeton University Press, Princeton (2019)
6. Gaudou, B., et al.: COMOKIT: a modeling kit to understand, analyze, and compare the impacts of mitigation policies against the COVID-19 epidemic at the scale of a city. Front. Public Health **8** (2020)
7. Taillandier, P., et al.: Building, composing and experimenting complex spatial models with the GAMA platform. GeoInformatica **23**(2), 299–322 (2019)
8. Organisation for Economic Co-operation and Development. Coronavirus special edition: Back to school. Trends shaping Education Spotlight 21 (2020). Accessed 5 June 2020
9. World Health Organization. Considerations for school-related public health measures in the context of COVID-19 (2020). Accessed 15 Dec 2020

10. Daudé, E., et al.: ESCAPE: exploring by simulation cities awareness on population evacuation. In: ISCRAM (2019)
11. Helbing, D., Molnar, P.: Social force model for pedestrian dynamics. Phy. Rev. E **51**(5), 4282 (1995)
12. Chapuis, K., Taillandier, P., Gaudou, B., Drogoul, A., Daudé, E.: A multi-modal urban traffic agent-based framework to study individual response to catastrophic events. In: Miller, T., Oren, N., Sakurai, Y., Noda, I., Savarimuthu, B.T.R., Cao Son, T. (eds.) PRIMA 2018. LNCS (LNAI), vol. 11224, pp. 440–448. Springer, Cham (2018). https://doi.org/10.1007/978-3-030-03098-8_28
13. The Lancet Respiratory Medicine. COVID-19 transmission-up in the air. The Lancet. Respiratory Medicine (2020)
14. Klompas, M., Baker, M.A., Rhee, C.: Airborne transmission of SARS-CoV-2: theoretical considerations and available evidence. Jama (2020)
15. Howard, J., et al.: An evidence review of face masks against COVID-19. In: Proceedings of the National Academy of Sciences, vol. 118, no. 4 (2021)
16. Tang, S., et al.: Aerosol transmission of SARS-CoV-2? evidence, prevention and control. Environ. Int. **144**, 106039 (2020)
17. van Doremalen, N., et al.: Aerosol and surface stability of SARS-CoV-2 as compared with SARS-CoV-1. New Engl. J. Med. **382**(16), 1564–1567 (2020)

Quantifying the Effects of Norms on COVID-19 Cases Using an Agent-Based Simulation

Jan de Mooij[1]([✉]), Davide Dell'Anna[1], Parantapa Bhattacharya[2],
Mehdi Dastani[1], Brian Logan[1], and Samarth Swarup[2]

[1] Intelligent Systems, Information and Computing Sciences, Utrecht University,
Utrecht, The Netherlands
{a.j.demooij,d.dellanna,m.m.dastani,b.s.logan}@uu.nl
[2] Biocomplexity Institute and Initiative, University of Virginia, Charlottesville, USA
{parantapa,swarup}@virginia.edu

Abstract. Modelling social phenomena in large-scale agent-based simulations has long been a challenge due to the computational cost of incorporating agents whose behaviors are determined by reasoning about their internal attitudes and external factors. However, COVID-19 has brought the urgency of doing this to the fore, as, in the absence of viable pharmaceutical interventions, the progression of the pandemic has primarily been driven by behaviors and behavioral interventions. In this paper, we address this problem by developing a large-scale data-driven agent-based simulation model where individual agents reason about their beliefs, objectives, trust in government, and the norms imposed by the government. These internal and external attitudes are based on actual data concerning daily activities of individuals, their political orientation, and norms being enforced in the US state of Virginia. Our model is calibrated using mobility and COVID-19 case data. We show the utility of our model by quantifying the benefits of the various behavioral interventions through counterfactual runs of our calibrated simulation.

Keywords: Large-scale social simulation · Norm reasoning agents · Computational epidemiology

1 Introduction

In social systems in general, and in the science of epidemiology in particular, human behavior has always been recognized to play a crucial role [9]. This is especially true in the COVID-19 pandemic since, prior to the availability of vaccines, efforts at containing the epidemic have emphasized behavioral changes, such as mask wearing, physical distancing (e.g., keeping 6 ft apart), and social distancing (e.g., working from home, schooling from home). Compliance with these recommendations has varied widely, both spatiotemporally and demographically [12]. In most places, these non-pharmaceutical interventions (NPIs) were implemented

© Springer Nature Switzerland AG 2022
K. H. Van Dam and N. Verstaevel (Eds.): MABS 2021, LNAI 13128, pp. 99–112, 2022.
https://doi.org/10.1007/978-3-030-94548-0_8

starting in March 2020. For example, in the US state of Virginia nine Executive Orders (EOs) were implemented between March and July 2020. Were some of these EOs more effective than others in limiting the spread of COVID-19? More generally, what determines the effectiveness of NPIs? Does their timing and sequence matter? These are all important questions to answer for developing effective mitigation plans for the next major epidemic. In this work, we propose an agent-based simulation approach for these problems, focusing on an analysis of the EOs implemented in Virginia.

Computational models of disease spread, including agent-based simulations, have become quite sophisticated. However, incorporating realistic models of human behavior in these simulations remains a challenge [5,10]. Most models assume a certain level of compliance with a behavioral intervention, and apply it uniformly at random [16]. In reality, however, compliance can be highly non-uniform as it depends on a number of factors, including: demographics, peer influence, political orientation, risk assessments, and beliefs about the efficacy of the behavior [2,4]. To improve epidemic simulations, we therefore need methods for the realistic modeling of behavior.

Belief-Desire-Intention (BDI) models developed in the MAS community, particularly those incorporating normative reasoning, are a natural fit for this problem [15]. However, it has been challenging to find appropriate data to calibrate such behavior models in simulations. Our approach is to use cellphone-based mobility data and a synthetic population [1] to create a data-driven simulation which is sufficiently detailed that the effects of behavioral responses to the EOs can be evaluated. To address the challenges of scaling, we adapt the BDI-based multiagent programming technology, 2APL [6,7], to support discreet time steps and deferral of action execution. We integrate this new library, Sim-2APL, with a new distributed agent-based simulation framework we call PanSim. This aspect of the work is presented in our companion paper [3]. In the current paper, we focus on the simulation design and evaluation. Our main contribution here is a framework that allows detailed investigation of the effects of non-pharmaceutical interventions through the use of multiple sources of data and appropriate behavioral models for agents.

2   Simulation Design

In this section, we describe our COVID-19 simulation, the key components of which are illustrated in Fig. 1. We start with a synthetic population of the US state of Virginia, where agents have realistic demographics, weekly activity schedules, and activity locations drawn from real location data. In our simulation, each individual in the synthetic population is represented by a norm-aware Sim-2APL agent (Sect. 2.2) which reasons about whether to comply with the various EOs that were implemented in Virginia (Sect. 2.3). The agents interact via a disease model implemented in the novel PanSim distributed environment (Sect. 2.4). In Sect. 3 we show how we calibrate the parameters of our simulation with real-world data, while in Sect. 4 we evaluate our simulation by comparing the disease progression when different norm interventions are put in place.

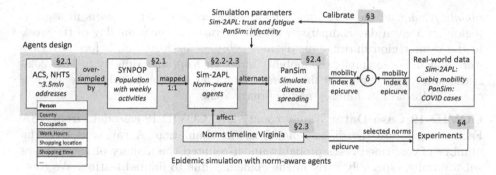

Fig. 1. COVID-19 simulation setting.

2.1 Data Sets Used in the Simulation

We use four data sets in this work, as described briefly below.

Synthetic Population of Virginia, USA: Agents in our simulation are drawn from a synthetic population of the state of Virginia, USA. This synthetic population has been constructed from multiple data sources including the American Community Survey (ACS), the National Household Travel Survey (NHTS), and various location and building data sets, as described in [1]. This gives us a very detailed representation of the region we are studying (multiple counties within Virginia). Agents are assigned demographic variables drawn from the ACS, such as age, sex, race, household income, and political orientation. In each county c, we label each household as Democratic with probability equal to the percentage of Democratic voters in the 2016 U.S. presidential elections in county c, and Republican otherwise. Agents are also assigned appropriate typical weekly activity patterns by integrating data from the NHTS. For each activity, each agent is assigned an appropriate location, using data about the built environment from multiple sources, including HERE, the Microsoft Building Database, and the National Center for Education Statistics (for school locations).

Mobility Data: In order to model the changes in mobility due to various Executive Orders (EOs) implemented between March and July 2020, we use anonymized and privacy-enhanced cellphone-based mobility data provided by Cuebiq. This data set contains location pings generated from the cellphones of a large number of anonymous and opted-in users throughout the USA. Cuebiq collects data with informed consent, anonymized all records and further enhanced privacy by replacing pings corresponding to home and work locations with the centroids of the corresponding Census blockgroups. We aggregate the data to the county level as follows. First we calculate the average *radius of gyration* for cellphone users in the county. The radius of gyration is given by $r = \sum_l d(l, l_c)/k$, where l is the location (latitude and longitude) of the user, l_c is the centroid of all the locations visited by the user on that day, k is the number of locations visited by the user on that day, and d is the Haversine distance. We then calculate a *mobility index* as the percentage change in average r over all users in a given region on a given day compared with the average for the same day of the week in the same region during January and February of 2020, i.e., before any EOs were issued. For example, the mobility index for a specific Monday in May 2020 is the percentage change in the average r on that day compared to the average over all Mondays in January and February 2020.

COVID-19 Case Data: We use county-level COVID-19 case data from USA Facts to calibrate the disease model in our simulation. A caveat is that the number of confirmed cases probably under-counted the number of actual cases substantially, especially early in the epidemic, due to limited testing. We compensate for this in the simulation calibration by choosing a scale factor of 30, i.e., we assume that the actual number of cases was 30× the reported number of cases. This arbitrary choice can straightforwardly be changed without affecting the methodology in our work.

Executive Orders in Virginia: We use a data set on Executive Orders that were implemented in each state in the USA [14] from the Johns Hopkins Coronavirus Resource Center [11]. From this we extract the ones that were implemented in Virginia in the period between March 1st and June 30th, 2020. In the simulation, EOs are represented by *norms* that agents may obey or violate, as described in Sect. 2.3. We quantify the benefits of these EOs through counterfactual runs of our calibrated simulation in Sect. 4.

2.2   Agents Activities and Deliberations

Each agent in the synthetic population is characterized by its weekly activity schedule, a set of typical daily activities over the course of one week. The schedule defines the location, start time and duration of all agents' activities as one of 7 distinct high level *activity types*: HOME, stay at or work from home; WORK, go to work or take a work-related trip; SHOP, buy goods (e.g., groceries, clothes, appliances); SCHOOL, attend school as a student; COLLEGE, attend college as a student; RELIGIOUS, religious or other community activities; and OTHER, any other activity, including recreational activities, exercise, dining at a restaurant, etc. For example, one activity in an agent's schedule could state "SHOP at location l between 7 p.m. and 8 p.m." These activity types categorize a larger number of low-level activity types, including but not limited to those describing the categories above. The high level activity types are what the agents use for reasoning, while the lower level activity types – which we do not use for reasoning because they are not guaranteed to have been sampled accurately during the creation of the synthetic populations – are only used to assign the location and activity time and duration according to the activity schedule. Each simulation step corresponds to one day, and at each simulation step, each agent retrieves and performs the activities from its activity schedule for the day of the week corresponding to that step.

We interpret each activity in an agent's daily schedule as a (to-do) goal for the corresponding Sim-2APL agent. For each activity (i.e. goal) in its daily schedule, the agent generates a plan based on its goal, identifies any norms applicable to the activity, and decides whether it will obey or violate the norm(s) (See Sect. 2.3 below). If there are no applicable norms, or if the agent decides not to obey the norm, the agent uses the default plan for the to-do goal, i.e., the planned daily activity. However, if the agent decides to obey an applicable norm, the default plan for the daily activity is transformed into a norm-aligned plan. For example, if a norm specifies a mask should be worn in public places, the SHOP activity in the example above will be transformed into a SHOP activity with a "wearing a mask" modality.

2.3 Reasoning with Norms

We consider 11 norms representing a subset of the Executive Orders implemented in the state of Virginia (US). We distinguish regimented norms (R) that cannot be violated by agents, from non-regimented norms (NR) where agents may autonomously decide whether to comply with the norm or not. In addition, some norms have parameters that further specify the applicability of a particular instance of the norm to the activity itself or to the agent considering that activity. For example, the *type* parameter of the *BusinessClosed* norm specifies the type of business to which the norm instance applies (e.g., an instance may specify that only Non-Essential Business (*NEB*) should close), while the *size* and *type* parameters of the *SmallGroups* norm specify the maximum size of groups permitted in a context of a particular type (e.g., no more than 10 people are allowed in a *public* space). The *type* parameter of *SchoolsClosed*, finally, specifies the grade levels that are closed (e.g., *K-12* specifies all K-12 level schools are closed, i.e. the norm applies only to activities of type SCHOOL when the agent performing the SCHOOL activity is attending K-12 level education). The norms are summarized in Table 1 and briefly explained in Table 2. Figure 2 shows the date on which each norm came into force.

Factors Influencing Agent Decisions. If a regimented norm applies to an activity of an agent, the agent simply obeys the norm. If a non-regimented norm applies, the agent's decision whether to obey or violate the norm is influenced by a number of factors determined by the agent's beliefs and preferences regarding the activity. For example, in deciding whether to maintain physical distancing in a particular shop (i.e., to obey a *MaintainDistance* norm during a SHOP activity in a particular shop), agents take into account how many other agents they have observed maintaining physical distancing (*dist*) in the shop in the past, and their *trust* in the government[1]. Note that a norm may not be applicable to (relevant for) certain activities or agents, e.g., the norm *WearMaskPublInd* is not applicable to WORK or SCHOOL. Each factor is represented by a real value in the interval [0, 1], and the factors are summarized in last five columns of Table 1.

---

[1] Our choice of the factors influencing the agents' decisions, as well as of the norms mentioned above, should be considered as a 'proof of concept' to illustrate our framework. In more realistic simulations, elicitation of the most relevant factors in a well-designed study would be paramount. This is left for future work.

Each agent's initial *trust* in the government is determined by sampling a beta distribution $Beta_v(\alpha_v, \beta_v)$ (with $v = R$ for Republican and $v = D$ for Democrat), where $\alpha_v = \mu_v \cdot \kappa$, $\beta_v = (1 - \mu_v) \cdot \kappa$. The means μ_R and μ_D are determined by calibration (explained in Sect. 3); $\kappa = \alpha_v + \beta_v = 100$ characterizes the spread of the distribution, and, for simplicity, is fixed for both distributions. To simulate the decreasing compliance with measures that in reality manifested over time, agents in our simulation decrease their trust in the government by a constant factor f per simulation step after t_f simulation steps (days). Both t_f and f are fixed for all agents and are determined through calibration. The factor *acc* specifies the probability that an agent can be accommodated to work from home (in our simulation $acc = 0.45$ [8], and is the same for all agents). The factors *mask*, *dist* and *symp* specify the fraction of other agents encountered at a certain location who were wearing a mask, maintaining physical distancing, and who were (visibly) symptomatic, respectively. Symptoms are only visible if an agent is actually infected (determined by the disease model PanSim, see Sect. 2.4), but not all infected agents are symptomatic. The factor *all* specifies the number of agents encountered at a given location in excess of the maximum number of agents allowed by the norms currently in force.[2]

Table 1. Which activities are affected by regimented (R) and non-regimented (NR) norms, and the factors influencing the decision to comply with each norm.

Norm	Id	Param	Type	Activity types transformations					Influencing agents believes					
				WORK	SHOP	OTHER	SCHOOL	RELIGIOUS	trust	symp	acc	mask	dist	all
AllowWearMask	n_1	–	NR	mod	mod	mod	mod	mod	x			x		
BusinessClosed	n_2	type	R	del										
EmplWearMask	n_3	–	R	mod										
EncourTelework	n_4	–	NR	del					x	x	x			
MaintainDistance	n_5	–	NR	mod	mod	mod	mod	mod	x				x	
RedBusinessCapac	n_6	perc	R			del								
SchoolsClosed	n_7	type	R				del							
SmallGroups	n_8	size, type	NR	del	del	del	del	del	x	x				x
StayHome	n_9	appl	NR	del	del	del	del	del	x					
TakeawayOnly	n_{10}	–	R			short								
WearMaskPublInd	n_{11}	–	NR		mod	mod		mod	x			x		

Violating or Obeying a Norm. To determine whether to obey or violate a norm n when performing an activity *act*, the agent calculates a probability $p(n, act)$ of obeying n at the current simulation step, given by:

$$p(n, act) = \frac{1}{1 + e^{(-k \cdot (x - x_0))}} \qquad (1)$$

---

[2] Due to space limitations, we refer to the code repository for the specific details of the factors: https://bitbucket.org/goldenagents/sim2apl-episimpledemics.

where x represents the evidence for complying with n computed as the *average* value of the factors (excluding the *trust* factor) that support the compliance with n when performing *act*, $x_0 = 1 - trust$ represents the agent's distrust in the institution that issued n, and k is the logistic growth rate or steepness of the curve ($k = 10$ in our simulation). Note that when the trust in the institution is extreme (e.g., x_0 is close to 0 or 1), the decision to comply with the norm becomes more "resistant" to evidence supporting norm compliance. For example, if the agent has no trust in the institution (i.e., $x_0 = 1$), the probability of complying with a norm that depends only on the factor *mask* is 0.5 when 100% of other agents do wear a mask, but drops off steeply as the value of *mask* declines (when 75% of other agents do wear a mask, the probability to comply with the norm drops to approximately 0.07 for $k = 10$). However, if the trust value is more balanced (e.g., $x_0 = 0.5$), the decision to comply with the norm relies more on the supporting evidence.

Table 2. A brief explanation of the norms enforced in our simulation and of their parameters.

Id	Interpretation	Parameters
n_1	Mask wearing is allowed and encouraged	–
n_2	Businesses of type *type* are closed	$type \in \{NEB\}$: the type of business, NEB = Non Essential Business
n_3	Employees working in retail must wear a mask during work activities	–
n_4	Telework is encouraged	–
n_5	Physical distance of 1.5 m should be maintained	–
n_6	Capacity of business should be reduced to *perc*	*perc*: percentage of business capacity
n_7	Schools of type *type* are closed	$type \in \{K12, HE, K12 \text{ or } HE\}$: the type of school, $K12$ = primary and secondary education HE = Higher Education (HE)
n_8	The maximum allowed size of groups of type *type* is *size*	$type \in \{public, private, all\}$: the target settings, either public, private or both (*all*); $size \in \mathbb{N}$: maximum size of groups
n_9	Stay at home if belong to category *appl*	$appl \in \{sick \text{ or } age \geq 65, all\}$: the group of agents to which the norm applies, either people sick or older than 65 (*sick or age $\geq$ 65*), or everyone (*all*)
n_{10}	Only take away allowed for restaurants	–
n_{11}	A mask must be worn in public indoor settings	–

When an agent violates a norm with respect to a scheduled activity, the norm is ignored for that activity and the agent adopts the default plan for the activity (the to-do goal of the agent). When an agent obeys a norm with respect to an activity, the activity is subject to a transformation. We distinguish three types of transformations of activities:

- *mod*: the modality (in our model either wearing a mask or practicing physical distancing) of the activity is changed. For example, when the norm *Wear-MaskPublInd* is obeyed for the *SHOP* activity, the agent performs that activity while wearing a mask. In the code, the modality is a flag that is interpreted by PanSim and affects the susceptibility or infectivity of an agent (see Sect. 2.4).
- *del*: the activity is cancelled. When an activity is cancelled, it is transformed into a HOME activity, unless the agent can shift the next scheduled activity. For example, if an agent is scheduled to go to WORK, but its working place is closed, the agent will stay HOME, unless in its daily schedule there is a consequent activity (e.g., a SHOP activity) that can be performed earlier.
- *short*: the activity is shortened. For example, when obeying a *TakeawayOnly* norm, the agent will spend less time at the restaurant.

The *Activity Types Transformations* shown in Table 1 specify how the norms affect each activity type. If no transformation is indicated in Table 1 for a pair ⟨norm n, activity type at⟩, the norm n does not apply to activities of type at.

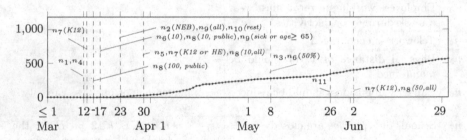

Fig. 2. Cumulative number of combined recorded cases in the counties of Goochland, Fluvanna, and Charlottesville (blue line). Red and green lines are introduction of new restrictions and relaxations of previous ones. (Color figure online)

2.4 Environment Design

To model the spread of COVID-19, we implemented a novel distributed agent-based epidemic simulation platform, which we call PanSim. In PanSim, a simulation progresses in discrete timesteps. When a Sim-2APL agent decides to visit a location, it interacts with other agents visiting that location, and observes the visible attributes exhibited by these agents such as: coughing, wearing mask, social distancing, etc., allowing it to modify its behavior based on its observations at subsequent timesteps. The probability of symptomatic and asymptomatic agents transmitting or becoming infected per unit time (5 minutes) under different action modalities such as the wearing of a mask or physical distancing, is given by the probabilistic addition of all individual interactions of that day. To simulate cases being introduced from outside, we artificially expose 5 agents during the first 5 days of the simulation, and 3 more agents each simulation day after.

The novelty of PanSim lies in the fact that, unlike previous epidemic simulation frameworks, PanSim has explicit support for modeling human behavior, increasing the number and type of social phenomena that can be modeled, and allowing disease progression to be driven by explicit colocation rather than statistical likelihood of contact between agents. The colocation in turn is the result of locations and times that individual agents – implemented in any agent programming language – can explicitly choose for their activities. PanSim further allows scaling up the number and complexity of agents and visits by distributing the simulation across multiple compute nodes, where each node simulates a distinct set of agents and locations. PanSim synchronizes its instances across compute nodes by sharing only the data relating to agents visiting a location simulated on another node, ensuring all its instances remain synchronized throughout the simulation with minimal communication. Both the framework and experiments showing the scalability are described in detail in the companion paper [3].

3 Calibration

We calibrate the behavior and disease parameters independently from each other in two distinct processes. For this reason, the best parameters for either model were not yet available when calibrating the other. In each process, the parameters for the model not being calibrated were fixed to our best estimations (based on results of earlier trial runs) of the values. In other words, the parameters for the disease model were fixed in the process in which we calibrated the behavior model, and vice versa. Both calibration processes are performed by means of Nelder-Mead (NM) minimization [13]. NM iteratively refines an initial configuration of parameters until it finds a local optimum that minimizes a given objective function, in this case the Root Mean Square Error (RMSE) between observations in the simulation and the real world. Calibration was performed using data from the counties of Charlottesville (41119 unique agents in the synthetic population, 83.25% of which voted Democratic, 16.75% Republican), Fluvanna (24109 unique agents, 45.35% Democratic, 54.65% Republican), and Goochland (20922 unique agents, 37.55% Democratic, 62, 45% Republican) for a total of 86150 agents, 61.55% Democratic, 33, 45% Republican. These counties have been selected for their proximity, number of agents, and variation in voting preference. For each set of parameters selected by NM, we run 5 different simulations in order to account for non-determinism in the simulation.

Agent Parameters. We calibrate the four parameters of the agent model introduced in Sect. 2.3, i.e., the *means* μ_D and μ_R of the two beta distributions

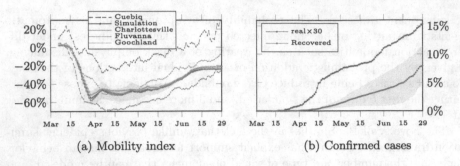

(a) Mobility index   (b) Confirmed cases

Fig. 3. The mobility index observed in the simulation plotted against that recorded by Cuebiq in each simulated county (a), and percentage confirmed cases (×30) of the population plotted against that of the recovered agents in the simulation (b).

from which we sample the trust attitudes of Democratic and Republican agents, respectively, the fatigue factor f, and the time step t_f in the simulation at which the fatigue becomes active. We calculate the RMSE between the mobility index in our simulation and in the real-world Cuebiq data (calculated as per Sect. 2.1). We apply a smoothing to the mobility index of each day by averaging it with the mobility index of the 6 preceding days in order to smooth out the intrinsic difference in the weekly repeated mobility trends between the synthetic population and Cuebiq data. We perform these simulations with the disease model parameters fixed to $inf_s = 0.00045$ and $inf_a = 0.0003375$ (best estimate).

Disease Model Parameters. The two parameters of the disease model that are calibrated are the infectivity of symptomatic (inf_s) and asymptomatic (inf_a) agents. We calculate the RMSE between the cumulative infection case count in the three simulated counties and the number of recovered agents in our simulation. The agent parameters are fixed to $\mu_D = 0.776816$, $\mu_R = 0.106955$, $f = 0.0125$, and $t_f = 60$ (best estimate).

Calibration Results. For both calibration processes, we run NM until 10 consecutive configurations of parameters did not improve the objective function. The final parameters determined by our calibration are: $\mu_D = 0.704621$, $\mu_R = 0.004685$, $f = 0.0125$ and $t_f = 60$ for the agent model (RMSE: 17.6574), and $inf_s = 0.0000481$ and $inf_a = 0.0000241$ for the disease model (RMSE: 2052.0222). Figure 3 compares the mobility (Fig. 3a) and the number of recovered agents (Fig. 3b) resulting from these parameters with the real data. The agent parameter calibration found a relatively good fit for the decrease in mobility, including the increase in mobility after the first few weeks. However, the large differences between the different counties could not be reproduced by our simulation. The disease model calibration resulted in a slightly less aggressive spread of the disease than the (scaled) recorded case count in the first few months of the COVID-19 outbreak.

4 Quantifying the Effects of Normative Interventions

We perform an experiment with the calibrated models to understand the relative impact of the measures instigated by the institutions in Virginia on the behavior of its residents. Given the list of $n = 9$ normative interventions that took place in Virginia as per Fig. 2, we run 10 different experiments: in experiment Ei, for $0 \leq i \leq n$, we enact only the first i executive orders. For example, in experiment $E0$, no norm is enforced, i.e., we simulate a scenario where no behavioral intervention takes place; in experiment $E1$, we enact only the first EO, i.e., norms $\{n_1, n_4\}$ starting from March 12th; in experiment $E2$ we enact the first two EOs, i.e., $\{n_1, n_4\}$ starting from March 12th and also $\{n_7(K12)\}$ starting from March 13th, etc. In each experiment we compute the total number of agents that has been infected at the end of the simulation. This time, we include the county of Louisa in the simulation, for a total of 119087 agents. We run each experiment 5 times to account for non-determinism in the simulation.

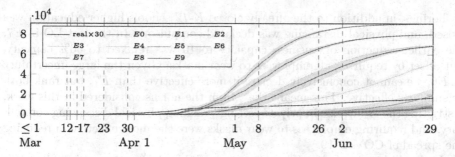

Fig. 4. Cumulative cases in $E1$-10, and in the real-world ($\times 30$, blue line). (Color figure online)

Figure 4 shows the number of recovered agents at each time step in the simulations (SIR plots available in the code repository), with the standard deviation between the 5 runs shown as the confidence interval. $E0$ shows that if no measures had been taken, the spread of COVID-19 would have been several times more rapid. The higher curves do not show exponential growth until the end of the simulation, since our simulation contained only 119087 agents. After a sufficiently large portion of the population has been infected it becomes increasingly hard for the disease to encounter susceptible agents, slowing the spread.

Table 3 shows the total number of agents that have been infected at the end of the simulation (including those not yet recovered). The experiment $E9$, where all the norms were enforced, shows the lowest number of total infections, with a reduction of 27% in cases compared the $E8$ – in which the maximum group size was completely lifted instead of relaxed from 10 to 50 people – and an 83% reduction compared to the experiment where no norms were enforced.

The largest decrease was from $E5$ to $E6$, closely follows by $E6$ to $E7$. In the last EO in $E6$ the maximum group size of 10 was also applied to private

Table 3. The average number of cumulative cases in each experiment

Exp.	Cumulative cases	Diff. w.r.t. E_{i-1}	Diff. w.r.t. E_0
E0	90983.6 ± 41.802		0.0%
E1	80711.0 ± 343.627	−11.29%	−11.29%
E2	71616.2 ± 241.017	−11.27%	−21.29%
E3	71760.6 ± 297.292	+0.20%	−21.13%
E4	64674.4 ± 445.714	−9.870%	−28.92%
E5	49118.0 ± 4162.414	−24.05%	−46.01%
E6	30505.0 ± 10202.892	−37.89%	−66.47%
E7	20599.0 ± 4423.636	−32.47%	−77.36%
E8	21195.6 ± 4044.473	+2.90%	−76.70%
E9	15569.6 ± 5144.708	−26.54%	−82.89%

gatherings, in addition to the already closed *K-12* schools higher education was closed, and physical distancing was declared compulsory. In the last EO in $E7$, the earlier reduction of business capacity to 10 was relaxed to 50% capacity, but offset by requiring all employees to wear masks. Given the large uncertainty in $E6$, we cannot conclusively declare it more effective than $E7$, but rank both as similarly effective. This means that, from the norms considered in this work, restricting the group size in private settings, making physical distancing compulsory, and requiring employees to wear masks were the most effective in reducing the spread of COVID-19.

It should be noted that for the purpose of this work, various simplifications have been applied to the actual norms enforced. Moreover, in practice the EOs (including relaxations) have been issued in response to the actual spread of COVID-19 at that time, while in our simulation they were fixed to their original dates. Nevertheless, these results show that behavioral responses of individual agents to normative interventions, and not just the effect of an assumed level of compliance, can be studied through our proposed simulation framework.

5   Conclusion

We presented a novel distributed agent-based simulation framework for large-scale multi-agent simulations of norm-governed behaviors in epidemics, and applied it to the case of COVID-19. We modeled a population of agents representing individuals from the state of Virginia, whose daily behavior was determined from multiple data sources, including the American Community Survey. We calibrated and validated the behavior exhibited by the agents, affected by the norms enforced in the state of Virginia (such as school and business closures, mask-wearing and physical distance interventions) using Cuebiq mobility data and the COVID-19 infection data. We used the model to compare the sensitivity of the COVID-19 outbreak size to the different normative interventions. In future work, we intend to evaluate the scalability of our framework, to introduce more complex agents dynamics, such as inter-agent communications, and to evaluate a number of different hypothesis about the COVID-19 pandemic.

Future work also includes improving the simulation calibration. We believe that reducing the arbitrary scaling of the observed number of cases from 30 to a smaller factor will result in better calibration. Improving the mobility calibration to reflect the variations in mobility index from one county to another may require further refinement of the behavior model. We are also working on scaling up to larger populations, such as all the 133 counties and independent cities in the state of Virginia, which add up to over 7.6 million agents, and evaluating more complex experiment designs.

More broadly, we believe that effective intervention to mitigate novel epidemics requires methods to evaluate the effects of normative interventions in detail, which in turn requires being able to model human behavioral choices and responses. Through the use of substantial real-world data, BDI models of agent reasoning, and a scalable simulation platform, we can come closer to this goal.

Acknowledgments. We thank Cuebiq; mobility data is provided by Cuebiq, a location intelligence and measurement platform. Through its Data for Good program, Cuebiq provides access to aggregated mobility data for academic research and humanitarian initiatives. This first-party data is collected from anonymized users who have opted-in to provide access to their location data anonymously, through a GDPR and CCPA compliant framework. To further preserve privacy, portions of the data are aggregated to the census-block group level.

PB and SS were supported in part by NSF Expeditions in Computing Grant CCF-1918656 and DTRA subcontract/ARA S-D00189-15-TO-01-UVA.

References

1. Adiga, A., et al.: Generating a synthetic population of the United States. Technical report, NDSSL 15-009, Network Dynamics and Simulation Science Laboratory (2015)
2. Becher, M., Stegmueller, D., Brouard, S., Kerrouche, E.: Comparative experimental evidence on compliance with social distancing during the COVID-19 pandemic. medRxiv (2020)
3. Bhattacharya, P., de Mooij, J., Dell'Anna, D., Dastani, M., Logan, B., Swarup, S.: PanSim + Sim-2APL: a framework for large-scale distributed simulation with complex agents. In: International Workshop on Engineering Multi-Agent Systems (2021)
4. Chan, D.K.C., Zhang, C.Q., Weman-Josefsson, K.: Why people failed to adhere to COVID-19 preventive behaviors? Perspectives from an integrated behavior change model. Infect. Control Hosp. Epidemiol. **42**(3), 375–376 (2021)
5. Chen, J., Lewis, B., Marathe, A., Marathe, M.V., Swarup, S., Vullikanti, A.K.S.: Individual and collective behavior in public health epidemiology. In: Disease Modelling and Public Health, Part A, vol. 36, pp. 329–368 (2017). Chapter 12
6. Dastani, M.: 2APL: a practical agent programming language. Auton. Agents Multi-Agent Syst. **16**, 214–248 (2008). https://doi.org/10.1007/s10458-008-9036-y

7. Dastani, M., Testerink, B.: Design patterns for multi-agent programming. Int. J. Agent-Oriented Softw. Eng. **5**(2/3), 167–202 (2016)
8. Dey, M., Frazis, H., Loewenstein, M.A., Sun, H.: Ability to work from home. Mon. Labor Rev. 1–19 (2020)
9. Ferguson, N.: Capturing human behavior. Nature **446**, 733 (2007)
10. Funk, S., et al.: Nine challenges in incorporating the dynamics of behaviour in infectious disease models. Epidemics **10**, 21–25 (2015)
11. Johns Hopkins Coronavirus Resource Center: Impact of opening and closing decisions in Virginia, new cases - Johns Hopkins. https://coronavirus.jhu.edu/data/state-timeline/new-confirmed-cases/virginia/. Accessed 07 Oct 2020
12. Katz, J., Sanger-Katz, M., Quealy, K.: A detailed map of who is wearing masks in the U.S. https://www.nytimes.com/interactive/2020/07/17/upshot/coronavirus-face-mask-map.html. Accessed 08 Oct 2020
13. Nelder, J.A., Mead, R.: A simplex method for function minimization. Comput. J. **7**(4), 308–313 (1965)
14. Northam, R.S.: Virginia Governor Ralph S. Northam - executive actions. https://www.governor.virginia.gov/executive-actions/. Accessed 07 Oct 2020
15. Swarup, S., Eubank, S., Marathe, M.: Computational epidemiology as a challenge domain for multiagent systems. In: Proceedings of the Thirteenth International Conference on Autonomous Agents and Multiagent Systems (AAMAS) (2014)
16. Verelst, F., Willem, L., Beutels, P.: Behavioural change models for infectious disease transmission: a systematic review. J. R. Soc. Interface **13**, 20160820 (2016)

MAS Network: Surrogate Neural Network for Multi-agent Simulation

Hiroaki Yamada[1][(✉)], Masataka Shirahashi[2], Naoyuki Kamiyama[3], and Yumeka Nakajima[2]

[1] Fujitsu Laboratories Ltd., Kawasaki, Japan
yamadah@fujitsu.com
[2] Graduate School of Mathematics, Kyushu University, Fukuoka, Japan
{shirahashi.masataka.317,nakajima.yumeka.456}@s.kyushu-u.ac.jp
[3] Institute of Mathematics for Industry, Kyushu University, Fukuoka, Japan
kamiyama@imi.kyushu-u.ac.jp

Abstract. Multi-agent simulation (MAS) plays an important role in analyzing our societies because it can model complexity in societies and assimilate a variety of social data. However, the execution of MAS is computationally expensive. When running numerous executions to determine optimal policy, it is crucial to develop a more computationally efficient mathematical model that is able to sufficiently substitute for the original simulation. In this paper, we propose a machine learning framework for developing neural network models, called *MAS network*, that can substitute for MAS. Furthermore, we propose an effective feature representation of agent parameters and a systematic dataset design for learning. We confirmed that the MAS network replicated the system dynamics of the simulation and that the MAS network accurately learned the sensitivity of output and input relation even at unknown parameter points.

Keywords: Multi-agent simulation · Surrogate model · Deep neural network · Pedestrian flow simulation

1 Introduction

Our societies are becoming increasingly complex. Multi-agent simulations (MAS) play a key role in the analysis of our societies. MAS models have sufficient flexibility to represent complexity in societies and to assimilate a variety of social data. Therefore, existing simulation models are used to analyze and improve social systems in the real world [12,13]. However, MAS has a disadvantage of long execution time, moreover, its execution is computationally expensive. Thus, when running numerous virtual experiments in MAS to determine an optimal policy (e.g., [2,11]), execution time becomes a problem. In practice, this type of optimization application repeatedly arises in daily or weekly planning tasks. It is crucial to develop a more computationally efficient mathematical model that is an adequate substitute for the original simulation model without losing the power of expression.

© Springer Nature Switzerland AG 2022
K. H. Van Dam and N. Verstaevel (Eds.): MABS 2021, LNAI 13128, pp. 113–124, 2022.
https://doi.org/10.1007/978-3-030-94548-0_9

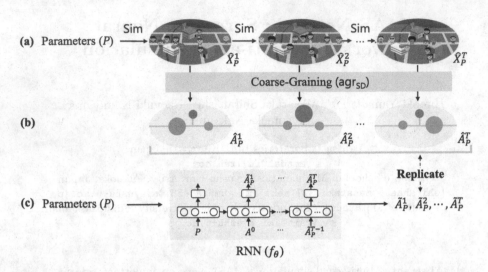

Fig. 1. Schematic of MAS network. (a) Multi-agent simulations (MAS), Sim makes future states of agents (positions of characters) based on their parameters and their past states. (b) The states of agents can be aggregated as population of each spot (sizes of circles), that is, we can do coarse-graining of the agent dynamics as population dynamics by the aggregate function, agr_{SD}. (c) MAS network, f_θ, learns the population dynamics for each parameters.

Here, we present a machine learning framework for developing computationally efficient mathematical models, called "MAS network", that can substitute for MAS (see Fig. 1). Our framework is based on a neural network-based surrogate model approach in physics, in which a simulator is mapped to a deep neural network through end-to-end learning using a variety of input and output data of the simulation. For example, [9] proposed a machine learning framework that can learn simulation models of various physical domains. In [4], the authors proposed an approximation model based on convolutional neural network for real-time prediction of non-uniform steady laminar flow (see also [7]). In [3], neural network surrogate models for animation based on physical principles are proposed. Training such neural networks on MAS with large state spaces of thousands of agents and complex dynamics of their interaction is difficult with standard end-to-end learning. In this paper, we introduce a method that represents simulations on the system dynamics level for training; that is, we attempt to capture aggregated population dynamics instead of individual agent dynamics.

The main advantage of our proposed framework is that it can achieve computational efficiency without losing valid resolution and valuable details. Generally, predicting the aggregated numbers is the primary objective of MAS, for example, predicting how many people are in a specific location, how many people belong to a particular social class, or how many people are infected with a contagion. Compared to pure system dynamics models, the advantage of a multi-agent simulation is the reproducibility of emergent phenomena arising from micro-level interaction. Through experiments, we confirmed that neural networks built on our framework could capture such valuable emergent details.

We evaluated our proposed MAS network by using several deep learning architectures, and we confirmed that these networks could sufficiently learn a pedestrian flow simulation. Our MAS network were able to learn the relationship between the simulator input, which is the set of agent parameters and environmental parameters, and the simulator output, which is the number of people in each location, indicating congestion. We showed that our method could predict congestion dynamics even when situations are unknown. Furthermore, we showed the reproducibility of emergent phenomena arising from micro-level interaction.

The contributions of this study are summarized as follows:

1. We propose a framework for constructing surrogate models of MAS.
2. We propose an effective feature representation of agent parameters.
3. We propose a systematic dataset design of MAS for the surrogate models.

2 Framework Definition

2.1 Multi-agent Simulation

We consider the MAS that is described as follows. The simulation has several parameters, and we denote by $\mathcal{P}$ the set of parameters. For example, in the pedestrian flow simulation, the parameters include, but are not limited to, the number of agents, the agents' preferences, the number of services, the processing speeds of the services. During the simulation, the simulation is given the input to the parameters, $P \in \mathcal{P}$. Based on the input, the simulation outputs the state, $X \in \mathcal{X}$, where $\mathcal{X}$ is the set of states of the simulation. For example, in the pedestrian flow simulation, each state, X, represents all agents' positions. The simulation outputs the state at the next time-step based on the input to the simulation, P, and the state at the previous time-step. Then, the simulation repeats this procedure from the first time-step to the last time-step.

That is, when we denote by $\mathcal{X}^*$ the set of finite sequences $(X^0, X^1, \ldots, X^t)$ of states in $\mathcal{X}$, the multi-agent simulation is represented by a mapping $\mathrm{Sim} \colon \mathcal{P} \times \mathcal{X}^* \to \mathcal{X}$. For each input to parameters $P \in \mathcal{P}$, the execution of the simulation until the time-step T is represented by the sequence $(X^0, \hat{X}_P^1, \ldots, \hat{X}_P^T)$ such that $\hat{X}_P^t = \mathrm{Sim}(P, (X^0, \hat{X}_P^1, \ldots, \hat{X}_P^{t-1}))$ for every integer $t \in \{1, 2, \ldots, T\}$ (see Fig. 1(a)). X^0 represents the initial state where no one has appeared in the simulation environment. For each input to parameters $P \in \mathcal{P}$ and for each positive integer T, the state sequence yielded by Sim is $\hat{\mathbf{X}}_P^{t_0:T} = (X^0, \hat{X}_P^1, \ldots, \hat{X}_P^T) \in \mathcal{X}^*$.

2.2 Coarse-Graining as System Dynamics

Usually, the MAS has many variables. Thus, the dimension of each state of the simulation, $X \in \mathcal{X}$, is substantial. Thus, when we predict the simulation dynamics, we focus on some aggregated information obtained from each state.

That is, we have to consider an appropriate aggregate function, $\mathsf{agr} \colon \mathcal{X} \to \mathcal{A}$, that maps each state of the simulation to some aggregated information, $A \in \mathcal{A}$. $\mathcal{A}$ is the set of the aggregated information. We define $\mathcal{A} := \{\mathsf{agr}(X) \mid X \in \mathcal{X}\}$. We denote by $\mathcal{A}^*$ the set of finite sequence $(\mathsf{agr}(X^0), \mathsf{agr}(X^1), \ldots, \mathsf{agr}(X^t))$ of aggregated information.

We introduce an aggregate function, $\mathsf{agr_{SD}}$, which coarse-grains state of the simulation from a system dynamics perspective. The function, $\mathsf{agr_{SD}}$, summarizes the state of the simulation, set explicitly of each agent state, into a set of several agent population states (see Fig. 1(b)). The idea behind this is that MAS can be captured as stocks and flows systems. The stock is the number of agents belonging to each population and flow is the states transition from one population to another population. An aggregated information, A, is an N length real vector representing the states of N agent populations. For example, in the pedestrian flow simulation, when we input a set of each agent state, $\mathsf{agr_{SD}}$ outputs the numbers of agents in each spot, where each population is related to each spot. The definitions of each population can be arbitrary according to objective and simulation type, such as the number of people in (station, shop, intersection, ...), (upper class, middle class, worker class, ...), (susceptible, infected, recovered, ...), or so on. For each input to parameters $P \in \mathcal{P}$ and each positive integer T, the aggregated information of $\hat{\mathbf{X}}_P^{t_0:T}$ by $\mathsf{agr_{SD}}$ is $\hat{\mathbf{A}}_P^{t_0:T} = (\mathsf{agr_{SD}}(X^0), \mathsf{agr_{SD}}(\hat{X}_P^1), \ldots, \mathsf{agr_{SD}}(\hat{X}_P^T)) \in \mathcal{A}^*$.

2.3   MAS Network

We denote by f_θ the surrogate model with parameters θ. MAS network as a surrogate model is mapping from the input to the simulation and the history of the agent population states until the current time-step to the states at the next step, $f_\theta : \mathcal{P} \times \mathcal{A}^* \to \mathcal{A}$. For example, in the pedestrian flow simulation, the MAS network is given the input to the simulation and the number of agents in the spots from the first time-step to the $(t-1)$th time-step, and then it predicts the numbers of agents in the spots at the tth time-step. For each input to parameters $P \in \mathcal{P}$, the prediction of the surrogate model until the time-step T is represented by $(A^0, \tilde{A}_P^1, \ldots, \tilde{A}_P^T)$ such that

$$\tilde{A}_P^t = f_\theta(P, (A^0, \tilde{A}_P^1, \ldots, \tilde{A}_P^{t-1})) \tag{1}$$

for every integer $t \in \{1, 2, \ldots, T\}$ (see Fig. 1(c)). For each input to parameters $P \in \mathcal{P}$, for each positive integer T, the state sequence yielded by f_θ is $\tilde{\mathbf{A}}_P^{t_0:T}(f_\theta) = (A^0, \tilde{A}_P^1, \ldots, \tilde{A}_P^T) \in \mathcal{A}^*$.

Our goal is to find a surrogate model that can approximate the state sequence yielded by the simulation and the aggregated function, $\hat{\mathbf{A}}_P^{t_0:T}$. In machine learning approach, assuming some probabilistic model (e.g., neural networks) f, we obtain the surrogate model by solving

$$\min_\theta \max_{P \in \mathcal{P}} L(\hat{\mathbf{A}}_P^{t_0:T}, \tilde{\mathbf{A}}_P^{t_0:T}(f_\theta)), \tag{2}$$

where L is a loss function that calculates a difference between state sequence yielded by Sim and $\mathsf{agr_{SD}}$, $\hat{\mathbf{A}}_P^{t_0:T}$, and state sequence predicted by f_θ, $\tilde{\mathbf{A}}_P^{t_0:T}(f_\theta)$.

3   Implementation

3.1   Neural Network Architecture

We use a type of neural network called a recurrent neural network (RNN) as a probabilistic model, f_θ. An RNN consists of a recurrent layer, $h^{t+1} = \sigma_{\theta_1}(h^t, x^t)$, and a fully connected layer, $y^{t+1} = \phi_{\theta_2}(h^{t+1})$, where h^t is the hidden state, x^t is the input of the network, y^{t+1} is the output, and θ_1, θ_2 are parameters of each layer. Recursive form of the RNN fits MAS network's that predicts the next population state from the parameters and past population states (Eq. 1).

We tested our framework using three RNN architectures: long short-term memory (LSTM) [5], sequence-to-sequence (seq2seq) [10], and attention [1]. An LSTM is an RNN with two hidden states, a cell state vector functioning as long-term memory and a hidden state vector functioning as short-term memory. In LSTM, the number of hidden layers was 2 and the number of nodes in the hidden layer was 128. A seq2seq is an architecture that consists of two RNNs: an encoder network and a decoder network. In seq2seq, a gated recurrent unit (GRU), which has the same functions as LSTM and is more computationally efficient than LSTM, was used for the encoder network and the decoder network; the number of hidden layers was 1, and the number of the hidden nodes was 128. Attention model is an extension of seq2seq, where the decoder generates an output sequence using its hidden state plus the hidden state of the encoder at all times-step. In the attention model, network parameters were the same as those of seq2seq.

3.2   Loss Function and Optimization Procedure

For a variety of P, we computed the mean squared error (MSE) of the simulated state sequence, $\hat{\mathbf{A}}_P^{t_0:T}$, and the predicted state sequence, $\tilde{\mathbf{A}}_P^{t_0:T}(f_\theta)$, as loss, that is,

$$L(\hat{\mathbf{A}}_P^{t_0:T}, \tilde{\mathbf{A}}_P^{t_0:T}(f_\theta)) = \frac{1}{TN} \sum_{t=1}^{T} \sum_{n=0}^{N} (\hat{a}_P^{t,n} - \tilde{a}_P^{t,n})^2, \qquad (3)$$

where $\hat{a}_P^{t,n}$ and $\tilde{a}_P^{t,n}$ are real numbers representing the number of agents on a spot, respectively. That is, $\hat{A}_P^t = \{\hat{a}_P^{t,0}, \hat{a}_P^{t,1}, \dots, \hat{a}_P^{t,N}\}$ and $\tilde{A}_P^t = \{\tilde{a}_P^{t,0}, \tilde{a}_P^{t,1}, \dots, \tilde{a}_P^{t,N}\}$. We optimized the model parameters θ over this loss using the Adam optimizer [6]. We performed 200 epoch training with a learning rate of 0.001. We implemented our models using PyTorch 1.7.1 [8]. It took approximately half a day to train a model on an NVIDIA Tesla V100 SXM2 (16GiB HBM2). We followed standard supervised learning procedures.

We generated simulation results on various parameters, then randomly divided them into training data (80%) and test data (20%). The training data was used to train the model by searching for the best model parameters that minimize the loss using the Adam optimizer. The test data were used only to evaluate the performance of the trained model, where the metric of performance is MSE, which is same as the loss function (Eq. 3). In our simulation, the time-step, T, is 1000, and the state's size, N, is 6.

3.3   Input and Output Representations

Commonly, simulations have multiple parameters. In the MAS, there are parameters related to the agent and related environment. In the pedestrian flow simulation, the agent parameters are the preference, destination list, arrival time, and congestion avoidance tendency of each agent, which governs all the population dynamics. The environment parameters are each spot's number of the server, service time per visitor, and network, which strongly relate to the individual population. In that sense, the former are global parameters, and the latter are local parameters of each population. From this perspective, we design input features representations.

We define P as set of parameter vectors $\{P^0, P^1, \ldots, P^m, \ldots, P^M\}$. Each parameter vector corresponds to each parameter of the simulation. Each element of the parameter vector relates to each population, $P^m = \{p^{m,0}, p^{m,1}, \ldots, p^{m,N}\}$. We input the parameter vectors to an RNN sequentially (Fig. 2). Note that there are two types of parameter vector: agent parameters, i.e., global parameters, and environment parameters, i.e., local parameters. The agent parameters share value within the vector, and the environment parameters do not share value within the vector. That is, the agent parameters are $p^{m,0} = p^{m,1} = \cdots = p^{m,N}$, whereas, the environment parameters are $p^{m,0} \neq p^{m,1} \neq \cdots \neq p^{m,N}$.

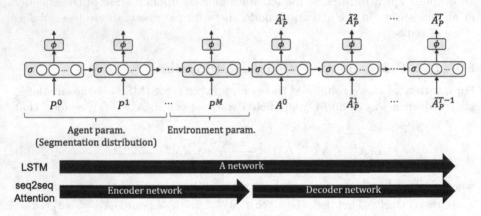

Fig. 2. Input and output of our RNN. The symbols below the σ functions are input to the RNN from left to right. A^0 is a N length zero vector. The symbols above the ϕ functions are the outputs of the RNN. We repeatedly applied ϕ and σ to an input sequence. The LSTM applies to the whole process. In the seq2seq and the attention, the encoder networks work only on encoding parameters, and the decoder networks work only on generating predictions. The decoder networks compute predictions through ϕ and π, using the encoder's hidden states at P^0 to P^M.

Preliminary experiments showed that an overlong parameter inhibited the learning process. In our simulation, the agent parameter's length reaches a thousand because the simulation has hundreds of agents and each agent has several parameters. Hence, we introduce a feature representation technique to perform dimensionality reduction of the agent parameters. We classify the agent into several segments according to their features' similarity and use the segments' distribution as the agent parameters. The procedure of this segmentation is as follows: 1) Calculation of the similarity of each agent using Euclidean distance of their features. 2) Clustering of the agents with K-means using the calculated distance. 3) Summarizing the number of agents in each cluster. 4) Replacing the agent parameter by the distribution of the cluster. We compared our segmentation feature representation and statistical dimensionality reduction techniques: principal component analysis (PCA) and autoencoder. The statistical techniques compute latent variables from a purely statistical perspective; thus, it is difficult to interpret the summarized values. Whereas summarized values computed by our segmentation feature representation is superior in interpretability.

We normalized all of the simulation's parameter, input and output element-wise to 0–1, using the minimum and maximum value training data.

4   Experimental Setup

4.1   Simulation Model

We tested our framework using a pedestrian flow simulation. The pedestrian flow simulation represents a simple street of a city consisting of six spots: three facilities, one intersection, one entrance, and one exit. Each facility provides service to visitors through a server, and the number of the servers and the service time per visitor are parameterized. The geography of the street is modeled as a queueing network, where each node represents each spot. The topology of the network is parameterized.

We prepared three pedestrian agents with different decision-making and interaction: migration agent, avoidance agent, and ori2dest agent. The pedestrian agents, which imitate shopper, tourist, or worker behavior, repeat the following sequence of actions: First, the agent arrives at the street. Next, the agent selects a facility to visit next from among its destinations. Furthermore the agent moves to the facility. If no one is waiting in the facility's queue, the agent can immediately receive a service; otherwise, the agent waits in line. After receiving the service, the agent removes the facility from its destination list and selects the next facility. This sequence of actions is repeated until the destination's set is empty; the agent then leaves the street.

Three types of agents have differences in the decision and the interaction. **Migration agent** models people who avoid congestion using a smart device. The agent selects the next facility based on its preference, distance from the current position to the facility, and degree of congestion. Specifically, agent i at position p computes its own utility $U_i(a, p)$ for each facility a by $U_i(a, p) = \alpha_i(a) + d(a, p) + \beta_i c_i(a)$. Then, the agent selects a facility that maximizes the utility as the next to visit. That is, the agent behaves following the discrete choice model that considers a congestion avoidance tendency. $\alpha_i(a)$ is the preference of pedestrian i for facility a; $d(a, p)$ is the travel cost between a

and p; and $c_i(a)$ is the congestion cost of a. β is a factor that determines pedestrian i's tendency to avoid congestion. The agent always decides sequentially and does not plan its route in advance. The agent can always get the latest congestion information from the intelligent device. **Avoidance agent** is another type of model representing congestion-avoidance behavior. The avoidance agent models people who avoid congestion but do not use a smart device to do so. Avoidance agent i at position p computes its own utility $U_i(a, p)$ for each facility a by $U_i(a, p) = \alpha_i(a) + d(a, p)$. Then, the agent selects a facility that maximizes the utility, similar to the migration agent. The avoidance agent does not consider congestion when it decides which facility to visit next. However, if a visited facility's congestion exceeds agent i's congestion threshold then i reselects the next destination upon arrival. In this model, the congestion threshold, γ_i, represents pedestrian i's congestion avoidance tendency. **Ori2dest agents** do not interact with each other. The ori2dest agent models people just moving from an origin to a destination, such as commuters and workers; the agent does not avoid congestion in any way. The ori2dest agent model is the same as that of the avoidance agent except the reselection behavior is eliminated.

4.2   Dataset Design

We tested our framework using three datasets generated by three simulation containing each type of agent. Each dataset consists of simulation results sampled from parameter space. Random sampling from the entire parameter space, $\mathcal{P}$, generates too sparse a dataset. In contrast, random sampling from limited parameter space can not produce a good surrogate model because space may not cover parameters that we want to predict. We introduce a method to define a sampling parameter space from what it could happen (scenario) and what we can do (policy). In the method, the sampling parameter space is defined by the two space's product: a scenario parameter space that covers all of the situations that we assume in the simulation and a policy parameter space that covers all of the policies that we want to test. In the pedestrian flow simulation, the former is the size of each segment (108 parameters), and the latter are each spot's number of the server, service time per visitor and network (48 parameters).

The dataset design procedure is as follows: 1) Enumerating the scenario parameters and the policy parameters. 2) Defining ranges of each parameter and slicing them by regular intervals. 3) Making candidate of parameters as a combination of each parameter's value. 4) Randomly sampling from the candidate and running the simulation. Each dataset consists of 10,000 simulation results generated from different parameters. We split the dataset as training data (80%) and test data (20%).

5   Results

Our results show that the MAS network can predict the simulation dynamics even with agents with a complicated manner of interaction (Fig. 3). The networks

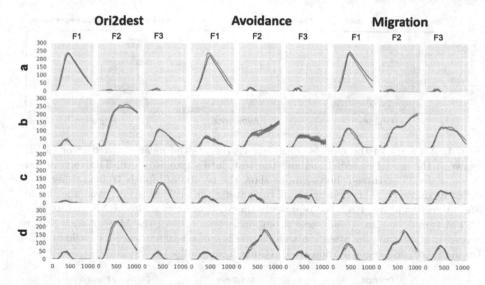

Fig. 3. Examples of the prediction results of the MAS network. Each panel shows the congestion dynamics of a facility. The horizontal axis is the time-step, and the vertical axis is the number of agents in the facility. The curves represent the ground truth (simulation output, gray) and prediction (red). Each row represents each parameter set's results (a–d). Each group of three columns is the results of a surrogate model trained using the specified type of agent (**Ori2dest**, **Avoidance**, **Migration**), and we made three surrogate models for each agent type. Each column is the results of each facility (F1, F2, F3). In the same row, the same simulation parameters were used, except for the agent model. All of the results were computed using the test data. The results were predicted by the attention architecture and segmentation feature representation. (Color figure online)

can predict valuable details, such as variation in population trends, that arise from micro-level interaction. For example, in Fig. 3b, the F2 curves changed by the different congestion avoidance tendency between the ori2dest and avoidance or the ori2dest and migration agent are reproduced. Moreover, the networks showed the capability of predicting radically different dynamics (Fig. 3a–d).

The MAS network using the attention architecture showed a lower MSE than the other architectures for all agent types (Fig. 4). LSTM lacks the expressive power necessary for learning the dynamics, whereas seq2seq has sufficient expressive power but requires more epochs to converge than the attention model (Fig. 5). Our task involved, roughly speaking, "translating" a series of simulation parameters to a series of degrees of congestion. LSTM is a general architecture mainly used for predicting unknown parts of a series from known parts of it (e.g., predicting future values from past time series), whereas seq2seq and attention, which belong to the encoder-decoder model, are architectures designed explicitly for translation tasks (e.g., machine translation). The difference in performance between the architectures may be due to their relative suitability for the

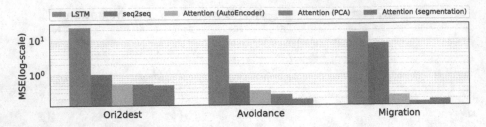

Fig. 4. Accuracy of the models. Each bar represents the mean squared error (MSE) between the model's predictions and the test data's ground truth. The vertical axis is log-scaled. The three-column groups show the results of models trained using three different datasets, generated by simulations using the ori2dest agent, avoidance agent, and migration agent. Each bar represents the MSE of an evaluated RNN architecture: LSTM (gray), seq2seq (blue), and attention (warm colors); the MSE of each feature representation using the attention architecture is separated: autoencoder (yellow), PCA (orange red), and segmentation (red). (Color figure online)

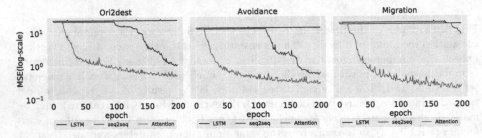

Fig. 5. Learning curves of the models. Each panel shows the learning curves of models trained using three different datasets using the ori2dest agent, avoidance agent, or migration agent. The horizontal axis is the epoch of training, and the vertical axis is the mean squared error (MSE) (log-scaled) in the test data. Each curve represents the MSE of an evaluated RNN architecture: LSTM (black), seq2seq (blue) and attention using segmentation representation (red). (Color figure online)

task. The segmentation feature representation, a feature representation method suitable for MAS, showed roughly the same MSE as the other dimensionality reduction techniques (Fig. 4 warm-colored bars). In the attention model, we can identify which elements in the input series are most related to predicting an element in the output series from the attention weight. We may reveal the input-output structure of the MAS as a complex system by analyzing the attention weight. We consider that our segmentation feature representation is vital for such advanced analysis, because interpretability of input values is a prerequisite for the analysis.

The MAS network correctly reproduced the output's sensitivity to input parameters even at unknown parameter points (Fig. 6). The network reproduced the main effects, for example, when the processing speed per visitor of F1 decreased, the queue length of F1 increased (Fig. 6, first row). Moreover,

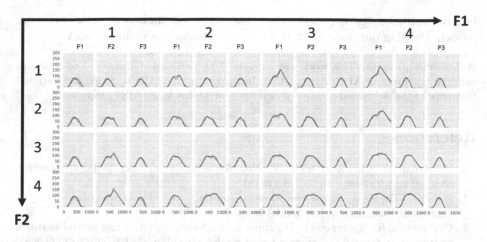

Fig. 6. Sensitivity of output to input. Each panel shows the congestion dynamics of each facility (F1, F2, F3) and each curves represents the ground truth (gray) and prediction (red). The horizontal axis is the time-step and the vertical axis is the number of agents. Each column shows the results of a simulation conducted with that F1's processing speed per visitor set as each value (**F1 : 1, 2, 3, 4**). Each row shows the results of a simulation conducted with that F2's processing speed per visitor set as each value (**F2 : 1, 2, 3, 4**). These results were predicted by a model trained by the migration agent dataset using the attention architecture and segmentation feature representation. Not all of the parameters are were included in the training data. (Color figure online)

the network reproduced the interaction effects. For example, when the processing speed of F2 was slow, the same manipulation caused F1's queue length to change and F2's queue length change (Fig. 6, fourth row).

6   Conclusion

We introduced the MAS network as a framework for constructing surrogate models for MAS. Our results provide evidence of their ability to learn population dynamics even if they contain emergent phenomena arising from micro-level interactions. We confirmed that the MAS network accurately learned output and input relation's sensitivity even at unknown parameter points. Our approach that builds a surrogate model using coarse-graining population information will have applicability to a domain where daily prediction and optimization are required (i.e., urban transportation management using MAS). The reason why the computational complexity of the predictors built by our framework is robust relative to the number of agents; for example, in the pedestrian flow simulation, where the computational complexity increases with respect to the number of spots, N, and is constant with respect to the number of agents. For example, we may compute optimal daily staff allocation of an airport terminal based on the user distribution forecast for the next day by using our surrogate models and black-box optimization technique. Because this study was limited in testing the toy model, applying our framework to real-scale simulations is future work.

Acknowledgments. This work was supported by Fujitsu Laboratories Ltd. Computational resources of AI Bridging Cloud Infrastructure (ABCI) provided by National Institute of the Advanced Industrial Science and Technology (AIST) were used.

References

1. Bahdanau, D., Cho, K., Bengio, Y.: Neural machine translation by jointly learning to align and translate. In: ICLR (2015)
2. Bufala, N.D., Kant, J.: An evolutionary approach to find optimal policies with an agent-based simulation. In: AAMAS, pp. 610–618 (2019)
3. Grzeszczuk, R., Terzopoulos, D., Hinton, G.: Neuroanimator: fast neural network emulation and control of physics-based models. In: SIGGRAPH, pp. 9–20 (1998)
4. Guo, X., Li, W., Iorio, F.: Convolutional neural networks for steady flow approximation. In: KDD, pp. 481–490 (2016)
5. Hochreiter, S., Schmidhuber, J.: Long short-term memory. Neural Comput. **9**(8), 1735–1780 (1997)
6. Kingma, D.P., Ba, J.: Adam: a method for stochastic optimization. In: ICLR (2015)
7. Kutz, J.N.: Deep learning in fluid dynamics. J. Fluid Mech. **814**, 1–4 (2017)
8. Paszke, A., et al.: Pytorch: an imperative style, high-performance deep learning library. Adv. Neural Inf. Process. Syst. **32**, 8024–8035 (2019)
9. Sanchez-Gonzalez, A., Godwin, J., Pfaff, T., Ying, R., Leskovec, J., Battaglia, P.W.: Learning to simulate complex physics with graph networks. In: ICML, pp. 8459–8468 (2020)
10. Sutskever, I., Vinyals, O., Le, Q.V.: Sequence to sequence learning with neural networks. Adv. Neural Inf. Process. Syst. **27**, 3104–3112 (2014)
11. Yamada, H., Kamiyama, N.: Optimal control of pedestrian flows by congestion forecasts satisfying user equilibrium conditions. In: PRIMA, LNCS, vol. 12568, pp. 299–314 (2020)
12. Yamada, H., et al.: Modeling and managing airport passenger flow under uncertainty: a case of Fukuoka airport in Japan. In: Ciampaglia, G.L., Mashhadi, A., Yasseri, T. (eds.) SocInfo 2017. LNCS, vol. 10540, pp. 419–430. Springer, Cham (2017). https://doi.org/10.1007/978-3-319-67256-4_33
13. Yamane, S., Ohori, K., Obata, A., Kobayashi, N., Yugami, N.: Agent-based social simulation for a checkout layout design of a specific supermarket. In: MABS, pp. 153–164 (2012)

Real-Time Inference of Urban Metrics Applying Machine Learning to an Agent-Based Model Coupling Mobility Mode and Housing Choice

Mireia Yurrita[✉], Arnaud Grignard, Luis Alonso, and Kent Larson

Massachusetts Institute of Technology, Cambridge, USA

Abstract. This paper describes the latest advancements in the Housing and Mobility Mode Choice module of CityScope, a data-driven tangible platform developed by MIT City Science (CS) to facilitate more participatory decision-making processes. The ultimate objective of the Module is to easily predict people's reactions to potential urban disruptions and policies by previously characterizing their behavioural patterns. The main phase of this work consisted of a generic Agent-Based Model coupling mobility mode and housing choice, which was calibrated and validated for the Metropolitan Boston Area and Kendall Square in Cambridge, US. However, the integration of such model onto the CityScope platform resulted challenging, due to the complexity of the represented dynamics. The present paper addresses this problem making use of machine learning to train a surrogate model that will enable the real-time visualization and analysis of the suggested actions. The real-time nature of the obtained urban metrics will allow to append this Module to the current easily-understandable CityScope feedback system, bringing different stakeholders together to consensually shape the most favourable urban scenario. This Module represents the first step towards the development of a dynamic incentive system where CS seeks to promote urban characteristics such as equality, diversity, walkability, and efficiency.

Keywords: Agent-based modelling · Real-time computing · Response surface methodology · Dynamic urban planning · Pro-social city development

1 Introduction

In line with the sustainable development goals established by the United Nations [19], MIT City Science Group (CS) aims at developing tools that will help bring different stakeholders together in an effort to make urban areas safe, inclusive, resilient and sustainable [1,19]. To this end, a new line of research within the CS Group seeks to develop a dynamic incentive system where dynamically reconfigurable set of pro-social incentives will focus on fulfilling citizens'

© Springer Nature Switzerland AG 2022
K. H. Van Dam and N. Verstaevel (Eds.): MABS 2021, LNAI 13128, pp. 125–138, 2022.
https://doi.org/10.1007/978-3-030-94548-0_10

aspirations [12,27]. An agent-based model was created as a first step towards the aforementioned incentive system [27]. Citizens' behavioural patterns when choosing their residential mobility mode and housing option were characterized and calibrated for the specific use case of the Metropolitan Boston Area and Kendall Square (Cambridge, US). The definition of such patterns enabled the prediction of citizens' reactions to various urban disruptions. Likewise, it opened the door to an in-depth study of the effects of modifying the urban configuration in the Square and applying various housing incentives.

The ultimate goal of this dynamic incentive system is its inclusion on CityScope, a data-driven tangible platform that helps different stakeholders—including a wide range of profiles like planners, politicians, industry partners, and citizens—reach an agreement on which are the most convenient urban actions to be taken [1,10]. It is thanks to its instant feedback system, which is, indeed, represented in a user-friendly way, that conflicting interests can be discussed and various potential solutions immediately tested. Nevertheless, in order to be able to facilitate consensus, it is necessary that the results of urban simulations are obtained real time. The agent-based model presented in [27] did not meet this criterion, which gave rise to the approach detailed in the present document. We suggest and develop a methodology where the original model will feed a machine learning algorithm that enables the immediate representation of the required urban metrics under a wide range of possible alternatives.

This paper is organized as follows. Section 2 describes the original agent-based model coupling mobility mode and housing choice and presents previous applications of the suggested real-time conversion methodology. Section 3 outlines the details of the procedure used for the creation of the actual surrogate model and illustrates the validation process. It also gives a detailed summary of the agents that constitute the real-time model, the behaviours of each of them and their dynamics. Section 4 gives some final thoughts on the effectiveness of the method and suggests future research approaches.

2 Background

2.1 Mobility Mode and Housing Choice ABM

In a previous paper, citizens' behavioural patterns regarding their mobility mode and housing choice were characterized using an agent-based model [27]. The definition of the parameters that affect their decision-making process allows the prediction of the effects that potential urban disruptions (in the form of extra housing units being built in the area) and policies (in the form of financial incentives over the housing rent price) might entail. This is, therefore, key when assessing the suitability of the suggested actions as part of the dynamic incentive system.

This agent-based model was based on the well-known Schelling segregation model [23]. Each "citizen agent" was given a random housing option in iteration 0 and in each subsequent iteration they would decide whether an alternative housing unit would best fit their needs. The scoring process used for assessing the appropriateness of each housing option included housing and mobility-related preferences. This approach was inspired by [9,16] and was adapted to each agents' income profile [4]. Both qualitative and quantitative criteria were considered when defining transportation and housing preferences. Mobility-related parameters included price, resulting commuting time, difficulty of usage, and social pattern, while housing-related factors consisted of price, commuting time—using the most convenient mobility mode—, zone preference, and diversity acceptance. Figure 1 displays the reasoning process that each "citizen agent" goes through when choosing their housing and, consequently, residential mobility mode.

In order to calibrate agents' decision-making parameters, an error minimization process was held. The base scenario, where neither additional housing area nor financial incentives were offered, was compared to current census [8] and transportation data [5] for Kendall Square (Cambridge, US) and the Metropolitan Boston Area. Two different errors were then defined: (1) housing error being the difference in income-profile-based spatial distribution (2) mobility error being the difference in the distribution of transportation usage. The preference parameters were adjusted so as to minimize the variations between simulation results and the real scenario. The hill climbing algorithm was used to explore the parameter space that would lead to a minimum amount of Root Mean Square Error. The housing error obtained after the calibration process accounted for 3.87% and the resulting mobility error accounted for 2.30%. The code of the main agent-based model and the one used for performing the calibration process are available on the following github repository[1].

GAMA Platform. The dynamics of the urban scenario were artificially reproduced using GAMA platform [11]. GAMA allows users to develop simulations that are spatially explicit where GIS data can be easily incorporated [25]. This same agent-based simulation platform has been effectively deployed on various previous CityScope projects, including Volpe [1], Andorra [10], and CityMatrix [28]. In this last project [28], GAMA platform was deployed to run computationally intensive transportation and energy simulations, and these results were then used to train a surrogate model.

2.2   Related Work

As stated in [27], the results obtained from the suggested ABM were not immediate and, thus, could not be directly integrated onto the CityScope real-time feedback system. Table 1 displays the wall-clock time (in seconds) needed for initializing the simulation and for performing the first four iterations. The number of "citizen agents" used in such simulation was 11,585, which corresponds the

---

[1] https://github.com/CityScope/CS_Dynamic_Urban_Planning

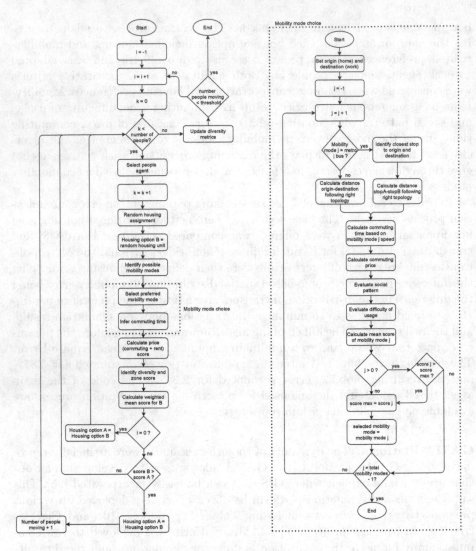

Fig. 1. Flow chart representing the housing and mobility mode evaluation process. In each iteration each "citizen agent" compares the score obtained by their current housing option A with respect to an alternative random housing option B. This score is calculated as a weighted mean value considering each agent's preferences regarding housing—price, zone, diversity acceptance, commuting time—and mobility mode—commuting time, commuting cost, difficulty of usage, social pattern—. The simulation converges whenever the amount of people willing to move to the alternative housing unit is below a certain threshold.

number of people working in Kendall Square according to the American Community Survey Data of 2017. These computations were held in a PC with an Intel Core i7-8565 CPU and a processor base frequency of 1.8 GHz.

Table 1. Wall-clock time needed for the initialization and first four iterations of the main agent-based model for 11,585 "citizen agents".

	Initialization	Iteration 1	Iteration 2	Iteration 3	Iteration 4
Wall-clock time [secs]	114.41	80.68	77.60	77.63	77.22

The issue of having individual models that are too computationally intensive directly compromises the real-time simulation architecture [24]. This kind of scenarios are fairly common in different areas of engineering [15] and architecture [26]. In engineering, computer simulated experiments play a key role when analyzing a wide range of alternatives for a design [15]. When these designs are being explored through expensive analysis codes such as Computational Fluid Dynamics (CFD) or Computational Structural Dynamics (CSD), creating approximation models, known as surrogate models, becomes important [13].

The surrogate model approach relies on sampled data to define input-output behaviours and to easily explore the space of design [13]. Aerospace [17,22], water engineering [3], architecture [26] or urban planning [28] are just some of the research areas where surrogate modeling methodologies have been deployed in recent years. In this last paper [28], a convolutional neural network (CNN) was trained with traffic and solar simulations and was then used as a surrogate model to foresee the effects of alternative actions and infer urban metrics real time. Due to the similarity of the treated issue, [28] is of special interest for the presented approach.

3   Architecture of the Suggested Methodology

In line with the aforementioned approaches, this section details (1) the steps followed to create the dataset out of what-if scenarios applied to the main ABM (batch experiments), (2) the usage of such dataset for training the machine learning algorithm that constitutes the surrogate model, (3) the validation of the surrogate model and (4) its usage in the real-time agent-based model. The methodology followed is graphically represented in Fig. 2 and the corresponding source code is publicly available on this github repository (see Footnote 1).

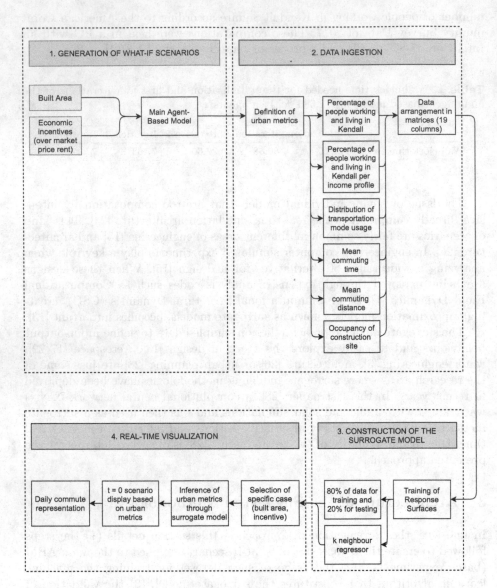

Fig. 2. Workflow of the suggested approach. The first step consists of a what-if-scenario generation step, where the main agent-based model presented in [27] is used to identify the consequences of having extra housing units built and financial incentives given over the market-driven rent price. For each what-if scenario urban metrics are calculated through the main ABM and arranged in matrices formed by 19 columns. The surrogate model (based on a k neighbour regressor) has been trained using 80% of the generated data and tested using the rest 20%. The real-time ABM uses this surrogate model to infer the t = 0 scenario for a certain input combination (built area, incentive given) and represents the daily commute of "citizen agents".

3.1   Batch Experiments. Generation of What-If Scenarios

In order to create a representative dataset covering a wide range of possible case studies, various what-if scenarios have been performed.

The inputs in each of these scenarios include the amount of area (in m^2) devoted to housing and the percentage of subsidy over the market price given to the citizens in the form of a pro-social financial incentive. It should be noted that these area and subsidy parameters only refer to the possible construction of new housing units in Volpe as mentioned in [27]. They have been assumed to be comprised of robotic micro-units (each of them would count with a $60\,m^2$ surface area) based on the CityScience Group vision and the subsidy percentage has been applied over the medium rent price in that area according to [20].

In the original mobility mode and housing model, once the iterative process has converged—meaning that the amount of people willing to move to an alternative housing option is below a threshold—each "citizen agent" eventually chooses a geolocated housing option and the most convenient available mobility mode for that residency. Nevertheless, for the real-time version of this same model, some general urban metrics have been defined as outputs. These will be calculated depending on the specific inputs (additional housing area and financial incentive) that characterize each what-if scenario. Outputs include: percentage of people working in Kendall Square that are actually living within the Square, percentage of citizens working in Kendall and belonging to income profile i that live in the Square $[i = 0(< \$30,000), \ldots, 7(> \$200,000)]$, percentage of usage of each transportation mode [car, bus, metro, bike, walking], mean commuting time, mean commuting distance, and the occupancy rate of the additional housing area. Such urban metrics have been chosen based on their usefulness for determining the suitability of urban actions within the framework of the CityScope radar [1].

3.2   Data Ingestion and Arrangement

The information extracted from the suggested what-if scenarios can be represented using Response Surfaces. This methodology identifies the influence of several input variables on performance measures, called responses, and facilitates their visualization thanks to its graphical perspective [18]. Figure 3 shows the Response Surface corresponding to the percentage of people living and working in Kendall for each of the studied cases. A hundred batch experiments have been performed following a 0.1 step in subsidy and 2E05 m^2 step in additional housing area.

This data has been structured using matrices of 19 columns. The first two columns correspond to the inputs (built area and financial incentive) while the rest of the columns represent each of the outputs of interest. As the information has been obtained following batch experiments with a constant step of increment, it has been necessary to randomize the data to prevent this uniformity from affecting the model training procedure [6]. Data rows were, thus, randomly shuffled fifty times.

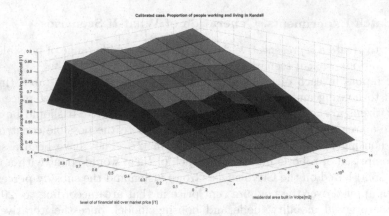

Fig. 3. Response surface resulting from the batch experiments performed to the original mobility mode and housing model with respect to the proportion of people working and living in Kendall. The x axis indicates the amount of residential area constructed in the Volpe site $[m^2]$, while the y axis indicates the level of financial aid given to the workers as a proportion of the total market prices for the area [/1]. The z axis is, precisely the percentage of people—of any income profile—working in Kendall that would end up living within a 20-min walking distance from their working place [/1].

3.3   Design of the Surrogate Model

The outputs resulting from the what-if scenarios have been deployed for training a k-neighbour regressor on Python. The Scikit-learn library [21] has been used for this purpose.

Training. 80% of the available rows have been used for training the model while the rest 20% was devoted to model testing following the Pareto Principle [7]. k has been set to 6, since this is the value that leads to the best accuracy score for our particular dataset. Figure 4 displays the R^2 obtained for different values of k, justifying our particular election. The effect of each neighbour in the final prediction has been weighted based on the distance to the point being evaluated. The idea behind the usage of a weighted k-nearest neighbour methodology is that the observations within the learning set that are close to the new observation should have a bigger influence than those that are far away [14]. In order to put equal weight on each covariate when computing the distances, it is necessary to standardize the values [14] and, thus, the extra housing area has been normalized—financial aid was already a rate between 0 and 1—.

Validation. Figure 5 shows the comparison between the simulated and predicted values for the first output, that is to say, the percentage of citizens working and living in Kendall. For this particular case a $R^2 = 0.979$ has been obtained and the Root Mean Square Error is 1.98%. In general terms, the mean value for R^2 has been 0.844 and RMSE has never exceeded 5.75%. The prediction capacity

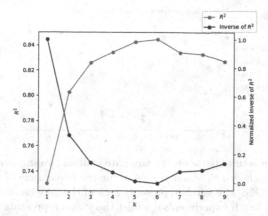

Fig. 4. R^2 and their normalized inverse values—these have been displayed to represent the characteristic elbow curve that determines the most suitable value for k—for different k neighbours tested. The best prediction capacity is obtained whenever the value of k is set to six, which justifies the election made in this document.

of such a surrogate model has been considered acceptable based on its similarity with the precision ($R^2 = 0.8$) obtained by [28]. All of the aforementioned computations have been performed using a PC with an Intel Core i7-8565 CPU and a processor base frequency of 1.8 GHz. Training and Validating the surrogate model (once the dataset resulting from the main agent-based model had been created) has required 102 min.

3.4 Real-Time ABM Description

Following the methodology that [28] presented, once the surrogate model has been defined, trained and validated, the urban metrics mentioned in Sect. 3 will be inferred real time for any input combination. This will constitute the t = 0 state for a simple agent-based model that represents the daily commute in the Square, adopting the approach presented by [9]. The time required for the initialization of the real-time ABM is 5.7 s and a mean of 34 ms for each step of the simulation (for an Intel Core i7-8565 CPU and a processor base frequency of 1.8 GHz), which enables the inclusion of this module in the CityScope platform [1].

Entities, State Variables, and Scales. The environmental variables include:

- **Building:** polygon representing the edifices within the Square [8]. Each building will be formed by the following attributes: *category:* type of usage given to the building in question—it might be residential, industrial, mixed use etc.—, *from_grid:* boolean parameter indicating whether the building belongs to the construction area or not—this variable is essential since at this point

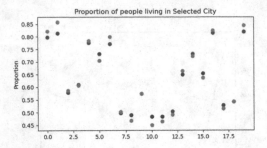

Fig. 5. Difference in results between the simulated values—orange—and the predicted values—blue—using the k-neighbour regressor for the percentage of people living and working in Kendall [/1]. The x axis represents each of the 20 what-if scenarios used for testing (20% of 100 batch experiments), whilst the y axis represents the proportion of citizens working and living in Kendall. The RMSE obtained for this metric has been 1.98%. (Color figure online)

financial incentives are only implemented for the housing units belonging to the grid—, and *is_entry_point:* boolean parameter indicating if the polygon accounts for an entry point to the Square or if it is a physical building—the percentage of people working and living in the Square will only be assigned physical buildings that are located within the 1 km × 1 km area surrounding the Square as their housing option—.

- **Entry point:** abstract species representing the entry points to the Square (parent: building). The percentage of people who are working in the Square but live elsewhere in each case will be assigned an entry point in iteration 0.
- **Road:** network of roads that agents can use to move around [8]. If their chosen mobility mode is the metro, they will only use these roads to get to the corresponding stop.
- **Metro line:** network of metro lines where "metro agents" will be able to move around [8]. The only attribute of this species is the *line* they belong to.
- **Bus and metro stops:** mobility hubs where "citizen agents" will head to in order to make use of buses and metros [8]. Attributes include: *waiting people:* number of "citizen agents" waiting for the correspondent vehicle to arrive, *route/line:* route (for buses) or line (for metros) that the stop belongs to [8].

The **agents species** that constitute this model include:

- **People:** these agents represent citizens who are working in the Square— 11,585 according to the American Community Survey Data of 2017—and who might live or not within the 1 km × 1 km area (the proportions are inferred from the surrogate model depending on the amount of additional area built and the given financial incentive). Their attributes include: *income_profile:* income profile they belong to, *mobility_mode:* mobility mode they chose— information extracted from the proportions obtained in the regressor—, *lives_in_Square:* boolean parameter defining whether this agent lives in the Square or commutes from an external point, *living_place:* building or entry

point that acts as the agent's living place depending on whether they live in the Square or elsewhere, *objectives:* list of trip objectives that the agent will complete throughout the day based on their hourly schedule, and *current_objective:* their current objective.
- **Bus and metro:** both "metro agents" and "bus agents" present the same attributes and dynamics with the exception of "metro agents" stopping in "metro stops" and moving around using the topology defined by "metro lines" and "bus agents" stopping in "bus stops" and moving around using the topology defined by "roads". Their attributes include: *stops:* list of hubs where these agents have to stop, *stop_passengers:* list of "citizen agents" waiting in the stop, *my_target:* stop these agents are heading to, and *route/line:* route (for buses) or line (for metros) that they are covering.

Process Overview. The dynamics of this model are driven by the behaviours of two main agents: "citizen agents" and "transit agents"—that is to say, "bus agents" and "metro agents"—. At each time step 'citizen agents' will: (1) Check their daily schedule to check whether they need to change their current location. (2) If so, move to their destination making use of their corresponding mobility mode and topology. As far as "transit agents" are concerned, their dynamics can also be narrowed down into three main steps: (1) Head to the next stop within their route or line (2) Collect the passengers that are waiting at that stop and make the ones who arrived at their destination descend. (3) Once 30 time steps are completed, move to their next destination.

Initialization and Input Data. The initialization of the model has relied on three main axes: the information extracted from the surrogate model, files containing GIS data, and *.csv* files containing the daily schedules of the profiles. The first piece of information enables the calculation of the percentage of people living and working in Kendall according to their income profile and depending on the amount of additional housing area that is being built and the given financial incentive. Thanks to the training and validation of the surrogate model, the urban metrics resulting from any combination of additional housing units built and given financial incentives that may not have been directly simulated using the main ABM can also be inferred. Additionally, information regarding the Volpe construction area occupancy rate, the distribution of usage of different mobility modes, mean commuting time and mean commuting distance is extracted. This information is key when generating "citizen agents" in iteration 0 and assigning them a specific housing and mobility option depending on their income profile. The second group of files includes (1) a shapefile containing the buildings that are currently available in Kendall Square [8], (2) a shapefile containing the road network of the Square [8], (3) a shapefile where the metro network of the area is included [2], (4) shapefiles with the mobility hubs (for metro and bus) [2], (5) a shapefile containing the entry points to the Square. When it comes to *.csv* files, a file containing an hourly schedule of "citizen agents" depending on their profile has been incorporated following the proposal in [9].

4   Discussion and Conclusion

In the present paper a methodology has been suggested and implemented for getting a real-time model out of a computationally expensive ABM evaluating additional housing offer and financial incentives—with a previous characterization of citizens' behavioural patterns regarding mobility mode and housing choice—. A surrogate model based on a k-neighbour regressor has been developed, trained, and validated. The information extracted from this model enables the identification of the following outputs: (1) the percentage of people working and living in Kendall according to their income profile and depending on the amount of housing area built and the financial aid offered, (2) the construction area occupancy rate, (3) the distribution of different mobility modes usage, (4) the mean commuting time and (5) the mean commuting distance. All of these metrics are of great interest when estimating the suitability of the suggested urban disruptions within the feedback framework of the CityScope platform [1]. In order to train such a model, batch experiments have been performed covering a hundred different what-if scenarios. This has led to a R^2 mean metric of 0.844, which proves an acceptable prediction capacity, in line with the results obtained in similar research approaches [28]. Should this measure be improved, a more abundant testing set should be created, taking into account the computational cost that this might entail. The aforementioned surrogate model has been used for feeding a simple ABM that represents the commuting patterns of people working in the Square according to the what-if scenario that is being evaluated. Although this real-time ABM is enough to graphically represent the differences between the suggested actions, should a more in-depth study of traffic jams or public transportation saturation be performed, further research into the metrics defining congestion in roads or overcrowding in mobility hubs would be necessary. It should also be noted that, when transferring this model onto the tangible platform, the extra housing area built in Volpe construction site would be the result of the amount and type of Lego bricks that different stakeholders ended up selecting, following the CityScope approach [1].

A final remark concerning further research into the development of the so called dynamic incentive system is also necessary. This paper, along with the original ABM coupling mobility mode and housing choice [27], have defined a methodology to evaluate the consequences of various urban disruptions related to housing and the corresponding financial incentives. The development of an equivalent model for other incentives which are not housing-related is the logical continuation of the present work. When a model embracing a wide range of incentives is created, a possible strategy for making the whole concept dynamic would rely on the pre-training of an algorithm capable of learning from the effects of static incentives. This algorithm would then be used for dynamically predicting the incentives needed to obtain the desired values of the defined metrics (which would, indeed, constitute a multi-objective optimization process).

References

1. Alonso, L., et al.: CityScope: a data-driven interactive simulation tool for urban design. Use case volpe. In: Morales, A.J., Gershenson, C., Braha, D., Minai, A.A., Bar-Yam, Y. (eds.) ICCS 2018. SPC, pp. 253–261. Springer, Cham (2018). https://doi.org/10.1007/978-3-319-96661-8_27
2. Massachusetts Bay Transportation Authority (MBTA). https://www.mbta.com/. Accessed Feb 2021
3. Bender, N.C., Andersen, T.O., Pedersen, H.C.: Feasibility of deep neural network surrogate models in fluid dynamics. Model. Identif. Control A Norw. Res. Bull. **40**, 71–87 (2019). https://doi.org/10.4173/mic.2019.2.1
4. U.S. Census Bureau: Census profiles. https://data.census.gov/cedsci/. Accessed Feb 2021
5. City of Cambridge: Parking and transportation demand management data in the city of Cambridge (2014). https://www.cambridgema.gov/CDD/Transportation/fordevelopers/ptdm. Accessed Feb 2021
6. Dietterich, T.G.: Ensemble methods in machine learning. In: Kittler, J., Roli, F. (eds.) MCS 2000. LNCS, vol. 1857, pp. 1–15. Springer, Heidelberg (2000). https://doi.org/10.1007/3-540-45014-9_1
7. Dunford, R., Su, Q., Tamang, E.: The pareto principle. Plymouth Stud. Sci. **7**, 140–148 (2014)
8. U.S. Government: United States Government's open data (2020). https://www.data.gov/. Accessed Feb 2021
9. Grignard, A., et al.: The impact of new mobility modes on a city: a generic approach using ABM. In: Morales, A.J., Gershenson, C., Braha, D., Minai, A.A., Bar-Yam, Y. (eds.) ICCS 2018. SPC, pp. 272–280. Springer, Cham (2018). https://doi.org/10.1007/978-3-319-96661-8_29
10. Grignard, A., Macià, N., Pastor, L.A., Noyman, A., Zhang, Y., Larson, K.: CityScope Andorra: a multi-level interactive and tangible agent-based visualization, pp. 1939–1940. International Foundation for Autonomous Agents and Multi-agent Systems (2018)
11. Grignard, A., Taillandier, P., Gaudou, B., Vo, D.A., Huynh, N.Q., Drogoul, A.: GAMA 1.6: advancing the art of complex agent-based modeling and simulation. In: Boella, G., Elkind, E., Savarimuthu, B.T.R., Dignum, F., Purvis, M.K. (eds.) PRIMA 2013. LNCS (LNAI), vol. 8291, pp. 117–131. Springer, Heidelberg (2013). https://doi.org/10.1007/978-3-642-44927-7_9
12. MIT Media Lab City Science Group: Algorithmic zoning. https://www.media.mit.edu/projects/algorithmic-zoning-dynamic-urban-planning/overview/. Accessed Feb 2021
13. Han, Z.H., Zhang, K.S.: Surrogate-based optimization. In: Real-World Applications of Genetic Algorithms (2012)
14. Hechenbichler, K., Schliep, K.: Weighted k-nearest-neighbor techniques and ordinal classification. Collaborative Research Center 386 (2004)
15. Jiang, P., Zhou, Q., Shao, X.: Surrogate-model-based design and optimization. In: Surrogate Model-Based Engineering Design and Optimization. STME, pp. 135–236. Springer, Singapore (2020). https://doi.org/10.1007/978-981-15-0731-1_7
16. Jordan, R., Birkin, M., Evans, A.: Agent-based modelling of residential mobility, housing choice and regeneration. In: Heppenstall, A., Crooks, A., See, L., Batty, M. (eds.) Agent-Based Models of Geographical Systems, pp. 511–524. Springer, Dordrecht (2012). https://doi.org/10.1007/978-90-481-8927-4_25

17. Mack, Y., Goel, T., Shyy, W., Haftka, R.: Surrogate model-based optimization framework: a case study in aerospace design. In: Yang, S., Ong, Y.S., Jin, Y. (eds.) Evolutionary Computation in Dynamic and Uncertain Environments. SCI, vol. 51, pp. 323–342. Springer, Heidelberg (2007). https://doi.org/10.1007/978-3-540-49774-5_14
18. Myers, R.H., Montgomery, D.C., Anderson-Cook, C.M.: Response Surface Methodology: Process and Product Optimization Using Designed Experiments (2016)
19. United Nations: Sustainable development goals. https://www.un.org/sustainabledevelopment/cities/. Accessed Feb 2021
20. PadMapper: Apartments for rent from the trusted apartment finder. https://www.padmapper.com/. Accessed Feb 2021
21. Pedregosa, F., et al.: Scikit-learn: machine learning in Python. J. Mach. Learn. Res. **12**, 2825–2830 (2011)
22. Queipo, N.V., Haftka, R.T., Shyy, W., Goel, T., Vaidyanathan, R., Tucker, P.K.: Surrogate-based analysis and optimization. Prog. Aerosp. Sci. **41**, 1–28 (2005). https://doi.org/10.1016/j.paerosci.2005.02.001
23. Schelling, T.: Models of segregation. Am. Econ. Rev. **59**, 488–493 (1969). https://EconPapers.repec.org/RePEc:aea:aecrev:v:59:y:1969:i:2:p:488-93
24. Stewart, P., Fleming, P., MacKenzie, S.: On the response surface methodology and designed experiments for computationally intensive distributed aerospace simulations, pp. 476–482. IEEE (2002). https://doi.org/10.1109/WSC.2002.1172919
25. Taillandier, P., et al.: Building, composing and experimenting complex spatial models with the GAMA platform. GeoInformatica **23**(2), 299–322 (2018). https://doi.org/10.1007/s10707-018-00339-6
26. Wortmann, T., Costa, A., Nannicini, G., Schroepfer, T.: Advantages of surrogate models for architectural design optimization. Artif. Intell. Eng. Des. Anal. Manuf. **29**, 471–481 (2015). https://doi.org/10.1017/S0890060415000451
27. Yurrita, M., et al.: Dynamic urban planning: an agent-based model coupling mobility mode and housing choice. Use case Kendall square. In: Arai, K. (ed.) Intelligent Computing. LNNS, vol. 284, pp. 940–951. Springer, Cham (2021). https://doi.org/10.1007/978-3-030-80126-7_66
28. Zhang, Y., Grignard, A., Aubuchon, A., Lyons, K., Lason, K.: Machine learning for real-time urban metrics and design recommendations (2018)

Changing Perspectives: Adaptable Interpretations of Norms for Agents

Christian Kammler[1]($\boxtimes$), Frank Dignum[1], Nanda Wijermans[2], and Helena Lindgren[1]

[1] Department of Computing Science, Umeå University, Umeå, Sweden
{christian.kammler,frank.dignum,helena.lindgren}@umu.se
[2] Stockholm Resilience Centre, Stockholm University, Stockholm, Sweden
nanda.wijermans@su.se

Abstract. For agent-based social simulations to be a powerful tool for policy makers and other decision makers in a given context (e.g. the current COVID-19 pandemic), they need to be socially realistic and thus, appropriately represent complex social concepts, such as social rules. In this paper, we focus on norms. Norms describe 'normal' behavior and aim at assuring the interests and values of groups or the society as a whole. People react differently to norms, and focus only on the parts that are relevant for them. Furthermore, norms are not only restrictions on behavior, but also trigger new behavior. Seeing a norm only as a restriction on certain behavior misses important aspects and leads to simulations that can be very misleading. Different perspectives need to be incorporated into the simulation to capture the variety of ways different stakeholders react to a norm and how this affects their interaction. We therefore present an approach to include these different perspectives on norms, and their consequences for different people and groups in decision support simulations. A perspective is specified by their goals, actions, effects of those actions, priorities in values, and social affordances. Through modeling perspectives we enable policy makers and other decision makers (the users) to be active in the modeling process and to tailor the simulation to their specific needs, by representing norms as modifiable objects, and providing textual and graphical representations of norms. This provides them with differentiated insights meaningful for the decisions they are faced with. We indicate the requirements for both the simulation platform as well as the agents that follow from our approach. Early explorations of our social simulation are showing the necessity of our approach.

Keywords: Norms · Social rules · Social simulation

1 Introduction

Social simulations are often seen as modern tools that can provide information on how people will react in changing circumstances. This can lead to new insights into key factors that determine the behavior of people in certain contexts

© Springer Nature Switzerland AG 2022
K. H. Van Dam and N. Verstaevel (Eds.): MABS 2021, LNAI 13128, pp. 139–152, 2022.
https://doi.org/10.1007/978-3-030-94548-0_11

(e.g. the current COVID-19 pandemic). Therefore, they can be very well used as tools to support policy makers and other stakeholders (the users of the simulation) to make well informed decisions in a domain.

This requires from the to ensure some measure of reality of the model they use. In this paper we will focus on the role of norms in social simulations. Norms describe 'normal' behavior and aim at assuring the interests and values of groups or the society as a whole [11]. They can arise from socially accepted behavior, social norms, but also directly imposed, legal norms. Furthermore, they are not only constraints on behavior. They can also motivate [2,12] and trigger new behavior [11].

Norms affect people differently and each individual takes only the parts into account that are relevant for them. as we will show with an example of a COVID decision context in Sect. 2. We show that seeing a norm only as a restriction on certain behavior misses important aspects and leads to simulations that can be very misleading.

Different perspectives need to be incorporated into the simulation to capture the variety of ways different stakeholders react to a norm and how this affects their interaction. Although norms have been studied in social simulations before e.g. [4,5,10], incorporating different perspectives on norms has not been done before.

Therefore, we present our approach to modeling different perspectives for social simulations in Sect. 3. We will first define what we mean by a perspective and detail what it entails connected to, e.g. goals, values, and social affordances.

Subsequently, we will show how using our approach impacts the interaction with the simulation from a user (decision-maker) point of view. Boshuijzen-van Burken et al. [1] showed the benefits and added value of such an user focused approach. Policy makers and other decision makers must be enabled to be active in the modeling process to tailor the simulation to their specific needs. To support them in gaining meaningful insights. To detail on our approach, we will derive requirements for each of the levels of the system (the user, the system and the agent).

2   Example

In the context of the current COVID-19 pandemic, we use the following (legal) norm as an example: a restaurant-size based restriction on number of guests. This norm may affect different agent groups in different ways, based on the target of the norm. Note that we are not striving for completeness in this example, we aim to use two of the affected groups, restaurant owners and guests, to show the complexity of a simple norm and the necessity for our new approach.

The **restaurant owner** considers one of the main functions of the restaurant to provide their income. Therefore, a restaurant owner may be focused on the financial impact of the norm, but may also (secondary) be focused on the social impact of the norm. Limiting number of guest has severe financial consequences for a restaurant owner. Fixed costs, e.g. rent, remain constant, but the income (fewer customers) is affected negatively and may trigger coming up with ways to compensate, e.g. extend opening hours, or bending the rule and allow a group of four people to enter even though only two seats are left (with the possible consequence of getting a negative reputation for doing so).

For the **guests**, the restaurant has mainly a social function. This can be the place where they gather together with their family and friends and enjoy some nice food together (social impact focus).

Since the norm is limiting the number of guests, some guests might decide to reserve a table, while other people might change their eating times. However, guests might also just keep on going to the same restaurant at the same time to see if they get lucky to find a table.

Another part of the guests behavior is based on the restaurants owner's reaction to the norm. Guests react and can adjust their behavior, based on certain actions taken by the restaurant owner. Some guests might stay away, if the restaurant owner is bending the norm, while other guests are fine with that and still come to the restaurant.

3 Adaptable Interpretations of Norms - Foundations

The restaurant example in the previous section shows that the same norm can have different impacts on different categories of persons. Thus each category will look at a norm from its own perspective. If these perspectives are not taken into account but the norm is seen only as a restriction of a certain state or action it leads to an oversimplification as illustrated in Fig. 1. Given this interpretation of the norm restaurants will restrict the number of guests, which leads to less income and therefore possible bankruptcy. This interpretation misses all the other kind of reactions the parties might have to the norm and subsequent behavior. When only having one perspective represented, such as the restaurant owner, the simulation can only be observed from their perspective and only their reactions to the norm can be shown, while the guest's point of view cannot be observed. Lowering the variable costs, for example, is then just another factor that is taken into account in addition to the restriction, with no additional insights.

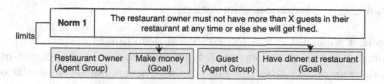

Fig. 1. Norm as a restriction. Arrows highlight that the achievability of the goal is limited by the norm

To allow different perspectives to play a role on how the norm affects the simulation results we need to model what different perspectives exactly are. This will be done in the following sections.

3.1 Perspectives

A guest (category) in a restaurant is supposed to have the goal of eating. Thus, when having the role of a guest, we attribute specific goals with connected actions to this role - and any person with that role. Therefore we expect a guest to order food, but not to go to the kitchen and cook. Furthermore, from a guests perspective, the objects in the context of the restaurant, such as a table, offer different social action possibilities, such as socializing with friends or family.

These are what we define as social affordances. In addition, we use values in the goal formation process, as different roles typically prioritize some values. E.g. a guest will prioritize having a good time, while a restaurant owner values providing good and ecological food.

Consequently, to represent different perspectives, we make different goals and actions available to the agents based on their role (i.e. the category they belong to). Furthermore, different perspectives lead to considering different effects of the same actions. The guest is interested if the eating leads to having a nice time, while the restaurant owner considers eating to lead to earnings. Finally, each perspective will attach different social affordances to the objects present leading to different available actions and interactions in a situation. Whereas the relation between goals, actions, and values have been used in agents before, e.g. [8,17], social affordances are a novel concept that we are introducing in this paper (see Sect. 3.3). We define a perspective as follows:

Definition 1. *A perspective is specified by goals (G), available actions (A), effects of those actions (EoA), social affordances (SocAffs), and priorities in values (PrioV).*

In the example the guest perspective can be instantiated as follows:
G_{guest} = {eat food, socialize with friends and family},
A_{guest} = {go to restaurant, reserve seat, order food, eat, pay, stay after eating, leave},
EoA_{guest} = {meet with friends and family, have place available, pleasure from eating food, lose money. socialize},
$SocAffs_{guest}$(table as example object) = {pleasure(-ability), socialize(-ability)},
and $PrioV_{guest}$ = {hedonism, stimulation}.

Note that we could give a formal logical definition of all terms, but refrain from doing so in this paper not to distract from the main goal of the paper to explain the way perspectives influence the way norms impact a simulation.

3.2 Perspectives, Values, and Goals

Values are evaluation criteria for events and behavior [15,16]. We use them in our context to determine which goals are important to achieve, and which actions are most desirable to take, to achieve the goal. Each perspective has its own priority between values.

For example: Restaurant owners that give priority to power and achievement are strongly money driven in their behavior. It leads to adopting goals that are likely to contribute to getting rich. Thus this restaurant owner will try to serve as many meals as possible against as little costs as possible. If a restaurant owner prioritizes environmental values, she will adopt goals that are in line with these values and e.g. has a goal to create vegetarian dishes.

3.3 Perspectives and Social Affordances

Different groups use objects differently. They look at them from a different perspective and have different purposes for them. A table in a restaurant is for the guests where they can sit, and for the restaurant owner where their guests are and eat. This means that the same resource, the table in a restaurant, is being being interpreted differently with regards to actions that can be performed by different roles.

These different perspectives on objects can be related to the notion of affordances. Affordances describe the "action possibilities provided to the actor by the environment"[1] The classical notion of affordances focuses on the physical options that are provided, e.g. the table is offering the ability to sit on it, sit-ability, and put an object on it, place-ability.

We view affordances as a *relation* between an object and the action possibilities that the object provides, i.e. the object affords the actions. We assume hereby that the object has the necessary properties to be suitable for the action. In the simulation, we have the set of n objects $O = \{o_1, o_2, ..., o_n\}$. We additionally assume that an agent has the necessary capabilities to perform the physical action (e.g. sitting). Leading us to define the physical affordances of an object as follows:

Definition 2. *The physical affordances (PhysAffs) of an object (o_i) describe the physical action possibilities, $\{\alpha_{physical}, \beta_{physical}, ...\}$, that the object ($o_i$) provides*

$$PhysAffs(o_i) = \{\alpha_{physical}, \beta_{physical}, ...\},$$

for any $o_i \in O$ where o_i has the necessary properties suitable for the actions.

The physical affordances for a table, for example, can then be formalized as: PhysAffs(table) = {sit, eat, drink,...}

Note that the set of physical affordances does not contain all actions one can perform with an object. It contains the actions one is "invited" to do with it, or "normally" do with it. E.g. one can saw the legs from a wooden table, but that is usually not thought as of an affordance of a table. In general the set of affordances can be subjective and context dependent. However, for the moment we use this simple definition which suffices for most social simulations.

People do not use objects in only a pure physical way. They choose their physical actions based on their role and the social effects of their actions (social

---

[1] https://www.interaction-design.org/literature/book/the-encyclopedia-of-human-computer-interaction-2nd-ed/affordances, accessed: 02/20/2021.

actions), e.g. people go to a restaurant to sit at a table together to socialize. This means that sitting together at a table in a restaurant offers socializing. Therefore, we have to move beyond the physical notion of affordances and look at the social interpretation of the use of the object next to the physical use. We call this *social affordances*. They describe the social use of the physical object.

To incorporate this social notion in the theory of affordances, we look at the purpose that the object fulfills for a person or a group. Dignum [6] states in his work on social practices that the purpose "determines the social interpretation [..] of certain physical situations" [6, p.2]. For example: The purpose of the table for the restaurant owner is that the guests can sit there and eat.

To define social affordances, we depart from Definition 2, having a physical object and adding the social aspects of time and location, and the role of the agent to formulate the social affordances that an object provides. The social meaning of the time (the social time) of an object refers to the association with it, e.g. the evening is associated with dinner time. Different times have different meanings and can therefore influence the available social affordances. This is similar for the social meaning of the location (the social location), e.g. a restaurant is a place to eat. We also need to look at the role of the agent, e.g. being a restaurant owner. Lastly, the role makes an agent belong to a group with the group's specific goals, values, and available actions.

With this as a basis, we can now define the social affordances of an object as follows:

Definition 3. *The social affordances (SocAffs) of an object (o_i) are the social effects of the physical actions performed (social actions), $\{\alpha_{social}, \beta_{social}, ...\}$, with the object ($o_i$). They are determined by the social time (SocT), the social location (SocL), the role of the agent (RoA) with the associated actions ($A(o_i)$), and the object (o_i) itself. The resulting formalization is then:*

$$SocAffs(o_i, SocT, SocL, RoA, A(o_i)) = \{\alpha_{social}, \beta_{social}, ...\},$$

for any $o_i \in O$ where o_i has the necessary properties suitable for the actions.

The social affordances of a table in a restaurant from a guest perspective can then be instantiated as follows:
SocAffs(table, dinner time, restaurant, guest, {sit(table),eat(table)}) = {having-pleasure, socialize}

This social view on objects enables to look how a norm affects the social affordances that an object provides for different agent groups. While the social affordances stay the same, specific actions might not be desirable anymore for certain agent groups, due to a norm. This interplay between social affordances (object-related actions) and norms (group-related action preferences) is crucial in our approach.

For example: After limiting the amount of people in a restaurant, guests might not be able anymore to stay after dinner for chatting, as the restaurant owner wants to make the table free so new guests can enter, eat there and subsequently spend more money. Thus, the ability to socialize is altered. Guests can now only socialize while eating and not afterwards. Furthermore, the possibility to relax is impacted, as guests have to leave faster and are not able to relax afterwards at the table.

Note that social affordances are different from norms, as they fulfill different functional roles. Social affordances describe the social effects of physical actions. These effects are defining what individuals expect when using those objects. Thus, they define the social actions possibilities that are offered by the object. Thus, they are different from norms, as they are not related to violations and are more centered around the individual.

In the next section we will investigate further how perspectives can help to describe the different ways a norm influences a simulation. It is important to note here that our definition covers only social affordances of physical objects. The future work we will look at norms and other social structures, and their affordances.

4   Using Perspectives with Adaptable Interpretations of Norms

With the definitions of the previous section, we can now investigate the impact of the introduction of a norm in a simulation. Based on the different goals, the norm will influence agents differently depending on their perspective. A norm can form a restriction for one goal, while other goals are unaffected. For example, limiting the number of people in a restaurant affects the guests and their ability to visit the restaurant, while the restaurant owner can still keep the restaurant open in the evening. In order to make sure the perspectives are well captured, we will enable the users of the simulation to be active in the modeling process, so they can tailor the simulation towards their needs, see different variations of what they want to do and to adapt norms on the fly. Therefore, norms are represented as modifiable objects which will be attached to the agents. The resulting user requirements will be described in more detail in, what we call, the user level in Sect. 4.1.

These requirements need to be supported by the system (the simulation itself). We call this the system level and it will be described in more detail in Sect. 4.2.

Finally, we will present the resulting agent requirements in, what we call. the agent level in Sect. 4.3.

4.1   User Level

Users (policy makers and other decision makers) need to gain meaningful insights from using the simulation. Therefore, they need to be able to tailor the simulation to their needs and thus take actively part in the modeling process. It is important to note here, that we focus on the adaptability of norms and see the existing perspectives as not modifiable (see future work). We identify the following requirements from the user side:

- Ability to observe the agent's behavior from different perspectives (UR1)
- Explanations of the simulation based on perspectives (and what they entail), incorporated social rules, such as norms, and the connections between the social rules (UR2)
- Ability to manipulate the simulation, ie. having the ability and the support to instantiate values, goals and available actions of the agents, add, alter, and delete norms prior to the start of the simulation, and on the fly (UR3)
- Present the above support in a form that is usable and not too complex. (UR4)

Each of these requirements, UR1 to UR4, will be explained in more detail now. Policy makers and other decision makers must be able to take different perspectives and observe the resulting behavior (UR1), such as the restaurant owner perspective or guest perspective.

For gaining meaningful insights from the simulation and its behavior, it is crucial to have detailed explanations of what is happening and why this is the case (UR2). The user must know which perspectives exist in the simulation. Therefore, it needs to be clear for every component in Definition 1 what it is. For example, for the restaurant owner perspective, what goals the restaurant owner has, such as getting income from the restaurant and keeping the restaurant open, and what their priorities in values are, such as having a priority in power and achievement.

When looking at the social affordances belonging to a perspective (UR2), we need to look at Definition 3. The user must have the information about the existing times in the simulation and what they mean (i.e. the social time), as it is the case for the locations, physical and social locations. It needs to be clear that evening means dinner time and that the restaurant is a place to eat. Going to the available actions for an object ($A(o_i)$), we can now see a connection to Definition 1, which entails all possible actions of a perspective. It needs to be clear for the user, which actions can be executed with which objects or if no objects are necessary to perform that action. The user must be informed that, when being at the restaurant table, the guest can order food, eat the food, stay after eating, pay, and leave the table.

A structured text form can be used here. However, textual descriptions can be vague and therefore, graphical support is needed. This enables the user to see connections between goals and actions quickly. Furthermore, having connections between actions and the objects they require shows possible impacts of norms that have the same object as the actions.

Furthermore, the user must be aware of which social rules exist in the simulation (UR2). When having a norm that is limiting the amount of people in restaurant, it needs to be made clear for the user that the objective of the norm is the restaurant. The objective is then used to highlight which agent groups are involved with the restaurant, such as the guests for example.

A framework that can be used here to represent norms in a more structured way, without being too formal, is the widely applied ADICO grammar by Crawford & Ostrom [3]. The grammar provides a general format for rules [17].

The need for and the level of explainability is also tightly connected to the complexity of the simulation which we discuss in UR4. To tackle this challenge, we use the experience that we gained in our ASSOCC[1] project where we provided an easy to use interface for our complex model, see therefore especially chapter [14] of our new book [7] for a detailed description.

Adding a new norm or changing an existing one is no trivial task and the user needs to be supported by the system to do so (UR3). While the ADICO grammar serves as a good starting point, it is not sufficient and a more detailed approach is necessary to formulate norms in such a precise way that they can be used in the simulation, through which the user needs to be guided. We adopt and extend the ADICO grammar in the following way, based on [9,12,18]:

- Attribute (A): Agent (group)
- Deontic (D) + aIm (I): Fulfillment/Violation condition
- Condition: Activation condition, deactivation condition
- Deadline (Dl)
- Repair (R)
- Or else (O): Punishment

An example of this new ADICDlRO can be found in Fig. 2 below. The figure also serves as a possible graphical representation of norms.

This graph provides a quick overview of the norms and shows that the restaurant owner is responsible to adhere to both norms (A). Furthermore, norms that share the same object (I_{Object}), and prominent punishments (here 1000$ fine) can be identified (same, dotted line). The graph also shows that the norm to have less guests in the restaurant negatively impacts (n-impacts, solid arrow) the goal of the restaurant owner to make money, as fewer guests can be present at the same time. The guests share the restaurant (I_{Object}) with the restaurant owner (shared, dotted line). Based on this shared relationship, guests can now look at the respective norm and all the relevant elements for them to see how that can potentially impact their behavior (looks at relationship, dotted arrow). They now see that their social affordances, in this example socialize-ability, are negatively impacted (n-impacts, solid arrow). Norm one results in fewer tables available, and norm two potentially alters the dinner time, due to the mandatory restaurant closure. Consequently, the figure shows that the two norms negatively impact the goal of the guests to have dinner at the restaurant (n-impacts, solid arrow) respectively. As the complexity of the graph can increase rapidly, the user must have the ability to turn different elements on and off. This is also the case for different norms and perspectives in general. One can also now see, how much complexity is necessary to model the behavior compared to the limiting view on norms as restrictions in Fig. 1.

Finally, taking different perspectives into account also has a high impact on the complexity of the simulation. The simulation needs to be as complex and as simple as the user requires it (UR4). If the simulation is too complex, it is not usable for the user. It may be too convoluted with parameters so that the users

---

[1] https://simassocc.org/.

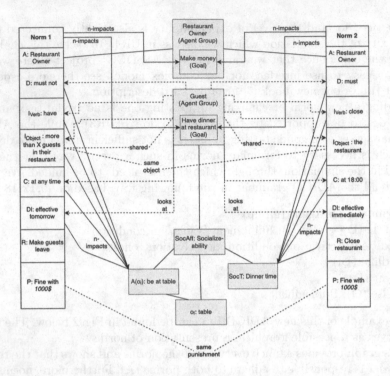

Fig. 2. Visual representation of norms.

are overwhelmed and the simulation becomes a black box, or it is so demanding that it cannot be run by the traditional machines that users have. However, if the simulation is not complex enough, then the desired effects and influences cannot be observed. Some people might decide to wait outside the restaurant until a table is free and this can lead to a queue in front of the restaurant. Such a possible queuing behavior needs to be modeled appropriately. Otherwise, this influencing factor is missed and no informed decisions can be made.

Taking these two sides together, it needs to be clear what the current limitations of the simulation are. Otherwise, the risk increases that users attribute elements and functions to the simulation that are not present. This is especially critical when abstractions and simplifications are made.

4.2   System Level

The system describes the simulation in itself. It needs to support the users with their goals. We therefore identify the following requirements for the system level:

Each of the elements in Fig. 2 need to be interactive. When clicking on an element, such as an I_{Object} or the user agent group, all connected elements are highlighted by the system. This enables the user to quickly identify connections and assess possible impacts.

Each norm column in Fig. 2 is represented as one modifiable object in the simulation. The system attaches the objects, the perspective object and the norm objects, to the agent so they can use it in their deliberation process. The distribution of the perspectives is determined by the user, prior the start of the simulation. The social affordances can be made public knowledge.

To support the user with modifying a norm and adding a new one, a 'lego-like' system, where each element of the ADICDIRO represents one building block. Each of these blocks requires a specific input, and together they make the desired norm change. This can then also be used to highlight at each step, based on the given input, which other elements are affected, such as goals, actions of an agent, or available social affordances. This means that the system needs to show for actions if they becoming forbidden or obliged, for goals if they become unachievable, and for social affordances if they get altered. Furthermore, agents that have these affected elements are then in a special focus to see if they change their behavior. Those events can be visually indicated during the run and logged in a table for further analysis. Furthermore, counters and other numerical tools can be utilized to measure how often certain actions, social affordances, and objects have been used and how a norm change or the introduction of a new norm influenced this number. A graph can then be used to see the development over time, and it becomes clear for the user whether the desired influence was achieved or not. However, such a 'lego-like'system needs to be designed very carefully. A good balance between giving the user freedom and limiting the input possibilities to prevent senseless input is necessary. Such a directed system can then also be used for supporting the user to set up the simulation.

Furthermore, the system needs to make sure that the information, when inspecting an agent, is provided in a meaningful way for the user. Thus, the inspection has to provide more than just values for the different variables, as in NetLogo [19] for example. It needs to be immediately clear from the inspection why the current actions have been chosen and which goal the agent is trying to achieve. Other objects in the simulation, such as the restaurant, need to be made inspectable as well. When inspecting an object, information needs to be provided for the user to see which actions can be performed with the object, and which norms are affecting this object.

4.3   Agent Level

Based on Fig. 2, we can see what elements need to be present in the agent's deliberation process to represent reactions to a new norm. The agent needs values and the ability to check that one goal aligns more to a value than another one. Work from [7,8] can be used here as a starting point.

Furthermore, an agent should be able to make alternative plans to reach a goal when an action becomes forbidden or obliged. It should also be able to reason with the available social affordances to check which alternative actions are available. When no actions are available anymore to reach the goal, the agent must be able to form a new plan to reach a different goal, based on the available actions. Ideas from previous norm aware approaches, for example [2,5,12], can be used here as a starting point. Such a planning behavior also takes place when the goals or actions are affected by the behavior of other agent groups.

Finally, agents need to be able to communicate with each other. When guests go to a restaurant to meet their friends, the friends need to be there as well. Thus, the agents need to be able to coordinate themselves in some way.

5 Preliminary Exploration

We are currently in the early stages of developing a social simulation of our model using NetLogo [19]. We are targeting the following scenario: Restaurants are offering three different time slots for eating, early evening (18:00–20:00), middle evening (20:00–22:00), and late evening (22:00–0:00). This changes the available social affordances, and the social time (SocT) of having dinner specifically. The dinner time is now extended, as guests can eat between 18:00–0:00 (6 h), instead of only eating between 18:00–20:00 (2 h).

Furthermore, the restaurant owners have daily fixed costs, e.g. for rent and electricity, and variable costs for each guest, e.g. cost of food, service costs and cleaning the dishes. Guests pay a fixed amount of money for their dinner and we assume that they have enough money for their dinner. To explore how guests react to the new eating time slots and if they change their dinner time (due to the altered social time (SocT)), we distinguish the following cases: norm as restriction, and norm as trigger of new behavior.

For both of these cases, we assume that people stay at the restaurant for one time slot, and they want to go once every week to the restaurant. Furthermore, we only look at the weekends, i.e. Friday to Sunday, as these are the most common days for people going to the restaurant. Table 1 shows the early explorations that we were able to make so far. We focus on the restaurants' financial situation, i.e. their capital and how it changes over time, and the guest's satisfaction, i. e. could guests go to the restaurant or has their spot been denied.

Norm as restriction: Guests do not alter their behavior. They try to go out for dinner at their usual dinner time and if the restaurant is full, they can try again the next day, thus the action going to the restaurant is not available anymore until the next day. We assume that people try to go to the restaurant to have dinner during the early evening time, i. e. 18:00–20:00, similar to northern European countries, e.g. Sweden, where people have dinner at around 18:00.

Norm as trigger of new behavior: Guests alter their behavior. Similarly to the previous case, the agents try to have dinner at their usual dinner time (early evening). However here, the action to go to the restaurant is available for every time slot, enabling guests to make use of the altered social affordances. The changed social time (SocT) allows guests to relax their dinner time and also go to the restaurant at a later time if the restaurant is full at their desired time.

We can see from these early explorations how a small change in behavior, as a reaction to a norm, can result in a vastly different outcome. Of course, the restaurant owner can also adapt to the norm and e.g. make different time slots to accommodate more people, or offer a booking system.

Table 1. Norm as a restriction compared to norm as a trigger of new behavior.

Cases	Early explorations
Norm as restriction	Restaurant owners are losing money and eventually go bankrupt, as not enough guests are in the restaurant to cover their costs. Also, the guest satisfaction is lower, since not everyone can go to the restaurant within one week
Norm as trigger of new behavior	Guests also use later time slots to have dinner. This enables restaurant owners to allocate guests per day rather than per time slot. These two factors together result in a higher guest satisfaction, and healthy restaurant capital

While our current explorations are still in their very early stages using a basic example, they show the necessity of our approach. Seeing the norm as a trigger of new behavior resulted in different consequences for guests and restaurant owners, and thus, in a different type of policy-behavior dynamics. We use this as a starting point for more elaborate simulations going forward.

6   Conclusion

In this paper, we presented an approach to incorporate different perspectives on norms into the simulation to provide policy makers and other decision makers with meaningful insights to support them in their decision making. The results of our preliminary explorations showed the necessity of our approach.

A perspective entails individual and group specific goals, priorities in values, actions, effects of those actions, and social affordances. Having these, users (policy makers and other decision makers) can then see how norms impact individuals and groups differently.

Enabling the user of the simulation to be active in the modeling process, allows for tailoring the simulation towards their specific needs and to observe different variations of what they want to achieve.

For our future work, we will formalize the links between the norms and perspectives. Given the importance of having an implementation, we will focus on this. We will start with the implementation of the agents based on the ideas of [1,7,8,13]. We will also focus on making different perspectives adaptable and what support the users need to adapt them and to add new ones. Additionally, we will define social affordances for social rules.

References

1. Boshuijzen-van Burken, C., Gore, R., Dignum, F., Royakkers, L., Wozny, P., Shults, F.L.: Agent-based modelling of values: the case of value sensitive design for refugee logistics. JASSS: J. Artif. Soc. Soc. Simul. **23**(4) (2020)

2. Castelfranchi, C., Dignum, F., Jonker, C.M., Treur, J.: Deliberative normative agents: principles and architecture. In: Jennings, N.R., Lespérance, Y. (eds.) Intelligent Agents VI LNAI 1757. pp. 364–378. Springer, Cham (2000). https://doi.org/10.1007/10719619

3. Crawford, S.E., Ostrom, E.: A grammar of institutions. Am. Polit. Sci. Rev. **89**, 582–600 (1995)

4. Dechesne, F., Di Tosto, G., Dignum, V., Dignum, F.: No smoking here: values, norms and culture in multi-agent systems. Artif. Intell. Law **21**(1), 79–107 (2013)

5. Dignum, F.: Autonomous agents with norms. Artif. Intell. Law **7**(1), 69–79 (1999)

6. Dignum, F.: Interactions as social practices: towards a formalization. arXiv preprint arXiv:1809.08751 (2018)

7. Dignum, F. (ed.): Social Simulation for a Crisis: Results and Lessons from Simulating the COVID-19 Crisis. Springer, Cham (2021). https://doi.org/10.1007/978-3-030-76397-8

8. Heidari, S., Jensen, M., Dignum, F.: Simulations with values. In: Verhagen, H., Borit, M., Bravo, G., Wijermans, N. (eds.) Advances in Social Simulation. SPC, pp. 201–215. Springer, Cham (2020). https://doi.org/10.1007/978-3-030-34127-5_19

9. Li, T., Jiang, J., Aldewereld, H., De Vos, M., Dignum, V., Padget, J.: Contextualized institutions in virtual organizations. In: International Workshop on Coordination, Organizations, Institutions, and Norms in Agent Systems. pp. 136–154. Springer, Berlin (2013). https://doi.org/10.1007/978-3-642-00443-8

10. y López, F.L., Luck, M., d'Inverno, M.: A normative framework for agent-based systems. Comp. Math. Organ. Theory **12**(2–3), 227–250 (2006)

11. Mellema, R., Jensen, M., Dignum, F.: Social rules for agent systems. arXiv preprint arXiv:2004.12797 (2020)

12. Panagiotidi, S., Alvarez-Napagao, S., Vázquez-Salceda, J.: Towards the norm-aware agent: bridging the gap between deontic specifications and practical mechanisms for norm monitoring and norm-aware planning. In: Balke, T., Dignum, F., van Riemsdijk, M.B., Chopra, A.K. (eds.) COIN 2013. LNCS (LNAI), vol. 8386, pp. 346–363. Springer, Cham (2014). https://doi.org/10.1007/978-3-319-07314-9_19

13. Pastrav, C., Dignum, F.: Norms in social simulation: balancing between realism and scalability. In: Proceedings of the Fourteenth International Social Simulation Conference (2018)

14. Păstrăv, C., Jensen, M., Mellema, R., Vanhée, L.: Social simulations for crises: from models to usable implementations. In: Dignum, F. (ed.) Social Simulation for a Crisis, pp. 85–117. Springer Cham (2021). https://doi.org/10.1007/978-3-030-76397-8

15. Rohan, M.J.: A rose by any name? The values construct. Person. Soc. Psychol. Rev. **4**(3), 255–277 (2000)

16. Schwartz, S.H., Bilsky, W.: Toward a universal psychological structure of human values. J. Person. Soc. Psychol. **53**(3), 550 (1987)

17. Smajgl, A., Izquierdo, L.R., Huigen, M.: Modeling endogenous rule changes in an institutional context: The ADICO sequence. Adv. Complex Syst. **11**(02), 199–215 (2008)

18. Vázquez-Salceda, J., Aldewereld, H., Grossi, D., Dignum, F.: From human regulations to regulated software agents' behavior: connecting the abstract declarative norms with the concrete operational implementation. A position paper. Artif. Intell. Law **16**(1), 73–87 (2008)

19. Wilensky, U.: Netlogo. http://ccl.northwestern.edu/netlogo/, Center for Connected Learning and Computer-Based Modeling, Northwestern University, Evanston (1999), http://ccl.northwestern.edu/netlogo/

Exploration of Model Coupling Strategies in a Hybrid Agent-Based Traffic Simulation

Jean-François Erdelyi(ID), Frédéric Amblard(ID), Benoit Gaudou(ID),
Elsy Kaddoum(ID), and Nicolas Verstaevel(✉)(ID)

IRIT, Université de Toulouse, CNRS, Toulouse INP, UT3, UT1, UT2,
Toulouse, France
{jean-francois.erdelyi,nicolas.verstaevel}@irit.fr

Abstract. Traffic simulation is a tool used by urban planners to assess the impact of new urban designs and public policies on mobility. Over the years, numerous traffic models have been proposed, each model offering different levels of details and performances. Multi-level model coupling is an interesting approach to combine the advantages of complementary representations while limiting their drawbacks. In this paper, we design and evaluate the performances of hybrid traffic models combining a microscopic model (IDM) with a mesoscopic model (event-driven and queue-based). The results show that microscopic models have more diversity in terms of behaviors but reduce the vehicle average speed and mesoscopic models are more efficient in terms of computational time but display a higher vehicle speed. Their hybridization then enables to find a balance between scalability and the variety of the observed behaviors.

Keywords: Traffic simulation · Model composition · GAMA platform

1 Introduction

The sustainable management of mobility is identified as a key component for a well-functioning Smart City [25]. On one side, technologies are evolving offering new and more effective transportation modes [22]. On the other side, urban planners see mobility as an enabler for designing better cities, integrating social, environmental, and economical components [7]. Therefore, there is an increasing need for tools that allow to assess the impact of these disruptive innovations based on "what if" prospective studies [31].

Various traffic simulation models and software tools have been developed to specifically model, plan and analyze current traffic in terms of offer and demand [20]. Each tool is focusing on specific aspects of traffic modeling using dedicated modeling approaches. A microscopic simulation focuses on modeling each vehicle and its dynamics individually, whereas a macroscopic simulation focuses on aggregated information such as traffic density and traffic flow [16]. To study the

© Springer Nature Switzerland AG 2022
K. H. Van Dam and N. Verstaevel (Eds.): MABS 2021, LNAI 13128, pp. 153–167, 2022.
https://doi.org/10.1007/978-3-030-94548-0_12

impact of urban planning decisions, that requires to both observe large-scale traffic at the scale of a metropolis and focus on the microscopic traffic at the scale of a ward, it is necessary to design tools that can combine and switch between those different scales at runtime [13]. Furthermore, it is also interesting to combine those different models with other models to study for example the impact on environmental factors [24], or the individual response of citizens to catastrophic events [8].

Large-scale road traffic in a city, including individual choices in terms of mobility, is a complex system: it is composed of numerous heterogeneous entities with nonlinear interactions that are geographically distributed and can be modeled and/or observed at different levels [13]. The agent-based paradigm is thus a particularly suitable approach to model such complex phenomena [4] and to couple various models, being of the same phenomenon at different scales or different phenomena [11]. The key issues when coupling different models (in particular of the same phenomenon at different levels) are to control the side effects at the interaction between models and to avoid divergence of the results [2].

This paper studies the impact of coupling different models of traffic simulation within an agent-based framework. One microscopic (IDM [10]) model and one mesoscopic (event-driven and queue-based [9]) model have been implemented and coupled on a road network: moves of vehicles on each road segment can follow the former or the latter model. The main contribution of this paper is to evaluate the **impact of the hybridization** (*i.e.* the ratio of each model type) on simulation performances (computation time, vehicles' average speed, and vehicles' time to reach their target). In short term, the objective is to understand and quantify the pros and cons of this hybridization and to emphasize the need for an equilibrium between computation time of the simulation and variety of agents' behaviors, and identify challenges for dynamic model coupling. In long term, the objective is to propose a framework to offer the possibility of dynamic model coupling applied to mobility simulation.

The paper is organized as follows: Sect. 2 provides background on traffic simulation and models coupling, Sect. 3 gives details about the two traffic flow models and their coupling, Sect. 4 analyses the performance of the integrated coupling of these two models. Finally, Sect. 5 concludes with perspectives.

2   Related Work

Numerous road traffic models have been proposed. Each model is designed with a specific hypothesis, depending on the simulation objectives and computational limits. Those models can be classified into three modeling levels [14]:

1. **Microscopic** [12, 29]: such models describe individually the entities involved in the traffic (vehicles, pedestrians, etc.), their interactions, and lead to emerging phenomena (such as congestion). They are considered the most accurate and realistic. However, this representation has some limitations especially

when upscaling: the computation cost indeed evolves rapidly with the number of individuals [27, 28]. These models are also difficult to calibrate because of their large number of parameters.

2. **Macroscopic** [18]: All individual vehicles are here aggregated and such models focus more on macroscopic variables of average speed, flow, and vehicle density [15]. The observed behaviors are thus less precise. However, they are very effective for representing large-scale phenomena in space and time. These models often use probabilistic concepts, which makes them simple to describe and calibrate. About traffic, they use concepts from fluid mechanics, including the conservation laws [21] and differential equations.

3. **Mesoscopic** [6]: these models consider an intermediate representation between microscopic and macroscopic models [30]. Two main approaches can be found in the literature: either the individuals are grouped and thus individual behaviors are not taken into account, or the dynamics of the flow of entities is determined by a simplification of the individual dynamics and managed at the road level [3, 28]. The advantage of this approach is to have an intermediate between the microscopic fine representation of individual vehicles, but expensive and difficult to calibrate, and macroscopic inexpensive and simple simulations providing coarse results.

Each of these modeling approaches has thus its specificities: macroscopic models are particularly relevant for large-scale simulations (*e.g.* the scale of a metropolis) whereas microscopic ones can be applied to represent precise traffic in a small ward. When a model is designed for urban planning purposes, it would be interesting to be able to observe both levels. To this extends it appears necessary to combine different models.

Multi-level model coupling is a technique used to combine the advantages of complementary representations of the same system. There are three main types of model coupling [11, 19]: **integrated** (model as a new model from the combination of two, or more, models), **weak** (the model as a set of interconnected independent models), and **strong** (model as a set of parallel models sharing data during the simulation). Model coupling, even if it can be technically complex when the number of interactions increases, provides huge benefits in terms of modularity: coupled model could be switched to increase precision or conversely to reduce computational time. The coupling can also be *static* or *dynamic* [28]. When the coupling is **static**, the coupled models and the ways they interact are defined at the initialization of the simulation and cannot be changed at runtime. This is the most commonly used approach as it does not need to implement transfer functions at runtime. The **dynamic** coupling approach allows the system to switch between multiple representations dynamically depending on specific criteria, such as the CPU load or user needs.

In this paper, we focus on a static **hybrid traffic models**, *i.e.* a model coupling different (mesoscopic and microscopic) representations of the same phenomenon: we divide the roads into sections and a specific (microscopic or mesoscopic) model is associated to each of them, the transition is managed by the frontier between each section.

Several works have already investigated the possibility to design a hybrid model of traffic flow, coupling models at various scales (in general a microscopic model with a mesoscopic or macroscopic model). Such models are limited to 2 or 3 road sections, each section using either a microscopic or a mesoscopic model. The objective is to ensure the coherence between these various models: in particular that the number of vehicles or the flow speed is not altered at the transition between models [2]. [17] focuses on the compatibility between a micro and a macro model and in particular on the compatibility of a micro car-following model at the interface with a macroscopic model. [5] also investigates how to minimize the perturbations at the interface between 2 levels. [1] focuses more specifically on the switch from a macroscopic to a microscopic model by proposing probabilistic desegregation, which could open the door to dynamic hybrid models.

Whereas previous models only focus on the interfaces between a microscopic and a macroscopic model, we go one step further by investigating and quantifying the impact of the hybridization rate, *i.e.* the rate of mesoscopic road segments in a hybrid model.

3   Methodology

This section details the design of an agent-based traffic model of a highway road. The road is sliced into segments of 1 km, where each segment is using its own traffic model. The objective of the simulations is to study the impact of hybridizing different types of traffic models within the same simulation by analyzing vehicles' average speed, vehicles' time to reach their target, and computation time for each simulation. The rest of this section is organised as follows: Subsect. 3.1 introduces the two models used for modelling traffic: one microscopic model (IDM model [10]) and one mesoscopic model (event-driven and queue-based [9]), and Subsect. 3.2 describes the implementation of those models within the agent-based modeling and simulation GAMA platform [26] and the coupling mechanism.

3.1   Traffic Models

Micro Model: Intelligent Driver Model (IDM) [29]. The first model is a micro-simulation model that simulates the individual behavior of a vehicle on a road. IDM is a time-continuous car-following model that describes the evolution of the position and velocity of each individual vehicle: it models a vehicle acceleration and deceleration, following the principle that a vehicle tries to maintain a minimum gap with its front vehicle. The original version of IDM is used in this experimentation. However, a variation of the model can be found that includes other factors such as the human reaction time [10]. This model is described by [10] as follows.

The computation of the nth vehicle acceleration $\dot{v}_n$ is given by the equation:

$$\dot{v}_n = a_n \left(1 - \left(\frac{v_n}{v_n^0} \right)^4 - \left(\frac{s^*(v_n, \Delta v_n)}{s_n} \right)^2 \right) \tag{1}$$

where a_n is the maximum acceleration of the vehicle n, v_n is the nth vehicle velocity, v_n^0 is the desired speed of the vehicle n. s_n is the distance gap between two vehicles and is defined as: $s_n = \Delta x_n - l_{n+1}$, where s_n is the distance bumper to bumper, $\Delta x_n = x_{n+1} - x_n$ is the distance between the vehicles n and $n+1$, and l_n the length of the vehicle n.

The desired minimum gap of the vehicle n, s_n^*, is given by:

$$s^*(v_n, \Delta v_n) = s_n^0 + T_n v_n - \frac{v_n \Delta v_n}{2\sqrt{a_n b_n}} \tag{2}$$

where s_n^0 is the jam distance of the vehicle n which is the distance between vehicles in a traffic jam, T_n is the safety time gap of the vehicle n, $\Delta v_n = v_{n+1} - v_n$ the velocity difference of the vehicle n, and b_n the desired deceleration of the vehicle n.

The IDM model is characterized by the intuitive parameters displayed in the Table 1 (with the commonly used default values of parameters). It suffers some limitations such as non-realistic deceleration in case of emergency braking, and the safety gap is not enough to guaranty safety in critical situations.

Table 1. Common default values of parameters for the IDM model

IDM parameter	IDM parameter description	Default value
l_n	The length of the vehicle n (m)	5 m
v_n^0	The desired speed of the vehicle n (m/s)	30 m/s
s_n^0	The jam distance of the vehicle n (m)	1 m
T_n	The reaction time of the vehicle n (s)	1.5 s
a_n	The maximum acceleration of the vehicle n (m/s^2)	4 m/s^2
b_n	The desired deceleration of the vehicle n (m/s^2)	3 m/s^2

Meso Model: A FIFO Queue Combined with the BPR Flow Equation. The second model is an event-driven queue-based traffic flow model [9]. Vehicles are aggregated at the road level where each road has a maximum capacity and a maximum free-flow speed so, when a vehicle enters a road, its traveling time is computed according to the current road capacity and free-flow speed using the flow equation provided by [23].

To exit a road, a vehicle has to reach 4 conditions:

1. The vehicle is at the top of the FIFO queue.
2. The time spent by the vehicle in the queue is at least equal to the time computed by the flow equation when it entered the queue.
3. The outflow capacity of the road (the maximum number of vehicles that can travel through a road in an hour) is not exceeded.
4. The next road capacity is not exceeded.

The next road should be (by default) another meso road, in this experimentation, the next road could be also micro, Sect. 3.2 provides details about the micro-meso coupling.

The Bureau of Public Road (BPR) function is used to compute the flow equation [23]:

$$t = t_f * (1 + \alpha * (\frac{v}{c})^\beta) \tag{3}$$

where t is the traveling time, $t_f = R_n^d / v_n^0$ is the free flow traveling time, R_n^d the length of the road n, v_n^0 is the free-flow speed, v the road volume, c the road capacity. The α and β parameters are two parameters that have to be calibrated: common values of those parameters are $\alpha = 0.15$ and $\beta = 4.0$. Different values of α and β can be used to take into account variation in transport infrastructures such as intersection delay, stop or crosswalk.

The outflow capacity of a road is the maximum number of vehicles that can leave the road over one hour. To comply with the outflow capacity, a minimum time between two vehicles t_0 is computed using the following formula: $t_0 = 3600/\zeta$, where t_0 is the minimum time between two vehicles and ζ is the maximum number of vehicles that can leave a road in an hour. ζ value depends on the characteristics of the road. In this paper, ζ is fixed at 2000 veh/h which corresponds to the maximum number of vehicles that can exit a segment of a one lane highway. Therefore, whenever a vehicle exit a road, the next vehicle in line in the queue will have at least to wait for a minimum time of t_0 before exiting the road itself. This model has proven to be efficient in large-scale scenarios [9].

3.2   Implementation and Coupling Strategy

The two previous models have been implemented within the GAMA platform [26]. A third model (that is the object of this paper) has been implemented to couple the microscopic and mesoscopic models on a road, each road segment been controlled by one of the two traffic models[1]. The model is composed of two types of agents, roads and vehicles. Each vehicle moves from the origin of the road to its target, its moves are controlled by either the microscopic or the mesoscopic model depending on the road agent. Each vehicle agent is characterized by a location, speed, and acceleration and the set of parameters used in the IDM model. Each road agent is characterized by its length, maximum speed, and all the parameters related to the mesoscopic model.

An important point of the model is that, once it has been created, a vehicle agent remains in the simulation until it reaches its target: in particular, it is kept at the transition between the micro and the meso roads. The only difference between a vehicle in a meso or a micro road is the activation or not of the IDM behavior: on a micro road, the vehicle computes its own moves following the IDM model, otherwise, the vehicle is controlled by the road. At the entrance

---

[1] In the following, we will use "meso road" (resp. "micro road") to refer a road controlled by a mesoscopic (resp. microscopic) model.

to a meso road, the vehicle registers to the road and waits until the road agent
wakes it up when it can exit the current road and enter the next road.

Different combinations of traffic models can be tested by selecting the model
executed by each road agent, from a fully microscopic model to a fully mesoscopic
model. Therefore, four types of transitions between models have to be designed
to effectively couple the different models and handle the transition from one
model to the other:

- **From a mesoscopic model to a mesoscopic model.** In this context, no
  specific action is required. The vehicle exiting the road just registers to the
  new one.
- **From a microscopic model to a microscopic model.** To avoid side-
  effects at the interface between 2 micro roads, vehicles driven by the IDM
  model consider a set of contiguous micro roads as a single road, and the
  computation of the closest vehicle, etc. will take into account vehicles of the
  current road, but also of the next road.
- **From a mesoscopic model to a microscopic model.** The key issue here
  is to compute the vehicle speed at the entrance in a micro road.
  1. **Step 1**: as the vehicle is on a meso road, it does not have any speed in
     the sense of the IDM model. So a mean speed v_n is computed at first:
     $v_n = R_m^d/t_m^{meso}$, where t_m^{meso} is the time to travel the current meso road
     (considering the time in the jam, this is the true time spend on the road)
     and R_m^d its length.
  2. **Step 2**: it consists in detecting whether the vehicle is the *leader* of the
     platoon:
     - If there is no vehicle to follow, the vehicle is the *leader* and it enters
       the road with the mean speed computed above;
     - Otherwise the vehicle enters the next road with a speed that is the
       minimum between the mean speed (computed above) and the speed
       of the followed vehicle.
  3. **Step 3**: the IDM behavior is activated, so all the interactions and behav-
     iors are computed by the vehicle itself and the road agent is passive.
- **From a microscopic model to a mesoscopic model.** A vehicle from a
  micro road has to take into consideration some meso road capability as the
  inflow.
  1. **Step 1**: if the vehicle is the *leader* of the platoon and the first vehicle
     in the road, it computes the time to reach the meso road $t_r = \frac{\delta d}{v_n}$, where
     δd is the distance between the current vehicle and the end of the current
     road, and v_n the vehicle speed
  2. **Step 2**: the vehicle checks if the time to reach the next road (t_r) is
     compatible with the outflow duration of the road, which means, the time
     to reach the next road is higher than the outflow time from the previous
     vehicle.
  3. **Step 3**: if the outflow duration is compatible, the vehicle continues until
     the end of the current road, otherwise the vehicle is braking and comes
     back to Step 1.

4. **Step 4:** the IDM behavior is deactivated, the road takes the control of the vehicle.

4   Experiment and Results

The objective is to study the impact of hybridizing a microscopic and a meso-scopic simulation model on the performances of an agent-based traffic simulation. More precisely, we are interested in studying the heterogeneity of vehicle behaviors by monitoring average speed and time to travel in different traffic conditions (inflow value and rate of mesoscopic models), and the computational time required to execute the simulations.

4.1   Experiment Design

The simulation is initialized with a 10 km section of motorway (segmented by 1 km sections) with two optional exits and one main exit (Fig. 1). Each road agent is characterized by a length (1 km), a maximum speed (34 m/s), and a model that has to be chosen between the microscopic and the mesoscopic models. Each vehicle has its set of IDM parameters initialized with values from Table 1.

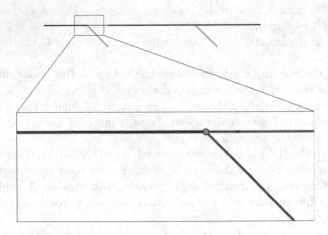

Fig. 1. Example of road configuration: blue roads are controlled by a microscopic model and green ones by a mesoscopic model. The main entrance (resp. exit) is located on the left (resp. right). (Color figure online)

The experiment configuration is as follows:

- A simulation step lasts 0.1 s;
- A simulation stops after 10 min (of simulation time);
- 80% of the vehicles are going from the main entrance to the main exit and 20% choose randomly an alternative exit among the two other ones.

We propose to explore the model according to two parameters:

- The **inflow of vehicles**: it allows to adjust the number of vehicles created each step: with an inflow of 1500, a new vehicle agent is created every 0.4 s. 5 values are evaluated: [1500, 1800, 2000, 2250, 2400] where 2000 corresponds to the max outflow. The objective is to study different traffic conditions including a low traffic inflow (1500 and 1800), the maximum free-flow inflow (2000), and congested flows (2250 and 2400).
- The **percentage of road hybridization**, that is the rate of meso roads (micro roads are considered as the reference). 11 values are explored from 0% to 100% with an increment of 10%. For each value, the roads executing the meso-model are randomly chosen.

To limit the effect of stochasticity, 20 replications (*i.e.* 20 simulations with the same parameters values) are executed. An exhaustive exploration is performed: all the combinations of the 11 values of hybridization and the 5 values of inflow are explored. A total of 1100 simulations 11 hybridisation values × 5 inflows × 20 runs) has thus been computed.

For each simulation, three indicators have been computed:

- **Mean travel time** of vehicles (in s) that exited the road during the simulation;
- **Mean speed** of all vehicles (in km/h);
- **Computation time** (in s) required to compute the 10 min simulations.

All simulations have been launched using a MacBook Pro with 2.3 GHz Intel Core i7 quad cores, 32 GB (3773 MHz) of RAM, and Intel Iris plus graphics (1536 MB).

4.2 Results

As the complexity of the microscopic model is influenced by the number of vehicles traveling in the road, we first study the effect of inflow on vehicle density (with 100% of micro roads). Figure 2 plots the mean density of vehicles in the road (the difference between the number of vehicles that entered the road and the number of vehicles that exited it during the simulations) for each inflow value. The horizontal and vertical axis are respectively the time and the density, and the color represents the inflow values. The results confirm that the higher the inflow is, the higher the density is. However, we see that densities for inflows of 2400 and 2250 are similar and close to the density of value 2000. The general tendency is linear from time 0 to time 330 and the curve is starting to flatten from that time. It corresponds to the moment when the first vehicles exit the road. The lower the inflow is, the stronger is this effect. It is the consequence of road congestion: with low inflow, vehicles are driving at a higher speed. Therefore, more vehicles manage to exit the road. Whereas at higher inflow values, vehicles need more time for exiting the road, leading to congestion.

On the left side, the Fig. 3 plots 3D graphs displaying the distribution of the mean speed of vehicles during the travel, the time needed to compute the

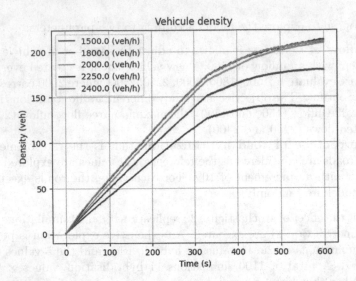

Fig. 2. Mean density of vehicles for each inflow value over time with 100% of micro roads.

simulation, and the time for vehicles to travel from origin to destination (only vehicles to the main exit). The x and y axes are the parameters *i.e.* percentage of road hybridization and inflow values, and the z-axis displays the computed metric *i.e.* speed, time to travel, and computation time. The bold line is the median value, and the top and bottom lines are respectively the limits of the first and third quartiles. To ease comparisons, the right side of Fig. 3 plots the evolution of the median value of each metric for each inflow value. The horizontal and vertical axis are respectively the hybridization percentage and the metric value, and the colors represent the different values of the inflow.

First, we can see that for any hybridization rate, an increase of the inflow leads to a reduction of the maximum speed. However, the full mesoscopic model (hybrid parameter at 1.0) produces higher speeds than the full microscopic model (hybrid parameter at 0.0). The range between Q1 and Q3 is narrower with the mesoscopic model. This could be explained by the fact that using a mesoscopic model, the vehicles tend to adopt the same behavior. On contrary, the distribution of speeds is more widespread with the micro model. As vehicles are influenced by proximity with others, and speed is influenced by acceleration and deceleration, each vehicle behaves differently. Nevertheless, we can notice that, for low inflows (below 2000), the distribution remains very limited, even for a mix of meso and micro roads (*e.g.* for the hybridization rate of 0.6).

We observe similar results with the travel times. The travel time is lower with the mesoscopic model than with the microscopic model. The distribution of the travel time is narrower with the mesoscopic model than with the microscopic model.

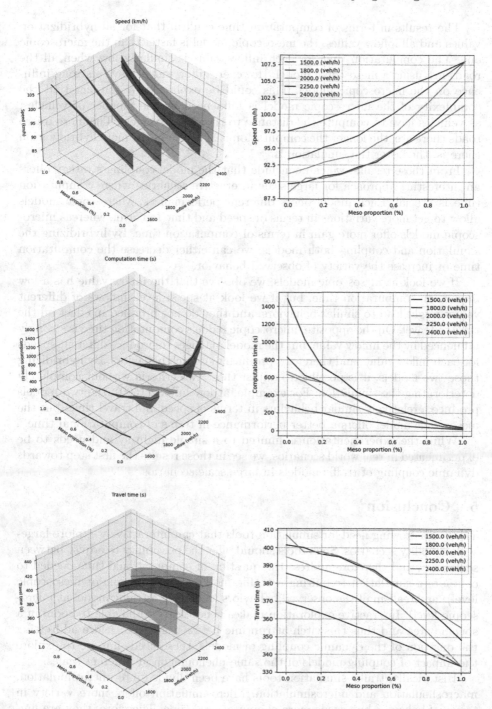

Fig. 3. On the left: the distribution of speed, computation time and time to travel for each inflow value. For each curve, the bold line corresponds to the median value, the top line the 3th quartile and the bottom line to the 1st quartile. On the right: only the median of the left values indicators.

The results in terms of computation time confirm that for all hybridization values and all inflow values, the mesoscopic model is faster than the microscopic one. The computation time for each inflow value is similarly low when all the roads are using a mesoscopic model. However, inflow values have a strong influence on the microscopic model. This could be explained by the fact that the complexity of the microscopic model is influenced by the number of vehicles, as vehicles have to compute the distance to the closest vehicle. The more micro roads there are, the longer the computation is. Therefore, the more hybridization there is, the faster the simulation is.

From those results, we can conclude that the model coupling strategy offers an interesting approach for large-scale interactive scenarios where computation time is crucial. Each model offers different performances. Microscopic models allow to get more variations in terms of speed and time to travel, whereas microscopic models offer more gain in terms of computation time. By hybridizing the simulation and coupling both models, we can either decrease the computation time or increase the variety of observed behavior.

If we look at mesoscopic models, we observe that the inflow value has a low impact on computation time, but if we look at speed level, inflows of different values might lead to similar behaviors, and they do not produce an effect on the time to travel. On the opposite, microscopic models computation time is strongly influenced by the inflow value, but the model manages to produce different speeds for each inflow value, and therefore, produce more rich behaviors. By hybridizing those two models, it is possible to adjust those two criteria without completely deteriorating the simulation. For example, at low inflow (1500), the two models produce a relatively similar behaviors in terms of speed and travel time, but the mesoscopic model offers a better performance in terms of computational time.

While the experimentation is limited to a simple highway and needs to be experimented in real world scenarios, we see in those results the first step towards dynamic coupling of traffic models in large scale scenarios.

5   Conclusion

There is a growing need for simulation tools that can interactively explore large-scale mobility scenarios. Such tools should offer the possibility to adjust between scalability, and therefore address the question of computational time needed to compute a simulation (requiring a traffic model at macroscopic or mesoscopic level), and realism of the observed behaviors (requiring a traffic model at microscopic level). Interactive exploration makes it necessary to be able to zoom in a specific area and thus to switch at runtime between models. Before addressing the question of the dynamic coupling of models, these needs impose to explore the impact of coupling models of the same phenomenon at different scales.

Historically, traffic simulation tools have been divided into microsimulation, macrosimulation and microsimulation. Microsimulation offers more variety in terms of behavior but needs more computational time. Therefore, they are limited to small scale simulation. On the other side, macrosimulation offers large scale scenarios, but individual behavior is aggregated.

To address this question, we present in this paper an agent-based traffic simulation in which mesoscopic and microscopic models are coupled. Through experimentation, we show that a hybridization strategy to adjust either the computational time or the variety of behavior is feasible. Simulations show the quantitative impacts of various rates of microscopic and mesoscopic models on the travel time, speed and computation times. In particular, we observe interesting results showing that in some inflow value ranges, both models behave quite similarly in terms of vehicle speed or travel time, but with a huge gain of computation time for the mesoscopic model. By dynamically switching between microscopic and mesoscopic models, it is, therefore, possible to adjust in real time the simulation to either increase its response speed or increase the variety of the observed behaviors. However, this switching will result in variations in terms of speed and time to travel. In addition, we would like to explore the possibility of calibrating the mesoscopic model online, using the well-known IDM (micro) model.

This work is a first step towards a dynamic coupling strategy for large-scale mobility scenario. Future work will include evaluation of the strategy in the real context of the two French cities of Bordeaux and Dijon, and evaluation of the performance in context where users dynamically change the model run by the roads. At longer term, we intend to develop a middleware framework to couple models at runtime according to users inputs or specific metrics (e.g. CPU load).

Acknowledgement. This work is part of the SwITCh (Simulating the transition of transport Infrastructures Toward smart and sustainable Cities, ANR-19-CE22-0003) research project funded by the French Research Agency.

References

1. Andreas, P., Siemens, A., Ronald, K., Hartmut, K.: Coupling of concurrent macroscopic and microscopic traffic flow models using hybrid stochastic and deterministic disaggregation. In: Transportation and Traffic Theory in the 21st Century. Emerald Group Publishing Ltd. Bingley (2002)
2. Banos, A., Corson, N., Lang, C., Marilleau, N., Taillandier, P.: Multiscale modeling: Application to traffic flow. In: Agent-based Spatial Simulation with NetLogo, vol. 2, pp. 37–62. Elsevier, Oxford (2017)
3. Barceló, J.: Fundamentals of Traffic Simulation, vol. 145. Springer, New York (2010). https://doi.org/10.1007/978-1-4419-6142-6
4. Bazzan, A.L., Klügl, F.: A review on agent-based technology for traffic and transportation. Knowl. Eng. Rev. **29**(3), 375 (2014)
5. Bourrel, E., Henn, V.: Mixing micro and macro representations of traffic flow: a first theoretical step. In: Proceedings of the 9th Meeting of the Euro Working Group on Transportation, pp. 610–616 (2002)
6. Burghout, W.: Mesoscopic simulation models for short-term prediction. PREDIKT Project Report CTR2005 3 (2005)
7. Cervero, R., Guerra, E., Al, S.: Beyond Mobility: Planning Cities for People and Places. Island Press, Washington (2017)

8. Chapuis, K., Taillandier, P., Gaudou, B., Drogoul, A., Daudé, E.: A multi-modal urban traffic agent-based framework to study individual response to catastrophic events. In: Miller, T., Oren, N., Sakurai, Y., Noda, I., Savarimuthu, B.T.R., Cao Son, T. (eds.) PRIMA 2018. LNCS (LNAI), vol. 11224, pp. 440–448. Springer, Cham (2018). https://doi.org/10.1007/978-3-030-03098-8_28
9. Charypar, D., Axhausen, K.W., Nagel, K.: Event-Driven Queue-Based Traffic Flow Microsimulation. Transp. Res. Record **2003**(1), 35–40 (2007)
10. Derbel, O., Peter, T., Zebiri, H., Mourllion, B., Basset, M.: Modified intelligent driver model for driver safety and traffic stability improvement. IFAC Proc. **46**(21), 744–749 (2013)
11. Drogoul, A., Huynh, N.Q., Truong, Q.C.: Coupling environmental, social and economic models to understand land-use change dynamics in the mekong delta. Fronti. Environ. Sci. **4**(2016)
12. Gazis, D.C., Herman, R., Rothery, R.W.: Nonlinear follow-the-leader models of traffic flow. Oper. Res. **9**(4), 545–567 (1961)
13. Haman, I.T., Kamla, V.C., Galland, S., Kamgang, J.C.: Towards an multilevel agent-based model for traffic simulation. Procedia Comput. Sci. **109**, 887–892 (2017)
14. Hoogendoorn, S.P., Bovy, P.H.: State-of-the-art of vehicular traffic flow modelling. Proc. Inst. Mech. Eng. Part I J. Syst. Control Eng. **215**(4), 283–303 (2001)
15. Lighthill, M.J., Whitham, G.B.: On kinematic waves II. A theory of traffic flow on long crowded roads. In: Proceedings of the Royal Society of London. Series A. Mathematical and Physical Sciences, vol. 229, pp. 317–345 (1955)
16. Lopez, P.A., et al.: Microscopic traffic simulation using sumo. In: 21st Internatinal Conference on Intelligent Transportation Systems (ITSC), pp. 2575–2582. IEEE (2018)
17. Magne, L., Rabut, S., Gabard, J.F.: Towards an hybrid macro-micro traffic flow simulation model. In: INFORMS Spring 2000 Meeting (2000)
18. Mohan, R., Ramadurai, G.: State-of-the art of macroscopic traffic flow modelling. Int. J. Adv. Eng. Sci. Appl. Math. **5**(2–3), 158–176 (2013)
19. Morvan, G.: Multi-level agent-based modeling - a literature survey. arXiv:1205.0561, November 2013, http://arxiv.org/abs/1205.0561, arXiv: 1205.0561
20. Pell, A., Meingast, A., Schauer, O.: Trends in real-time traffic simulation. Transp. Res. Procedia **25**, 1477–1484 (2017)
21. Popping, J.: An overview of microscopic and macroscopic traffic models. Doctoral dissertation, Faculty of Science and Engineering (2013)
22. Radu, L.D.: Disruptive technologies in smart cities: a survey on current trends and challenges. Smart Cities **3**(3), 1022–1038 (2020)
23. Roads, U.S.B.o.P.: Traffic Assignment Manual for Application with a Large, High Speed Computer. U.S. Department of Commerce, Bureau of Public Roads, Office of Planning, Urban Planning Division (1964)
24. Schulze, J., Müller, B., Groeneveld, J., Grimm, V.: Agent-based modelling of social-ecological systems: achievements, challenges, and a way forward. J. Artif. Soc. Soc. Simul. **20**(2) (2017)
25. Šurdonja, S., Giuffrè, T., Deluka-Tibljaš, A.: Smart mobility solutions-necessary precondition for a well-functioning smart city. Transp. Res. Procedia **45**, 604–611 (2020)
26. Taillandier, P., et al.: Building, composing and experimenting complex spatial models with the GAMA platform. GeoInformatica **23**(2), 299–322 (2019)
27. Taplin, J.: Simulation models of traffic flow. In: The 34th Annual Conference of the Operational Research Society of New Zealand, New Zealand, p. 12 (1999)

28. Tchappi Haman, I., Kamla, V.C., Galland, S., Kamgang, J.C.: Towards an multi-level agent-based model for traffic simulation. Procedia Comput. Sci. **109**, 887–892 (2017)
29. Treiber, M., Hennecke, A., Helbing, D.: Congested traffic states in empirical observations and microscopic simulations. Phys. Rev. E **62**(2), 1805–1824 (2000)
30. Vorraa, T., Brignone, A.: Modelling traffic in detail with mesoscopic models: opening powerful new possibilities for traffic analyses. WIT Trans. Built Environ. **101**, 659–666 (2008)
31. Wegener, M.: The future of mobility in cities: challenges for urban modelling. Transp. Policy **29**, 275–282 (2013)

The Recruitment Game: An Agent-Based Simulation

Siavash Farahbakhsh[1]([envelope])([iD]) and Mario Paolucci[2]([iD])

[1] Social Sciences Unit, Flanders Research Institute for Agriculture,
Fisheries and Food, Merelbeke, Belgium
`siavash.farahbakhsh@ilvo.vlaanderen.be`
[2] Laboratory on Agent-Based Social Simulation, Institute of Cognitive Science
and Technology, CNR, Rome, Italy
`mario.paolucci@cnr.it`

Abstract. While the studies on terrorism and radicalization are forego-ing, the socialization aspect of recruitment for terrorist organizations has stayed under-explored. In this paper, we develop an agent-based model simulating the socialization process of recruitment for terrorist organi-zations. In conceptualizing the socialization process, we implement an asymmetric game-theoretical model, with the two players of recruiter and target. The players have predominant strategies in which they differ based on their kinds. Our results show that initial ratios of different kinds in the population such as denouncer and vulnerable, in the simulation environment, have significant effects on the population of recruiters.

Keywords: Recruitment game · Agent-based modeling · Game theory · Terrorism

1 Introduction

The literature on terrorism and radicalization is very rich. Different aspects such as the role of communication (Bouko et al. 2021), networks (Martinez-Vaquero et al. 2019; Calderoni et al. 2021), ideologies (Kruglanski and Fishman, 2009; van den Hurk and Dignum 2019), typologies of terrorists (Horgan et al. 2018), recruitment strategic motivations (Bloom 2017), radicalization stages (Klausen et al. 2016), and strategic gains for social groups (Daniel et al. 2003; Sandler 2003, 2017; Skyrms 2014) are studied.

There is a consensus among scholars in this field that the emergence of terror-ism has less to do with socioeconomic factors such as wealth and education and they are associated mostly with ideologies and socialization (Horgan 2003; Turk 2004; Kruglanski and Fishman 2009). Joining a terrorist organization contains a socialization process, which relies on an *attraction-selection-attrition* frame-work (Schneider 1987; Bretz et al. 1989). Hence, potential targets for terrorist organizations, based on a shared reality and their attitudes, are attracted to an extremist or terrorist recruiter. Nevertheless, joining a terrorist organization

K. H. Van Dam and N. Verstaevel (Eds.): MABS 2021, LNAI 13128, pp. 168–179, 2022.
https://doi.org/10.1007/978-3-030-94548-0_13

contains risk-taking and arguably, strategy. That is, both parties, the potential target, and the recruiter, when facing each other, decide to act or not based on their risk evaluation, as they are aware of active efforts made by legitimate agents to prevent recruitment from happening.

Despite the existing rich literature on radicalization and terrorism, the sociological foundations of terrorism require further research. More precisely, besides a very few studies (van den Hurk and Dignum 2019; Calderoni et al. 2021; Martinez-Vaquero et al. 2019), computational models of terrorism's recruitment illustrating socialization processes of terrorist organizations are rare. In this respect, this study aims to *explore, with a computational approach, the mechanisms of a terrorism recruitment process through the lens of individual decisions and their collective outcome.*

In investigating our research question, we take an agent-based simulation approach (Edmonds and Meyer 2017; Epstein 2006). We build up a model of an environment where recruiters and potential targets, both possibly being snitches, interact and play a two-player asymmetric recruitment game. The game is initiated by recruiters in which they may target potential agents, and they wait for the targets' response.

In other words, we focus here on the social consequences of individual decisions, generated from individual traits, in a high-stakes recruitment game with hostile undercover agents. This is just one of several components needed to describe a real situation with high complexity and a strong dependence on individual paths and external drivers (e.g. terror events). Nevertheless, the part we study is a critical part that some other models neglected; having a better understanding of recruitment sustainability in abstract conditions might be an important ingredient for further, more situated studies.

More precisely, previous related models such as Calderoni et al. (2021), even though calibrated, employ as the main decision for a target to be recruited a simple threshold. Whereas, our model, with a game-theoretical approach, opens up the black box of that threshold, aiming to the understanding of the dynamism of interactions between recruiters and potential targets. Hence, our approach, which is presented here with a toy model, could be further applied as an add-on to existing radicalization-related simulation models.

In the next sections, first, we elaborate on the recruitment game simulation model. Second, we present the results of the model.

2   The Model

We propose here an agent-based model where interacting heterogeneous agents of two types – *recruiter, target*– coexist. The interaction between the recruiter and the target is formalized through a recruitment game. The recruitment game contains decisions and actions that a recruiter and a target must take together. The decision for both parties includes risk-taking, incentive, and penalty-related elements. Below we describe the model structure.

2.1   Structure, Initial Settings, Parametrization

Agents are either *residents* or *recruiters*. In this version of the model, agents
exhibit a fixed behavior, predetermined at startup. In the residents' population,
agents can be one of three kinds, vulnerable to the recruiters' offers, refusing
them, or even denouncing recruiters when they are approached. Similarly, in the
recruiters' population, the kind distinguishes true recruiters from undercover
agents aimed to fond out the vulnerable population.

The model is initiated as follows. We build the two groups of agents; residents
and recruiters. We assign kind to all agents depending on whether they are residents or recruiters. We ask the two groups to interact and play the recruitment
game. Below we elaborate the recruitment game as the main model dynamics.

2.2   Recruitment Game

With a game-theoretical approach, we design the interaction between the
recruiters and the potential targets. In designing the recruitment game, we first
assume the two players: *recruiter* and *target*. We further by the assumption that
in the first step, the game is initiated by the request of the *recruiter*. In the
second step, the target should respond to the recruiter's offer, which is to join
the terrorist organization, thus becoming a recruiter him/herself. Hence, our
modeling approach is to design a sequential asymmetric game, where the players do not have perfect information about the other player's potential responses
(Gibbons 1992; Sandler 2003). The rewards of the game depend on the actual
intentions of the players, which could be sincere or not. The recruiter could be
actually organizing terror acts, or she could be an undercover informant. The
target could also be a potential terrorist, a non-harmful citizen, or also be an
undercover agent. Targets that are not denouncers nor vulnerable simply refuse
to be recruited.

In formalizing the strategies of the two players, we rely on the variable kind,
and we define the following strategies for the players.

1. **Recruiter**'s possibilities based on its kind:
   (a) **Recruit** (*R*), when the recruiter asks the target to join the terror orga-
       nization.
   (b) **Undercover** (*U*), as the above, but in fact the recruiter is an undercover
       agent will remove the target if that decides to join.
2. **Target**'s possibilities, when approached by a recruiter, based on its kind:
   (a) **Denounce** (*D*), denouncing the recruiter and thus removing it from the
       game.
   (b) **Accept** (*A*), accepting the recruiter's offer to join a potential terrorist
       organization. This choice turns the agent to a recruiter.
   (c) **Refuse** (*A*), refusing to join the terrorist organization with no other
       effect.

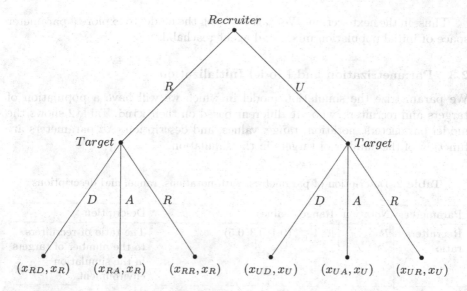

Fig. 1. Extended recruitment game

Based on the described groups, strategies, and sequences, we can draw the following game tree (see Fig. 1), which is an asymmetric game in an extensive form. The game tree can be formulated as a normal game.

Moreover, based on the presented game tree, Table 1 demonstrates the game transformation into a payoff matrix, where the row player is the recruiter and the column player is the target.

Table 1. Payoff matrix for the recruitment game, where x stands for the payoff gain e.g. x_{RD} is the gain of a recruiter who chose to *Recruit*, and then his/her target responded to *Denounce*

	D	A	R
R	(x_{RD}, x_R)	(x_{RA}, x_R)	(x_{RR}, x_R)
U	(x_{UD}, x_U)	(x_{UA}, x_U)	(x_{UR}, x_U)

Hence, the developed recruitment game is an asymmetric game. In order to assign utility values to the payoffs in Table 1, we would need agents to weigh internally the risk of being apprehended, perhaps in its simplest form as the cost of being caught times its probability. But how to calculate the cost of such a life-threatening event?

As an alternative to this calculation, in the present work, we examine the population structure of the game, assuming that playing the game would either affect the **kind** of the agent or remove it from the game, as in the specification above.

Thus, in the next section, We start by using the model to explore a parameter space of initial population mixes and agent reachability.

2.3   Parametrization and Model Initialization

We parametrize the simulation model in which we will have a population of targets and recruiters, who are different based on their kind. Table 2 shows the model parameters, notation, range, values, and description. All parameters are function of the number of targets in the simulation.

Table 2. Description of parameters, with notations, range, and descriptions

Parameter	Notation	Range	Values	Description
Recruiters ratio	R_r	[0, 1]	(0.1, 0.3, 0.5)	The ratio of recruiters to the number of targets in the simulation environment
Undercover ratio	U_r	[0, 1]	(0.1, 0.4)	The ratio of recruiters whose kind is *Undercover* over the total number of recruiters. The rest are true recruiters, their kind being *Recruit*
Denouncer ratio	D_r	[0, 1]	(0.025, 0.075, 0.125, 0.175)	The ratio of targets that incline toward denouncing targets in case of being approached. Their kind is *Denounce*
Vulnerable ratio	V_r	[0, 1]	(0.1, 0.25, 0.50, 0.75, 0.9)	The ratio of targets that are vulnerable in case of being approached. Their kind is *Accept*
+ Radius	θ	[0, 10]	(1, 3)	The distance that a recruiter, in its surrounding, can span to reach a potential target

3   Results

3.1   Global Sensitivity Analysis

To test our model, we take a global sensitivity approach and we ran simulations by varying all the combinations parameters. More precisely, following the ranges shown in Table 2, we varied R_r, U_r and D_r, in the $0-0.5$ interval with increments of 0.1, V_r in the $0-1$ interval with the increments of 0.1, and θ at the two values $\theta = 1$ and $\theta = 3$. We repeat each experiment 10 times letting it run for 200 steps, each step randomly activating all the recruiters. Knowing the repetitions and parameters, we ended up with 146410 observations. We expect that without the defense offered by denouncers and undercover agents, all vulnerable agents will eventually be recruited; to the contrary, when the opposition is strong, the recruiter's population will die out.

When plotting our global sensitivity results, we noticed that two factors can characterize the outcome variable; 1) the number of recruiters who survive in the simulation over time, and 2) the time when the recruiters population reaches its maximum. This time factor suggests three sub-patterns. The first pattern (a) is of uncontrolled growth until every agent is a recruiter. The second (b) is an initial surge that is later controlled and reduced by the defensive strategies (denouncers, undercover). Finally, the third pattern (c) shows a decrease of the recruiters at the onset, bringing to extinction. These patterns can usefully be distinguished by capturing the (last) moment when the number of recruiters reaches a global maximum. This is the last step for pattern (a), an intermediate step for pattern (b), and zero step for pattern (c). Thus, the time when a simulation reaches its maximum value for the number of recruiters can distinguish which of the pattern we are seeing.

Regarding the role of each parameter on the evolution of recruiters' population, on the first sight, it appears that all of the parameters have a visible influence. However, their effects are not uniform. This makes the ground to consider different value sets for each parameters in designing the experiments.

3.2 Experimental Design

Based on the global sensitivity analysis, we reduce the parameter values to the most sensitive regions for the outcome variable. The main experiment values are indicated in Table 2. The selected parameters values show $5 \times 3 \times 2 \times 4 \times 2 = 240$ parameters configurations, therefore, runs. In order to calculate how many repetitions for each configuration are needed, we applied statistical power analysis following Secchi and Seri (2017). The results suggested to repeat each configuration 43 times. Moreover, based on the sensitivity analysis, we decided to focus on the time steps below 50 as after this value, no major changes are visible. Hence, knowing the number of configurations, and repetitions, we ran our model 10320 times, and knowing the limiting time step, 526320 observations were resulted.

3.3 Experiment Results

We present our results in two steps. First, we show the evolution of recruiters population over time under different parameters configurations. Second, we focus on the growth of recruiters population until it reaches its maximum.

Recruiters' Population over Time: Figure 2 shows the evolution of recruiters' population over time under different conditions. Based on Fig. 2, it appears that all the parameters have observable effects on the evolution of recruiters' population over time. In the meantime, the trajectories are very different when comparing the two settings of the two settings of $\theta = 1$ with $\theta = 3$. In this regard, when the recruiters stay mostly in their neighborhood ($\theta = 1$), all the other parameters have an observable effect. More precisely, an increase in the denouncer ratio (D_r) and undercover ratio (U_r) leads to a lower recruiters' population. Comparing the effects of the denouncer ratio (D_r) and undercover ratio (U_r) based on the set values, one may argue that the denouncer ratio (D_r) has a more significant effect on the population of recruiters over time since by smaller changes in its set value the trajectory also changes.

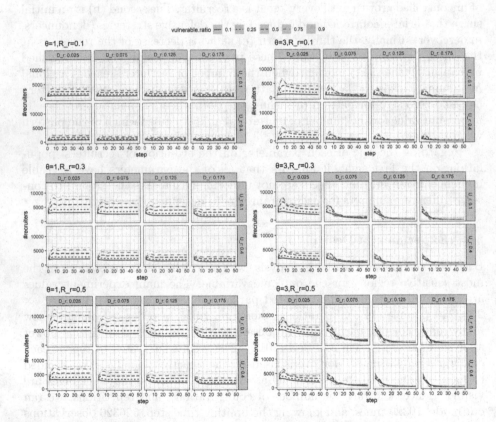

Fig. 2. Evolution of recruiters' population over time

The effect of recruiters ratio (R_r) appears linear. The more initial recruiters are in the model, the more recruiters population will remain at time step 50. This also holds for the V_r parameter. That is, when there are more vulnerable in the population, in general, there will be more recruiters at the end of the simulation.

On the contrary, when the recruiters move beyond their neighborhood ($\theta = 3$), most of the parameters effect disappear. Seemingly, by moving further, given the simulation space, recruiters are exposed to denouncers and undercovers with a higher probability. This will result in a recruiters' population disappearing (be caught) in a short time. This mechanism is specifically observable when $D_r \geq$ 0.075, which shows an effective level of denouncers in the population. Furthermore, at $\theta = 3$, $R_r \geq 0.3$ and $D_r \geq 0.075$, the peaks of recruiters' population start to disappear, shifting from pattern b to pattern c; a decrease of the recruiters right at the onset, bringing to extinction at the end of the simulation. Change in the peaks and patterns motivates us to look into also the peak of recruiters' population.

Recruiters' Population Maximum Growths: Figure 3 shows the growth of recruiters population until its reaches its maximum. More precisely, the outcome variable G_r we plot here is:

$$G_r = \frac{M_r - I_r}{T_m}$$

where M_r is the maximum of recruiters' population, I_r is the initial population of recruiters, and T_m is the time it takes in order for the recruiters population to reach its maximum. Thus, G_r summarizes both the time of the peak and its intensity.

We show the values of G_r in Fig. 3, that exhibits a general pattern, which can be observed on the diagonals of each sub-graph where there is a change from darker colors to lighter colors. The darker the color is, the smaller G_r is, with the peak intensity being low or reached late. In contrast, when the color is light, that means, the peak intensity is high, caused by showing a large growth of recruiters population in a short time. This sets ground on which bases to assess the growth of recruiters population and how to respond to it.

This representation might be used to decide policy intervention. For example, assuming that all parameter could be modified in small amounts at a comparable cost, the neighbors of a specific situation could be observed to decide which parameter has the stronger effect in each context. In practice, the simplest policy decision would be to move in the direction that brings about the darkest hue. As Fig. 3 suggests, at any radius (θ), the general pattern seems to be at a 45° diagonal, which shows the linear effect of recruiters' ratio (R_r) and vulnerable ratio (V_r). This suggests the more initial recruiters and vulnerable in the population will result in a higher G_r and peak intensity for the recruiters' population. In this line of argumentation, one may suggest that policy instruments should be implemented in order to decrease the vulnerable ratio (V_r) first, which could be seen as more of a mitigation approach. However, when it comes to decreasing the recruiter ratio (R_r), it may not be obvious how and when besides direct intervention by the governments.

Furthermore, when comparing the sub-graphs of Fig. 3 in a horizontal way, we can see the effect of the undercover ratio (U_r) parameter. The more undercovers are in the population, the less value of G_r, thus peak intensity for the recruiters' population. Hence, increasing the undercover ratio (U_r) is an effective instrument

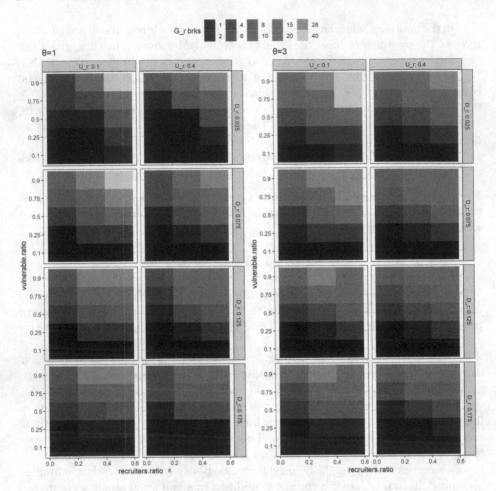

Fig. 3. Growth of recruiters' population until reaching its maximum

in tackling the peak of the recruiters' population. Nevertheless, this instrument can be seen as a costly solution as in order to have a significant effect the U_r needs to be increased by large steps (i.e. $U_r = 0.1 \rightarrow U_r = 0.4$). This means, not only there needs to be an investment in attracting the population to become undercover, but also a certain level of undercover is needed to have an effective strategy.

Similarly, the effect of the denouncer ratio (D_r) parameter can be seen when comparing the sub-graphs of Fig. 3 vertically. In general, an increase in the denouncer ratio (D_r) results in lower ranges of G_t and peak intensity for the recruiters' population. Its effect is particularly visible when one compares the setting of $D_r = 0.025$ with $D_r = 0.175$. Therefore, increasing the denouncer ratio (D_r) can be seen as an instrument, which unlike the undercover ratio (U_r) does not need a large increase to be effective. Increasing the denouncers' population

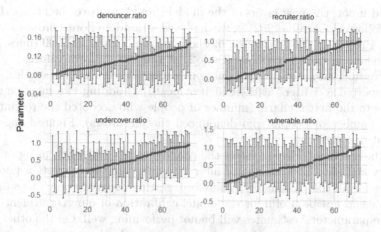

(a) Random Forest Cross Validation: summary statistic of recruiter's population

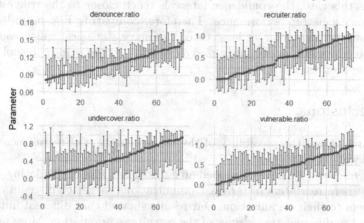

(b) Random Forest Cross Validation: summary statistics of recruiter's population, denouncers, and accept

Fig. 4. Cross validation results

could be seen as a mitigation plan aiming to attract a certain level of the population who are willing to take a risk and denounce the recruiters while ignoring possible networks (kinship, friends, etc.).

3.4 Calibration and Identification Approach

Following the sensitivity analysis, we plan to train our model for a potential calibration of this model. Using this model, one may access to some summary statistics, which could be at an abstract level e.g. the number of recruiters identified at the highest peak of terrorism in fragile neighborhoods, or the number of denouncing cases, etc. Therefore, our model parameters should fit potential data, and if not, the new layers of the model should improve the fitness. In this regard, following Carrella (2021)[1], we deployed a Random Forest cross-validation method. Practicing the calibration method, we ran our model 5000 times, where we set the model parameters (see Table 2) at random uniform values.

We consider two scenarios: 1) only one accessible summary statistics; (number of reported recruiters at their highest peak), 2) adding two more summary statistics to the first scenario (number of people who accepted the recruitment, and the number of people who denounced the recruiters). Figure 4 shows the results of this analysis.

On the one hand, Fig. 4a shows the confidence interval when using only one summary statistic. The confidence interval is large and it suggests a poor performance for all the parameters. Therefore, getting access to only one summary statistic could not be useful for the model calibration of our recruitment model to be the parameters' estimates will be not performing well. On the other hand, Fig. 4b shows the confidence interval when using only three summary statistics instead. In this case, the confidence intervals reach closer to the true estimates and it shows a better performance. Therefore, comparing Fig. 4a and Fig. 4b, one may suggest deploying at least three summary statistics, which could calibrate the recruitment model if it is used as an add-on to existing threshold-based recruitment models.

4   Conclusions

Our research shows the possibility of the implementation of recruitment games through agent-based modeling.

In this research, we have developed an agent-based model simulating an environment, where recruiters of terrorist organizations target civilians in order to attract them to their organization. Our results showed that different initial conditions lead to different trajectories of the recruiter's population. More precisely, the vulnerable and denouncer ratios appear to have significant effects on the recruiter's population. On the one hand, when there are either more vulnerable or recruiters in the population, more recruiters will result in the overall population. On the other hand, increasing the denouncer and undercover ratios results in a decrease in the recruiters' population. Furthermore, the effect of radius, the distance which a recruiter could go and reach a target has a very strong effect in which, when recruiters are willing to move further away and beyond their neighborhood, they will face higher probabilities of being exposed to other undercovers and denouncers, thus being caught leading to a decrease in recruiters' population.

Our results also put forward the attention on the peak intensity of the recruiters' population. This is particularly interesting as it emphasizes the moment that the recruiters' population together with its gravity in a sense how many recruiters are in the environment. With this context, the role of introduced

---

[1] https://carrknight.github.io/abm/2021/02/18/freelunch.html.

parameters could be seen as crucial in influencing the peak and the intensity of the recruiters' population.

References

Bloom, M.: Constructing expertise: terrorist recruitment and talent spotting in the pira, al qaeda, and isis. Stud. Confl. Terrorism **40**(7), 603–623 (2017)

Bouko, C., Naderer, B., Rieger, D., Van Ostaeyen, P., Voué, P.: Discourse patterns used by extremist salafists on facebook: identifying potential triggers to cognitive biases in radicalized content. Critical Discourse Studies, pp. 1–22 (2021)

Bretz, R.D., Jr., Ash, R.A., Dreher, G.F.: Do people make the place? an examination of the attraction-selection-attrition hypothesis. Pers. Psychol. **42**(3), 561–581 (1989)

Calderoni, F., Campedelli, G.M., Szekely, A., Paolucci, M., Andrighetto, G.: Recruitment into organized crime: an agent-based approach testing the impact of different policies. J. Quant. Criminol. (2021). https://doi.org/10.1007/s10940-020-09489-z

Carrella, E.: No free lunch when estimating simulation parameters. J. Artif. Soc. Soc. Simul. **24**(2), 7 (2021)

Daniel, G., Arce, M., Sandler, T.: An evolutionary game approach to fundamentalism and conflict. J. Ins. Theor. Econ. JITE **159**(1), 132–154 (2003)

Edmonds, B., Meyer, R.: Simulating Social Complexity. A Handbook. second edition, Springer, Heidelberg (2015)

Epstein, J.M.: Generative Social Science: Studies in Agent-based Computational Modeling. Princeton University Press, New Jersey (2012)

Gibbons, R.: A Primer in Game Theory. Prentice Hall Inc, Hoboken (1992)

Horgan, J.: The search for the terrorist personality. In: Silke, A. (ed.) Terrorists, Victims and Society: Psychological Perspectives on Terrorism and Its Consequences. Wiley Online Library, Hoboken (2003)

Horgan, J., Shortland, N., Abbasciano, S.: Towards a typology of terrorism involvement: a behavioral differentiation of violent extremist offenders. J. Threat Assess. Manag. **5**(2), 84 (2018)

Klausen, J., Campion, S., Needle, N., Nguyen, G., Libretti, R.: Toward a behavioral model of homegrown radicalization trajectories. Stud. Confl. Terrorism **39**(1), 67–83 (2016)

Kruglanski, A.W., Fishman, S.: Psychological factors in terrorism and counterterrorism: individual, group, and organizational levels of analysis. Soc. Issues Policy Rev. **3**(1), 1–44 (2009)

Martinez-Vaquero, L.A., Dolci, V., Trianni, V.: Evolutionary dynamics of organised crime and terrorist networks. Sci. Rep. **9**(1), 1–10 (2019)

Sandler, T.: Terrorism and game theory. Simul. Gaming **34**(3), 319–337 (2003)

Sandler, T.: Counterterrorism: a public goods approach. In: Buchholz, W., Rübbelke, D. (eds.) The Theory of Externalities and Public Goods, pp. 197–218. Springer, Cham (2017). https://doi.org/10.1007/978-3-319-49442-5_11

Schneider, B.: The people make the place. Pers. Psychol. **40**(3), 437–453 (1987)

Secchi, D., Seri, R.: Controlling for 'false negatives' in agent-based models: a review of power analysis in organizational research. Comput. Math. Organ. Theory **23**(1), 94–121 (2017)

Skyrms, B.: Evolution of the Social Contract, 2nd edn. Cambridge University Press, Cambridge (2014)

Turk, A.T.: Sociology of terrorism. Ann. Rev. Soc. **30**, 271–286 (2004)

van den Hurk, M., Dignum, F.: Towards fundamental models of radicalization. In: ESSA, pp. 67–79 (2019)

Fishing Together?
Exploring the Murky Waters of Sociality

Nanda Wijermans[1]([✉])[iD] and Harko Verhagen[2][iD]

[1] Stockholm Resilience Centre, Stockholm University, Kräftriket 2b, 10691
Stockholm, Sweden
nanda.wijermans@su.se
[2] Department of Computer and Systems Sciences, Stockholm University,
PO Box 7003, 16407 Kista, Sweden
verhagen@dsv.su.se

Abstract. Collective action research of natural resource use aims to understand why and when collective overuse arises. Agent-based simulations and behavioural experiments are part of the toolkit for this quest. In most agent-based simulation models however, individual and collective decision-making are discerned, but the crucial transition between these two stances is understudied. In this paper we formalise computational agents able to think and act from an individual, social, or collective stance using a combination of empirical findings and theoretical models on togetherness. To this end, we use a conceptual agent framework to adapt and extend an existing agent-based model designed to advance the understanding of group processes for sustainable governance of dynamic common pool resource environments. The findings of the paper are mainly a conceptual model and future research will further develop the framework as well as the agent-based model for further understanding of the processes involved.

Keywords: Togetherness · Collective action · Decision modes · Agent-based modelling

1 Introduction

Research on collective action regarding use of natural resource targets understanding and practices to avoid collective overuse. It covers a vast domain of empirical, experimental, and modelling work including agent-based simulations [21]. At the core lies the dilemma that individuals have to restrain themselves so that the collective (including that individual) can continue to benefit from a particular resource. Whether or not an individual feels part of a group or considers the effects of choices on other individuals has a profound influence on decisions and behaviour. For many challenges humanity faces, the difference between acting collectively versus individually is crucial, e.g. behaviour change to maintain available resources.

© Springer Nature Switzerland AG 2022
K. H. Van Dam and N. Verstaevel (Eds.): MABS 2021, LNAI 13128, pp. 180–193, 2022.
https://doi.org/10.1007/978-3-030-94548-0_14

The study of how large groups of people govern natural resources and how to improve this governance is one of the main topics within sustainability science. Among the most iconic and influential work is the work of Elinor Ostrom and her colleagues. Using empirical evidence, Ostrom challenged the then dominating view that over-exploiting of resources by communities is unavoidable, i.e. Hardin's tragedy of the commons [14]. She showed this theoretical construct had little to no relation to reality. Ostrom found communities are very much able to self-organise, and that a government (top-down) or privatisation are not the only ways of dealing with resources that are finite and freely accessible [19]. The ability of a community to self-organise and collectively avoid over-use of resources directly relates to a degree of togetherness in such a community. Findings regarding communities world-wide led to the identification of factors that contribute to successful self-organisation and resource management. These factors were further investigated using behavioural experimental and agent-based models to unpack the causal mechanisms underlying self-organisation and in particular factors that strengthen or weaken the capacity for collective action. Still much needs to be done to understand why, when, and how self-organisation works see e.g. [6,16]. Particularly when including/integrating the role of group dynamics, social identity etc., build on a social constructionist approach, where for instance these preference evolve through social interaction [9]. Or - to address the core of this paper - how do humans switch from one mode of decision making to another (e.g. individualistic versus collectivist)? Some work exists that reflects on the different decision mechanisms when reasoning from individual versus collective modes [26,27], and what makes one feel part of a group or not and to what degree one identifies with/has autonomy in such a group ([22,27]). The connection of these insights, ways of seeing and studying are the key to advancing our why, when, and how understanding of the emergence of collective action in common pool resource (CPR) problems.

How and when individuals transition to collectively oriented decision-making is understudied and undervalued. Many studies focus on the how and when of cooperation or coordination arise [17,21]. Their focus is on the factors and situations leading to collective action, rather than on the meta-level decision-making of switching between the individual and collective decision-making mode. This falls between the cracks of scholarly domains focusing on either individual or collective oriented individuals [9]. Most computational agent models currently in use to understand, reproduce, or predict human behaviour also fall short. Here, the starting point is often individual agents reasoning from an individual stance. To understand and address problems of collective action our computational agents need to be able to think and act individually and collectively, which requires the conceptual design to be based on understandings of being in either mode and how an agent transitions from one mode to the other. As agents in our work represent humans, we turn to the theories and models used to understand human behaviour and decision-making.

In this paper we share the design and formalisation of agents capable of transitioning between being individual, social, or collectively oriented when deciding on their behaviour based on empirical insights on 'togetherness'/collectiveness. This allows for agents being situated in a group in which decision-making and behaviour can (depending on the situation) be influenced by being aware of others (social) as well as by belonging to a group (collective). We adapt and extend an existing agent-based model designed to advance understanding of group processes for sustainable governance of dynamic common pool resource environments [24,30]. By using a combination of empirical findings and theoretical models on the (emergence of) togetherness, we develop a conceptual model, providing a set of decision trees reflecting the social and collective mode of decision making as well as the process by which these decision trees get activated. Finally, we will propose next steps in formalising but also in refining empirical data collection and experimental design. These steps underline one of the main points of this paper, namely the importance of continuous interplay between theoretical models, simulation models and outcomes, and empirical data for deeper understanding of social processes.

This paper is firmly located within agent-based social simulation, an area of research within agent-based simulation with a strong base in research traditions in the social and behavioural sciences as well as e.g. population ecology. In the modelling of the agent internal decision making and the interaction between the agents and their environment, theoretical models and empirical findings in these areas are used to build simulations that help understand or predict social level phenomena of interacting individual agents. We recognise that in what one may call main stream agent-based simulation research this coupling is less strong while in our research domain - agent-based social simulation -, the coupling is particularly strong. Thus, we will start with an overview of theories relevant for our research before moving to the empirical part of our work before connecting these two parts to the agent-based social simulation model under development.

2   Models of Individual and Social Decision-Making and Behaviour

Human behaviour and decision-making have been studied in various research areas. Amongst others in philosophy, and more in particular social ontology, however, these generally lack empirical grounding. Research areas that combine empirical research and theoretical models based on the empirical findings range from sociology (and related areas such as political science and anthropology) via social psychology to psychology. The explanatory model of these areas mirrors the collective, social, and individual level respectively. In agent-based systems some of these theories and models have been used, with a particularly strong position for individual-centred models (reflecting its connection to AI, which is in its turn closely connected to cognitive science). In these models, deliberation and goal-directed planning are key and the individual agent ranks action alternatives according to an all encompassing utility function to choose the best alternative. Philosophically, agent research has its primary home in the belief-desires-intentions (BDI) approach which has a similar take on agent reasoning.

At the core of BDI is the idea of (human) agents being primarily planning agents [3] and has a philosophical base in the work of amongst others Michael Bratman. Given that there are concerns about the possibility of BDI models to learn [20] or to interact with other agents in a multi-agent environment [10] it is surprising it has become so popular in agent research. In the following we will present a few relevant agent decision-making models from the different areas.

In sociology, a long-lasting debate has been about the so-called micro-macro link [1] which expresses the need for investigating the relationship between the individual agent and interaction between individuals and the society at large of which it is part as expressed in institutional, cultural, and societal aspects. The debate includes how concepts on each of the two levels can play a role in explaining and predicting behaviour.

Rational choice theory is one of the main models in use which places all emphasis on individualistic decision-making, in the line of methodological individualism based on the stance of Max Weber where individual actions that are driven by intentions are the base for any effects on a social level. It is close to the idea of *homo economicus* as used in economic theory to explain individual choices. The model of decision-making is that of utility maximisation. The BDI model is a perfect mapping of this stance.

On the other hand of the spectrum we find *homo sociologicus*, first branded by Dahrendorf [7], where individual behaviour is steered by the social role the individual plays and thus follows the norms that apply. A later take on the homo sociologicus from philosopher and social ontologist Margaret Gilbert describes this as agents acting based on their self-identification as a member of a social group constituted by a set of norms [11, 23]. To quote the opening sentence from her later collection of essays:

> We are social individuals: beings both independent and interdependent, units that are unified into larger wholes. Living together, we live our lives in terms of two distinct standpoints: the personal standpoint and the collective standpoint [12].

The notion of togetherness is crucial for the way people in a community decide and behave, and therefore important to include in the formalisation of mechanisms of collective action. The work done in sustainability science on collective action stresses this importance of togetherness by focusing on the ability of communities to self-organise, however needs to connect beyond the institutional level of collective action only.

Social psychology on the other hand, focuses on individual decision making while being part of a group. Agent models are rarely endowed with a sensitivity to togetherness in their decision making process and thereby lacking a crucial decision pathway to behave collectively. In related social ontological models, the model of reasoning is team reasoning [2, 25] which addresses issues of collective rationality and collective intentionality as an extension of game theory. This level brings us closer to a multi-agent perspective.

The micro-macro distinction excludes the meso-level of shared social space while not sharing collective intentions. There is something between being individual (making decisions independent) and being part of a collective (making decisions from a collective stance). An example of theories spanning all three levels of sociality is the social identity approach [22], as developed in social psychology. This is close to the stance Margaret Gilbert presented in the previous paragraph.

The models presented so far apply the same decision-making model in all contexts and circumstances. All decision-making is still goal-directed in nature. This leaves out situations in which there is no deliberation, where actions have a habitual origin. These may well be the rule and deliberation may be the exception, as formulated by philosopher Alan Goldman at the opening of [13]:

> Days, weeks, months go by in which I engage in no real deliberation about what to do. ... In none of the(se) ordinary situations is there deliberation in anything like the way philosophers typically describe: listing and weighing of reasons on each side of a contemplated action, assigning rough numerical values to reflect the weights, summing and reflectively forming the intention to perform the action with the greatest weight of reason behind it.

This habitual level of decision-making is part of the Consumat framework [15]. This framework is firmly based in psychological theories and explains that different decision-making models apply in different contexts, mainly depending on the individual evaluation of its previous choices and the (un)certainty regarding the information to which it has access. The Consumat framework is however weak in its take on social aspects. A more elaborate framework is the Model Social Agent, as developed by Carley and Newell [4]. In this framework, social science concepts characterising different levels of sociality and agent-internal frameworks, mainly from the cognitive sciences, are combined to create a space over different types of behaviour that follow from the agent model and situation. The Model Social Agent framework is particularly strong in its encompassing of subtly different social theories. Both frameworks inspired the development of the Contextual Action Framework for Computational Agents (CAFCA) [8] which we will use in this paper.

CAFCA distinguishes two dimensions of decision-making context that together frame what models of reasoning can be applied in the resulting context as it is seen by the agent, see Fig. 1. One dimension describes the type of reasoning: habitual, strategic (goal-driven) or normative. The other dimension pinpoints the level of sociality in individual, social, and collective. In the individual mode the agent interprets the decision as independent of others. In the social mode agents recognise other agents in the situation but sees oneself as distinct from or in competition with them. In the collective mode the agent does not only recognise others but perceives itself as belonging to the others, as a member of a collective or team.

		SOCIALITY DIMENSION		
		INDIVIDUAL	**SOCIAL**	**COLLECTIVE**
REASONING DIMENSION	**HABITUAL**	Repetition	Imitation	Joining-in
	STRATEGIC	Rational choice	Game theory	Team reasoning
	NORMATIVE	(institutional) rules	(social) norms	(moral) values

Fig. 1. Contextual Action Framework for Computational Agents (CAFCA) applied to common theories [adapted version of [8]]

3 Empirical Exploration on Togetherness

We collected empirical data to further develop our model in a framed field experiment in the form of a dynamic common-pool resource (CPR) game designed to capture behavioural responses of resource-dependent small-scale fishers to potential resource scarcity [18]. The experiment is a so-called 'pen-and-paper experiment' in which 4 participants (fishers in our case) sit at a table, get information on paper, and are accompanied by an experiment leader who guides them through the game rounds. The group plays for the duration of 14 rounds, a duration of which the participants are not aware. In each game round the group of 4 fishers could: i) communicate face-to-face, ii) individually and anonymously harvest resources by writing down how much resource units they want, and then iii) were informed by the experiment leader about the resulting fish-stock (after harvesting and renewal of the resource). Based on how they played they received payment for each unit of resource after the game. This set-up is common for behavioural experiments on CPR use.

To unpack the role of togetherness empirically, we qualitatively examined group dynamics processes in this behavioural experiment of collective action situation of natural resources. More specifically, after six of the 42 the behavioural experiments with the Thai fishers in different coastal communities, debriefing interviews were conducted with the experimenter team to get a feel for the group dynamics to support the formalisation process. The choice for which group depended on the availability of the experiment team (afternoon session only) and the presence of the first author (first half of the field experiments). The aim of the project for this data collection is to formalise the influence of perception of change in the resource on their actions via their internal characteristics and processes. We asked questions about the group dynamics, their perceptions and attributions, but also on whether they felt like a group, whether this changed throughout the experiment etc. In five of the six debrief interviews group-feel could be discerned.

3.1   Inspiration and Reflections on Togetherness of Thai Fishers Participating in Behavioural Experiments

When analysing the interviews from the angle of togetherness we notice how the individual-social-collective way of looking at decision making and behaviour allows for describing the situations that occurred.

Group A: A Collective and an Individual. In this particular group, participant #3 always took more than the others, while pretending they didn't understand. The other three however (participants #1, #2, #4) felt like a psychological group, they talked, strategised and attempted to convince #3 to adapt their behaviour. Over time they suspected #3 of taking too much and this changed the group dynamics. From that point onward #4 also took more, whereas #2 starts to take even less to compensate for #3.

Reflections. Group A can be described in many ways. On group level as a badly functioning group, and one may even say this was not a psychological group, there was no togetherness. However, there clearly was a subgroup (majority) that started out as a well functioning group and they were severely affected by the one person that took out too much. The effect led to entirely different changes in mode: some went more deeply in the collective mode by restricting oneself even more (damage-control for the group) while others removing oneself from the collective by taking out more (damage-control for self). These are core nuances that remain hidden when describing this situation as a non-cooperative group or as erosion of cooperation in presence of defection.

The other reflection concerns the concept of a collective. Does this imply a group in which all feel part of the same group or a majority that feels part of the group? What do we mean when we talk about collectives? It is thus important to distinguish between the thinking/decision-making and the behaviour regarding the level of sociality (individual-social-collective). The thinking/decision mode relates to what is valued or in focus, e.g. the group vs individual gains, how considering other individuals plays a role in the decision. The behaviour can be completely in line with the decision mode, but can also be different, e.g. an individual shows behaviour that can be considered motivated for the collective but actually is based on social motives. Particularly in changing situations (e.g. times of polarisation), the importance of unpacking the underlying factors and processes and understanding the why under behaviours is crucial for starting to anticipate behavioural change and differences in collective commitments.

Group B: Tragedy of Cultural Rules. This groups seemed to be trapped in their mechanisms around age and influence, and the group happened to have a large age gap. The elder group members have influence, but limited knowledge and engagement. The group members with adequate knowledge had no influence as they were younger and thus resorted in either no engagement (participant #1) or kept trying to talk and involve the others (participant #4), but were ignored. This resulted in very little to no communication and repeated depletion of the resource. Nonetheless, apart from #3 who trusted everyone, all participants indicated to feel part of the group. The Thai research team attributed this to the participants bonding in the village. And #3 did trust everyone, but felt not part of the group because they just moved out of the village.

Reflections. This particular group underlines the importance of cultural sensitivity, but also at the role of age or being part of a particular generation in the (in)ability of forming a psychological group (all feel part of the group). This group also points at the important of understanding the different reasons for why someone (doesn't) feel part of the group.

Group C: Group with Conflict. Group C can be considered a group that had a group-feel even while conflicts occurred. When the situation turned bad, the group pulled together to think and act as a group, even though it was too late to make the fish stock increase. There was a conflict when there was a big unexpected drop in resource. Participant #2 got angry with participant #4. As a consequence, the group stopped communicating for a while causing the fish to decrease too much to allow replenishment despite renewed communication about the strategy. In the beginning everyone followed participant #4, who was always taking more than agreed. After the conflict everyone followed the suggestions of participant #2. There were more tensions, as #4 wanted to end the game because wanting to take time to pray (religion), whereas participant #2 wanted to play as long as possible. Also, participant #2 told participant #4 "Don't be greedy" because participant #4 always said he wanted to catch a lot.

Reflections. In this group many things are going on. Firstly, the participant #4 clearly has two groups in mind they feel part of and by the sound of it, the other (religion-defined) group affects their behaviour in the strongest sense (wanting to end the game). Secondly, participant #2 upholds strong value of fairness/focus on the optimal range of fish stock and normatively points out when someone is not behaving appropriately and tries to make the person behave appropriately in the collective.

4 Formalising Fishing Together

The empirical narratives provided in the previous section serve as inspiration for realistic group(-feel) situations and dynamics without claiming to be complete or representative. They help us think and advance type of agent formalisation, theories and other empirical knowledge we need to include the transition to and from collective to improve realism of our agents and real life complexity in our empirical understandings.

To formalise collective decision making, we depart from an existing model of human collective action in a common pool resource dilemma, called Agen-

tEx [30]. AgentEx refers to the family of models that seek to (causally) understand collective action and sustainable resource use, while combining behavioural
experiments and agent-based modelling (ABMs). The way the approaches are
combined depends on the focus on the project and model. For example, in the
AgentEx-I the aim was to explain a behavioural experimental result that theory
could not explain. The AgentEx-I model was developed after data collection,
where the agents embodied a possible explanation. In a follow up project, on
the other hand, the data collection of and around behavioural experiments was
designed to serve the empirical needs to design the agents, aiming to unpack the
role of perception on (collective) decision making.

In parallel, we used CAFCA to reflect on the dimensions of decision-making
in the AgentEx-I model (see Fig. 2) we realised that the model could in CAFCA
terms couldn't produce collective behaviour (as indicated by the grey cells containing 'AgentEx') (see [30] for more details of such analysis). As it makes sense
to include collective decision making to study collective action problems, we
developed a conceptual model of AgentEx-I that reflects collective decision-
making using the qualitative inspirations described in the previous section. This
extension complements the individual (decisions independent of others) and
social (decisions are affected by the agent itself and the fact that other agents
act and exist in the world as well) with collective decision making (decisions
are affected by relationships with other agents in the group the agent is part
of) in the AgentEx model. Other possible extensions would include the habitual
and normative level respectively, if applicable. For this, we need more and other
empirical data though.

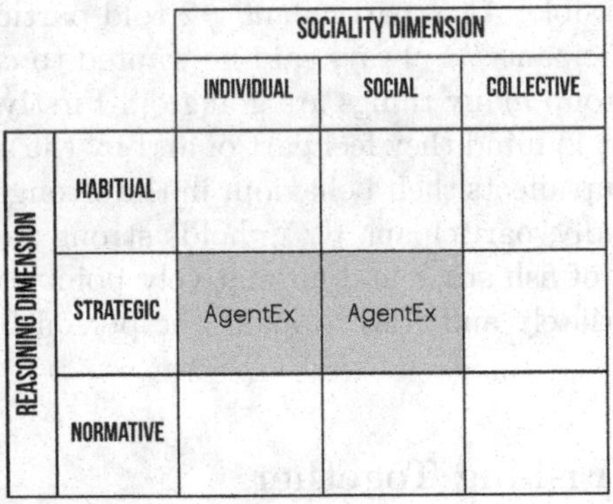

		SOCIALITY DIMENSION		
		INDIVIDUAL	SOCIAL	COLLECTIVE
REASONING DIMENSION	HABITUAL			
	STRATEGIC	AgentEx	AgentEx	
	NORMATIVE			

Fig. 2. Contextual Action Framework for Computational Agents (CAFCA) applied
to agent-based model of common pool resource group dynamics - AgentEx. AgentEx
shows to reside on the strategic level on the reasoning dimension, whereas on the
sociality dimension it can show behaviour on all levels of sociality, but its reasoning
resides on the individual and social level of sociality.

4.1 AgentEx+Collective—A Conceptual Model

In AgentEx-I, the behavioural outcomes could be 'take more than an equal share', 'take the equal share' and do not take anything out. Each of these types of behaviours are the result of different motivations and their connected decision-making. There is a strong distinction between following the strategy of the group versus one's own strategy. The decision making is at its heart utility maximising (going for the highest gains), with some individual attributes (high trust, and social preferences) that prevent an individual from pursuing short-term maximal personal gain. This is reflected by the white decision points on left side of the AgentEx decision tree in Fig. 3.

A key take away of the empirical inspirations on the role of togetherness is that feeling part of a group is essential in the way decision making takes place. CAFCA departs from the presence of different decision modes connected to how an individual relates to others in the sociality dimension being either individual (independent of others), social (in competition or cooperation with others) or collective (collaborative, together with others). The combination of these insights lead us to include collectives decision making path in the decision tree, in the form of an top node that discerns between whether on feels part of the group or not.

The further refinements of the collective decision tree branch toward behaviour was also informed by the stress in the empirical inspirations on both (not) feeling part of a group and the role of one's perception of others feeling part of the group. The latter was illuminated by the different ways participants dealt with how others experienced group feel. For example, suspicion of others taking out too much resulted in acting to do 'group damage control' while others performed individual damage control, in which the group feel of others made a person weaker or stronger connected the to group and acted accordingly. Based on these, we formalised the collective decision tree branch and connected to the individual and social decision tree branches. In Fig. 3 these complementary decision paths are reflected by the dotted lines.

5 Discussion and Conclusion

In this paper we argue for the importance of including and formalising collective decision-making mechanisms in agents and take some first formalisation steps. We contribute by formalising how such a collective decision-making mechanisms may look like using an existing model of collective action in a natural resource use context (AgentEx). More specifically we 1) made use of qualitative empirical insights gained by debriefing interviews after a behavioural field experiment of the same decision context of the model; 2) made a formal suggestion for collective decision-making mechanism in the form of a decision tree branch integrated in the AgentEx decision tree.

Within and beyond the study of collective action there is an unrecognised need for the formalisation of agent-based social simulations able to represent different modes of decision making depending on the context of sociality they

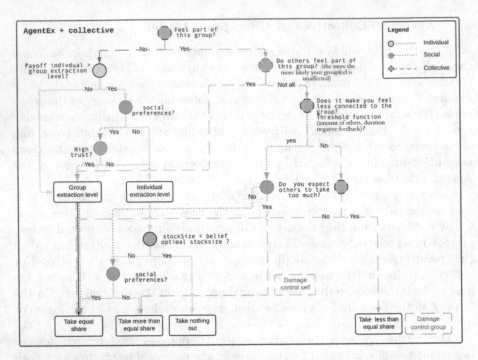

Fig. 3. Decision tree AgentEx (left branch) complemented with collective decision mode pathways (top decision point and right branch), where the different modes of decision making - individual (solid yellow lines), social (dotted purple lines) and collective (dashed blue lines), can lead to the same behaviour for different reasons.

are in and mechanisms to adapt accordingly. Modelling decision making is often trapped in rational actor thinking, while the social sciences suggest many alternative ways and insights on how decisions are made depending on the context [5]. For the sake of social realism and context sensitivity, agent-based simulation modellers working on models reflecting real-world human interaction need to advance to formalising other ways of describing decision making, to encompass both individual agency and collective agency. This boils down to modellers engaging with social sciences and integrate (and thereby value) theoretical insights and empirical insights of a 'qualitative' nature. Not only will this support model building, but also exploring and extending the ability to reflect different social realities that are important in supporting the complex challenges we face as humanity.

While taking a small step in this grand ambition, it paves a way to go. Providing tools that critically assess decision situations with CAFCA, but also demonstrate the inclusion and formalisation of such 'low attention' areas such as collective minded decision-making in agents. We will continue taking baby steps towards our grand challenge, and consider the following points in advancing the formalisation of collective decision-making in agents:

Further Development of AgentEx: As a next step we will implement this conceptual model of collective decision making in AgentEx and explore the role of different initial conditions for the group member to feel part of the group [0, 25%, 50%, 75%, 100%] and compare these with the old AgentEx outcome for a baseline situation. We will check the effect on both cooperation and sustainable resource use to see the implications of this inclusion. Directly after, we would focus on togetherness dynamics. To conceptualise, formalise and test the role of changing group feel based on the outcomes of the group. E.g. good/bad resource state increases/decreases, participation of others in conversation yes/no etc.

Empirical Insights on Reasoning: In this paper we deepened the sociality dimension of CAFCA for the formalisation of collective action, by reflecting on what level of sociality (individual, social, collective) decision making is represented. However, a decision context is defined by the sociality and reasoning dimension. What are reasoning modes used by who, when, and why in the context of collective action for natural resource use. In particular, do the reasoning modes relate to the different ways they have been modelled in CAFCA (automatic, strategic or normative) or do they follow other types of decision models e.g. following Weber's taxonomy of decision-modes calculation-based, recognition-based, role-based or affect-based) [28,29]? For future data collection we thus aim at including questions regarding the mode of decision-making of the participants. This will enable us to the unpack the decision context and its formalisation, thereby identifying the relevant decision context for this application domain and enable the agents to switch decision mode (based on reasoning and sociality).

CAFCA in Context: While using CAFCA in an application domain using AgentEx, we encountered some aspects that require reflection on CAFCA - as CAFCA has been developed from an application domain neutral stance. We realised that a behavioural outcome in AgentEx (taking out nothing) is influenced by the relation a person may feel for nature or a natural resources, e.g. not wanting a fish stock to be depleted, forest to disappear etc.). While applying the analytical framework to reflect on the sociality dimension (individual, social, collective) to a social-ecological decision situation, this social-ecological aspect of sociality is missing. It triggered a thought experiment, would there be another branch with top node that reflects the (dis-)connection to nature that potentially affects decision-making and behaviour via a deliberate path from ones values/morals to behaviour. It concerns unpacking quite a complex black box, beyond the scope of this paper, but worthwhile to explore as relevant for the inclusion to this model.

References

1. Alexander, J.C., Giesen, B., Münch, R., Smelser, N.J. (eds.): The Micro-macro Link. Univerity of California Press (1987)
2. Bacharach, M.: Interactive team reasoning: a contribution to the theory of cooperation. Res. Econ. **53**(2), 117–147 (1999)

3. Bratman, M.: Rational and social agency: reflections and replies. In: Vargas, M., Yaffe, G. (eds.) Rational and Social Agency: The Philosophy of Michael Bratman, pp. 294–343. Oxford University Press, USA (2014)
4. Carley, K., Newell, A.: The nature of the social agent. J. Math. Sociol. **19**(4), 221–262 (1994)
5. Constantino, S.M., Schlüter, M., Weber, E.U., Wijermans, N.: Cognition and behavior in context: a framework and theories to explain natural resource use decisions in social-ecological systems. Sustain. Sci. **16**(5), 1651–1671 (2021). https://doi.org/10.1007/s11625-021-00989-w
6. Cumming, G.S., et al.: Advancing understanding of natural resource governance: a post-Ostrom research agenda. Curr. Opin. Environ. Sustain. **44**, 26–34 (2020). https://doi.org/10.1016/j.cosust.2020.02.005
7. Dahrendorf, R.: Homo Sociologicus: ein Versuch zur Geschichte. Westdeutscher Verlag, Bedeutung und Kritik der Kategorie der sozialen Rolle. Köln und Opladen (1958)
8. Elsenbroich, C., Verhagen, H.: The simplicity of complex agents: a contextual action framework for computational agents. Mind Soc. **15**(1), 131–143 (2016)
9. Faysse, N., Mustapha, A.B.: Finding common ground between theories of collective action: the potential of analyses at a meso-scale. Int. J. Commons **11**(2), 928–949 (2016). https://doi.org/10.18352/ijc.776
10. Georgeff, M., Pell, B., Pollack, M., Tambe, M., Wooldridge, M.: The belief-desire-intention model of agency. In: Müller, J.P., Rao, A.S., Singh, M.P. (eds.) ATAL 1998. LNCS, vol. 1555, pp. 1–10. Springer, Heidelberg (1999). https://doi.org/10.1007/3-540-49057-4_1
11. Gilbert, M.: On Social Facts. Princeton University Press, Princeton (1992)
12. Gilbert, M.: Living Together: Rationality, Sociality, and Obligation. Rowman & Littlefield Publishers, Lanham (1996)
13. Goldman, A.H.: Reasons from Within: Desires and Values. Oxford University Press, Oxford (2009)
14. Hardin, G.: The tragedy of the commons. Science **162**, 1243–1248 (1968)
15. Jansen, M., Jager, W.: An integrated approach to simulating behavioural processes: a case study of the lock-in of consumption patterns. J. Artif. Soc. Soc. Simul. **2**(2), 21–35 (2000)
16. van Laerhoven, F., Schoon, M., Villamayor-Tomas, S.: Celebrating the 30th anniversary of Ostrom's governing the commons: traditions and trends in the study of the commons. Revisited. Int. J. Commons **14**(1), 208–224 (2020). https://doi.org/10.5334/ijc.1030
17. Lange, P.A.M., Joireman, J., Parks, C.D., Dijk, E.: The psychology of social dilemmas: a review. Organizational Behav. Hum. Decis. Processes **120**(2), 125–141 (2013). https://doi.org/10.1016/j.obhdp.2012.11.003
18. Lindahl, T., Schill, C., Jarungrattanapong, R.: Beijer Discussion Paper 276: The role of resource dependency for sharing increasingly scarce resources: Evidence from a behavioural experiment with small-scale fishers. Beijer Discussion Paper Series (2021)
19. Ostrom, E.: Revisiting the commons: local lessons, global challenges. Science **284**(5412), 278–282 (1999). https://doi.org/10.1126/science.284.5412.278
20. Phung, T., Winikoff, M., Padgham, L.: Learning within the BDI framework: an empirical analysis. In: Khosla, R., Howlett, R.J., Jain, L.C. (eds.) KES 2005. LNCS (LNAI), vol. 3683, pp. 282–288. Springer, Heidelberg (2005). https://doi.org/10.1007/11553939_41

21. Poteete, A.R., Janssen, M.A., Ostrom, E.: Working Together: Collective Action, the Commons, and Multiple Methods in Practice. Princeton University Press, Princeton (2010)
22. Reicher, S.D., Spears, R., Haslam, S.A.: The social identity approach in social psychology. In: The SAGE Handbook of Identities, pp. 45–62. SAGE Publications Ltd., 1 Oliver's Yard, 55 City Road, London EC1Y 1SP United Kingdom (2010). https://doi.org/10.4135/9781446200889.n4
23. Newall, M.: Convention. In: What is a Picture? LNCS (LNAI), pp. 9–18. Palgrave Macmillan UK, London (2011). https://doi.org/10.1057/9780230297531_2
24. Schill, C., Wijermans, N., Schlüter, M., Lindahl, T.: Cooperation is not enough—exploring social-ecological micro-foundations for sustainable common-pool resource use. PLoS One **11**(8), e0157796 (2016). https://doi.org/10.1371/journal.pone.0157796
25. Sugden, R.: The logic of team reasoning. Philos. Explor. **6**(3), 165–181 (2003). https://doi.org/10.1080/10002003098538748
26. Verhagen, H.: Norm autonomous agents. Ph.D. thesis, Stockholm University (2000)
27. Verhagen, H.: Simulation of the learning of norms. Soc. Sci. Comput. Rev. **19**(3), 296–306 (2001)
28. Weber, E.U., Ames, D.R., Blais, A.R.: 'How do I choose thee? let me count the ways': a textual analysis of similarities and differences in modes of decision-making in China and the United States. Manage. Organization Rev. **1**(1), 1–32 (2004)
29. Weber, E.U., Lindemann, P.G.: From intuition to analysis. In: Plessner, H., Betsch, C., Betsch, T. (eds.) Intuition in Judgment and Decision Making, pp. 1–17. Psychology Press, New York (2011)
30. Wijermans, N., Schill, C., Lindahl, T., Schlüter, M.: AgentEx (2016). https://doi.org/10.25937/js95-6d78

Author Index

Printed in the United States
by Baker & Taylor Publisher Services

Printed in the United States
by Baker & Taylor Publisher Services